Exploring Industry and Enterprise

Exploring Industry
and Enterprise

Exploring Industry and Enterprise

A practical guide for students of economics, industry and business enterprise

Robert Dransfield
Shell Research Fellow, Centre for Industrial Studies

David Needham
Lecturer in Business Studies, Darlington College of Technology

CASSELL

Cassell Publishers Limited
Artillery House
Artillery Row
London SW1P 1RT

First published 1989

British Library Cataloguing in Publication Data
Dransfield, Robert
  Exploring industry and enterprise: a
  practical guide for students of economics,
  industry and business enterprise.
  1. Great Britain. Business enterprise
  I. Title   II. Needham, David
  338.6'0941

  ISBN 0-304-31575-3

Typeset by Witwell Ltd, Southport
Printed and bound in Great Britain
by the Bath Press, Avon.

Contents

official trade union organisation; The unofficial union organisation; Trade
unions and disputes; The Trades Union Congress; Employers' associations;
Professional associations; ACAS; The government and industrial relations.

Acknowledgements

The Centre for Industrial Studies is a meeting-place for a wide range of members of the community interested in developing education/industry links. It is not surprising that producing a publication investigating industrial and economic society requires the collaboration of a wide range of individuals and groups. We should like to thank the following:

Contributors

John Elliott	–	Marketing East Midlands Electricity
Chris Lee	–	Interviewing at Marks & Spencer
Peter Nuttall	–	Employment
Paul Read	–	New technology in industry

Newspapers

We would particularly like to thank *The Independent* and *The Grantham Journal* for their excellent contributions. We also thank the following:

The Daily Mirror
The Dewsbury Reporter Series
The Harrogate Advertiser
The Peterborough Evening Telegraph
Pravda International
Which?
Yorkshire Evening Press

Schools and Colleges

Lincolnshire County Council were a great help in making introductions — particularly their inspectors Peter Fletcher and Val Charles.

The schools and colleges that tested and used the materials were:

Branston Community College, Lincoln
Darlington College of Technology
De Aston School, Market Rasen
Kesteven and Grantham Girls School

Kings School, Grantham
North Border School, Bircotes
Robert Manning School, Bourne
Waingels Copse School, Reading

Individuals

Steven Burtt
Ben Cribb
Marilyn Elliott
Jim Farley
Andre Finney
Mike Goodjohn
Elaine Lilley

Akio Morita
Christopher Rowney
Malcolm Scott
Mike Thomas
Christine Yeaman
Robert Young

Companies and other groups

Belfast Development Agency
British Nuclear Fuels plc
British Standards Institution
Burtts of Lincolnshire
Carousel
Concept Graphics
Darlington Council
Deltacam Systems Ltd
Durham County Council
East Midlands Electricity Board
Friends of the Earth
Greater Nottingham Co-operative Society Ltd
Greenpeace
The Highlands and Islands Development Board
Hilary Morgan

The Labour Party
Linpac, Huntley Boorne and Stevens
Lloyds Bank plc
Merlin Ecology Fund
Mitchell Packability
Napcolour Ltd
Nestlé
NUPE Publications
Pedigree Petfoods
The Prudential
South East Wales Development Agency
Shell UK
The Tin Council
York Development Agency

The cover photographs are reproduced with kind permission of Shell Education, Shell Livewire and Sandra Gibson.

Introduction

■ Question

Study the four scenes in Figure 1 (overleaf). Which
of the scenes would you expect to provide themes
for investigation in a course on industrial studies?
Explain your answer.

Millions of people around the world are involved in creating goods and services which are
used to meet our needs and wants. Industrial
society produces the goods and services on
which the quality of our lives depend.

There are many ways in which individuals
contribute to the well-being of others: the refuse
collector makes the streets clean and tidy; the
supermarket shelf-filler displays goods so that
they can be seen and picked up easily; the child-
minder makes it possible for others to go out to
work or to enjoy their leisure; the factory worker
helps to provide manufactured goods. All these
people are concerned with helping to improve
the welfare of society.

Industrial society is therefore based around
the process of creating value - through paid and
unpaid activities, through manufacturing and
service industries.

Modern industrial societies like the United
Kingdom and the United States of America are
said to be in their third wave of development. In
the first stage these countries were mainly based
on agriculture; the second stage was dominated
by manufacturing industry. Today, as we
experience the 'third wave', the service sector has
become increasingly important, and more and
more people are employed in service occupations.

Interdependence

Interdependence means that the parts of a
system need and depend on each other. Today,
more than ever before we live in a globally
interdependent economy. Individuals and
groups are parts of communities, communities
are parts of nations, and nations are parts of the
global economy, as can be seen in Figure 2.

What is happening in the world economy can
- and frequently does - have a direct effect on
each of us. A small clothes manufacturer in East
London will have to compete with similar
manufacturers in Eastern Europe and the Far

Figure 2 Interdependence in a global economy.

Figure 1 Different aspects of modern life: prosperity and poverty, industrial expansion and industrial decline.

East. When they buy raw materials from other local companies they may be buying cotton from East Africa and machinery from South Korea. If technology improves in Taiwan this might lead to unemployment in London and vice versa.

On a more local scale, individuals and organisations are interdependent in a wide variety of ways, as illustrated in Figure 3. Individuals play a number of roles in industrial society as buyers, sellers, employees, employers, taxpayers, voters and many more.

Industrial organisations also interact with a wide network of other groups and individuals.

Figure 3 A firm in its environment illustrating interdependence.

For example, a small packaging firm in Cardiff has to deal with raw material suppliers, its customers and competitors and its employees and the trade unions to which they belong. It uses business services such as banks, insurance companies, the Post Office and British Telecom. It employs industrial services such as a cleaning company and builders. It pays taxes to the government and is inspected regularly by factory and health officials. The business must also pay attention to complaints from a local residents' pressure group regarding lorries parking in the neighbourhood.

Investigation

This book sets out to encourage students to carry out investigations into the way that an industrial society operates.

Investigation involves asking questions, and trying to make use of information to increase our understanding. It involves trying to weigh up and understand different statements and points of view. For example, if Mrs A says that unemployment is not a problem you would need to try to understand:

1. what she means by the statement;
2. why she might make the statement.

You would then need to carry out the same process for Mr B who says that unemployment is a problem.

By taking apart such statements and other information, and by exploring the cause and effect of a variety of activities, you should develop a clearer insight into the way that society functions.

Industrial society is made up of many complex arrangements. At best our understanding of how it operates will be very limited. Through carrying out investigations we hope to find out a little bit more – to try and understand more clearly. We rarely come across right or wrong answers – more often there are alternative ways of doing things and alternative points of view.

This book encourages you to think through a wide number of real-life situations. Each chapter contains text which is broken up by case studies and questions. Every chapter also contains coursework suggestions and classroom coursework activities.

You will find a number of questions frequently appear:

1. Who loses out and who benefits from a particular activity?
2. How and why do they benefit/lose out?
3. What is meant by fair? (Fairness means different things to different people.)
4. What is meant by best? (This can mean different things to different people in different circumstances.)

There are no right and wrong answers: such issues are open to discussion. In the media, and in everyday discussion, people frequently make judgements concerning industrial society. This book sets out to provide a wide range of situations through which you can investigate industrial society.

Opportunity cost

Opportunity cost means the next best alternative that is sacrificed when we carry out a particular action. Individuals, groups, communities and nations are continually making decisions. When you make a decision to buy one thing you sacrifice alternatives: when you decide to buy a record the real cost to you is the things that you have to give up.

At the beginning of this introduction you were shown four photographs and asked which ones you would expect to be themes for a course in industrial studies. The answer is that they all are. Industrial society is a decision-making society – decisions are constantly being made about what to produce, how to produce, and who gets the rewards. A derelict piece of land in an inner city is a scarce resource in the same way as is a modern factory unit. Decisions have to be made about how to use these scarce resources – the derelict land could become a supermarket or housing for homeless families. When a decision is made some people will benefit and others will lose out. Different people will have different views about what is fair and what is best.

CHAPTER 1
Setting up a small business enterprise

In 1988 there were more than a million businesses with annual sales figures of less than £100,000. There were a further 300,000 businesses with sales between £100,000 and £1 million per year. In percentage terms, 68% of all businesses fall within the description of a small business, that is to say one with sales of less than £100,000.

As you can see, a lot of businesses are small ones! Not surprisingly, these businesses provide much employment. Latest figures suggest that businesses employing fewer than 100 people provide 50% of all UK jobs.

Perhaps more significantly, almost 1 million new jobs have been created in this sector between 1982 and 1988. Small business has therefore become a vital force in the United Kingdom economy, and one that is becoming more important as we continue to see a decline in the importance of 'heavy industries' (large-scale producers of basic raw materials, such as coal and iron ore, and manufactures such as steel, railway girders and ships) and in the numbers employed in these industries.

In 1988 it was estimated that there would be over a quarter of a million new businesses starting up. Unfortunately, however, the failure rate is also high. Only 70% are likely to survive the first year, 50% the first five years and a mere 30% will survive ten years.

Small businesses provide a good starting point for a course in industrial studies. They face all the problems common to large organisations and they are easy to investigate and explore. Small businesses also provide an excellent topic area for fieldwork inquiries.

Identifying a business opportunity

There are many reasons why people choose to set up their own business. Most people at some time or another have said things like: 'If only someone sold "x" here they could make a fortune', or 'I have got a great idea for a new product...'. In business it also helps to be at the right place at the right time.

Business opportunities usually arise if someone:

1. spots a gap in the market;
2. develops a hobby into a paying business;
3. copies an existing idea that is already in demand;
4. takes over an existing business.

■ Case Study: The greengrocers

Ramesh and Vinod Gehlot have set up their own greengrocers shop in Reading. Their parents had always had a business of one sort or another and the two boys had helped out. They worked hard and managed to get some savings together. After leaving school the most obvious choice seemed to be to carry on working for their parents or to go into some sort of office job.

Instead Ramesh and Vinod decided to form a partnership. They found an area of Reading where there would be a lot of customers and little competition. They pooled their savings, borrowed a small sum from relatives and took out a bank loan.

The main costs of running the business are the rent and rates, the cost of stock, and the hire-purchase repayments on their van.

Figure 1.1 Ramesh and
Vinod Gehlot –
greengrocers.
Soure: Kim Hooper.

■ Case Study: The jeweller

At school Elizabeth Clare had been particularly
interested in art and pottery. She liked working with
small objects and had started making her own ear-
rings. Many of her friends had liked them and had
commissioned Elizabeth to make similar ones.
Strangers started to ring her up to try and place
orders. At art college Elizabeth specialised in
jewellery making in her final year. The college
encouraged her to put on an exhibition at a gallery
in London.

A number of teenage magazines featured stories
about Elizabeth and a local jeweller suggested that
if she would like to set up in business then he
would lend her some money.

Elizabeth now produces a range of jewellery
items. She sells them to high-quality jewellers and
has just started to work on a mail-order catalogue.

■ Activity

The two case studies above illustrate the ways in
which people spot business opportunities.

Working in groups of two or three, make a list of
six business ideas that you think would work in
your area. Pick out the best two ideas from your list

Figure 1.2 Elizabeth Clare – jeweller.
Source: Kim Hooper.

and discuss in your small group why you think they are good ideas.

The groups then present their two best ideas to the rest of the class. A list of all the ideas should be displayed at the front of the room. When all the ideas have been listed the class should vote for the best idea.

Market research

Before setting up in business it is vitally important to find out as much information as possible about the market.

You need to find out what potential customers want and how much they are prepared to pay for different goods and services. You need to find out what competition there is and how rival firms operate. You might think that you have the best product in the world but unless people know about you and are prepared to buy your product, then setting up an enterprise will be a waste of time and money.

Planning ahead – cash flow forecasting

Before setting up in business it is essential that you put together a business plan setting out your strategy. The business plan should show that you are knowledgeable about your markets, and quite clear about your financial needs. An important part of your business plan will be your cash flow prediction.

It is essential that you estimate what you think your cash flow will be in the months ahead. You need to work out what your incomings and outgoings will be. If your payments remain higher than the inflow of cash there is no point in setting up in business.

Table 1.1 Cash flow chart.

	Jan. (£)	Feb. (£)	Mar. (£)	Apr.
Starting balance	(200)	(100)	0	100
Incomings	200	200	200	200
Outgoings	100	100	100	
Closing balance	(100)	0	100	

(N.B: Negative balances are shown in brackets.)

A simplified cash flow chart is shown in Table 1.1. The business estimates that it will start off

with an overdraft of £200. In January the business expects to sell £200 worth of goods and to make purchases of £100. As a result it is calculated that at the end of January the business overdraft will be reduced to £100. This minus figure is then carried forward to the beginning of February and the cash flow rolls on. All expenditures and revenues should be included in the projection. The business is then able to check its progress against the cash flow chart.

■ Case Study: The signwriter

Suzanne Thorpe is 24 and has just set up in business as a signwriter. Suzanne studied art at college and went on a business course before deciding to set up. She did some market research in her local town, Harrogate, to check that there was a sufficient demand for her product and that competition would not be too fierce. She then applied to join and was accepted for the government-run Enterprise Allowance Scheme. She operates her business from home, using a shed adjoining the house for her carpentry and artwork.

	Jan	Feb	Mar	Apr	May	June
Opening balance						
Incomings Sales Enterprise Allowance						
Total income						
Outgoings Purchases of materials Telephone Vehicle tax and insurance Petrol Heat and light Wages Advertising Stationery Sundries						
Total outgoings						
CLOSING BALANCE						

Figure 1.3 Outline for cash flow chart for Suzanne Thorpe.

*Figure 1.4 Suzanne Thorpe
– signwriter.*

Suzanne will charge £9 an hour for her work. She calculates that she will be working for 50 hours a month in January, February and March. As business picks up Suzanne will take on more contracts so that after March she expects to be working on average 125 hours per month.

Suzanne will be able to claim the Enterprise Allowance throughout the year. She will receive £160 from the scheme in January, February, April and June and £200 in March and May.

In January, Suzanne will purchase a stock of materials worth £300. In the following months she will only purchase £50 worth of materials per month. Suzanne hopes to pay herself a wage of £400 per month.

Suzanne has bought an old van for the business. The tax and insurance for the vehicle will be spread over the first four months at £58 per month. Petrol is estimated at £50 for the first three months, rising to £75 per month for the rest of the first year.

£15 per month will be set aside to pay the telephone bill, and £25 is estimated to cover the heating and lighting bills which must be paid in March and June (quarterly bills).

Suzanne will not advertise until March because she expects to get some good press coverage in the first two months. In March she will spend £100 on advertising in the local paper.

Finally, Suzanne will set aside £10 per month for stationery and £10 per month for sundries (any other items of expense).

Questions

1. Fill in Suzanne's cash flow forecast (assuming she starts with an opening balance of £500).
2. Are there any items that you can think of which might be missing from the forecast?
3. Why might Suzanne's actual figures stray from those given in the forecast?

Sources of finance

Anyone investing money in a new business has to be convinced that the future benefit is worth the risk.

Seeking finance is the first step you should take in actually setting up your business. You will need to know how much capital is required to get your business started and to keep it operating for at least the first year.

Savings are an obvious way of putting money into a business. You may also be able to *borrow* from family and friends.

If you do not possess the amount needed you may choose to try for a *loan*. A loan is a sum of money lent for a given period of time. Repayment is made with interest. Your own high street bank manager is often the best person to approach. The lender of money needs to know all the business opportunities and risks involved. In addition the bank needs to be sure that you are able to safeguard the money lent. Finally, the bank needs to arrange a way of getting some or all of the money back if things go wrong.

Another way of borrowing is to arrange an *overdraft* facility with a bank. This means that you can take out more money from your account than you have put in. The bank will fix a maximum limit for the overdraft. Interest will be charged on how much you are overdrawn on a day-to-day basis.

Small businesses sometimes qualify for *grants*. Government and private funds are sometimes made available to businesses that meet certain conditions. For example, grants and loans are sometimes available to firms setting up in rural areas or where there is high unemployment.

It is also possible to attract extra finance by taking on a *partner* or by selling *shares*. The problem caused by bringing in extra people is that profits have to be shared and you might find it more difficult to take quick decisions.

A further way of raising capital that has become more popular in recent years has been that of *venture capital*. Larger businesses with cash to spare have been putting funds into small- and medium-sized businesses.

Once a business is up and running there are various ways of financing its running costs. Expensive items of equipment can be *leased*. Rather than buying the equipment the business

hires it from a leasing company. This saves having to lay out sums of money and the small business does not have to worry about having to carry out major repairs itself. Motor vehicles, machines, and office equipment are often leased.

Hire-purchase is an alternative way of purchasing items of equipment. With a leased item you use and pay for the item but never own it. With hire-purchase you put down a deposit on an item and then pay off the rest in instalments. When the last instalment has been paid you become the owner of the item.

Another common way in which firms can finance their business in the short term is through *trade credit*. In business it is common practice to purchase items and pay for them later. The supplier will normally send the purchaser a statement at the end of each month saying how much is owed. The buyer is then given a period of time in which to pay. If payment is made within a set time a cash discount will often be granted.

Most small businesses will regularly be owed money by a selection of people who have been supplied with goods and services on credit. The problem here is that this will leave the business short of ready cash to buy in fresh materials and to pay its bills. One way of getting round this is to sell your debts to a factoring company. By *factoring* your debts you will have ready cash to carry on other business activities. Suppose, for example, you are owed £2,000. The factoring company would take your bills and give you, say, half of what you are owed immediately, i.e. £1,000. The factoring company will then collect the £2,000 in the course of time. It will then give you another £700 at a later date keeping £300 in commission for itself. (These are only imaginary figures.)

■ Questions

What sources of finance would you consider to be appropriate in the following examples? (Explain your answers.)

1. Amjad Jinjua is setting up a computer software business. He has calculated that the business will be short of cash for one week only when it is first set up.
2. Diane Goodchild has a decorating business. She

does not as yet own a motor vehicle. She would like to buy a second-hand van which she has seen recently, costing £3,000.

3. Kay Kerr has a photography business. She currently owes other people £2,000 and is owed £10,000. One of her suppliers is threatening to sue her for the money she owes.

4. *The Grantham Journal* is a local newspaper with a readership of 30,000. It would now like to spend £40,000 on new computer technology.

5. Sanjay Desai is a signwriter. He would like to purchase a new lorry. He wants to own the lorry eventually but cannot afford to pay outright at the moment.

6. Sally Davis would like to acquire a new typewriter for her secretarial agency. She wants to be able to 'flog the machine to death' without having the responsibility of owning or repairing the machine.

7. Winston Alexander runs a small corner-shop. He would like to expand the size of the shop and share the responsibility of running the business.

8. Julie Head has a landscape gardening business employing six people. She would like to employ ten more people and to buy a fleet of three small vehicles.

■ Case Study: The freelance accountant

Valerie Davis had worked for 15 years as an accountant with a large company. In 1989 she decided to branch out on her own. She made some enquiries to clients that she already dealt with and they gave her guarantees of work which would give her an income of at least £25,000 in her first year.

She then worked out how much money she would need to set up in business. Her main costs would be: rent and rates for an office £4,000 per year, cost of computer and office equipment (purchased outright) £11,000, other running expenses (phone, petrol, etc.) £5,000.

In the short term she calculated that she needed £11,000 for her first month of trading. She only had £5,000 of savings.

■ Question

What do you think would be the main sources of finance that Valerie would have considered? What steps might she have taken to get the finance?

Figure 1.5 Valerie Davis – freelance accountant. Source: Kim Hooper.

Production methods

Two major processes should come together in the preparation of a good or service for market:

1. market research to find out what people want to buy, and how and where they want it;
2. product design and development to look at different ways of producing a good or service.

Very often these two areas will combine to produce one or a number of prototypes, i.e., examples of what might be produced. For example, in a small biscuit manufacturers:

1. the market research department first finds out that there is a demand from the public for a new cherry-flavoured biscuit;
2. the product design team then works out various methods by which it can be made, prototypes are produced and the new biscuit is pre-tested before pre-production runs are made and tried out on the public.

Actual production can then take place. These stages in the production process are illustrated in Figure 1.6.

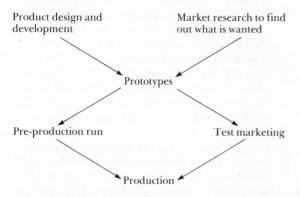

Figure 1.6 Stages in the production process.

There are several different methods of producing goods and services.

Job production

This involves the production of single, individual items. For example, a boat-builder might get an order to produce a one-off yacht, or a hairdresser may be asked to create a style for one person for a special occasion.

Firms might specialise in producing one-off jobs such as customised motor bikes.

Batch production

This means the production of batches of similar products. For example, a baker might produce batches of jam doughnuts, cream buns, Eccles cakes and so on.

Flow production

With this method, production parts are passed on from one stage of production to another in a regular flow. Each stage adds to the product.

Mass production

This is the production of products on a large scale. This sometimes involves flow production, but there may be only one stage in the production process.

■ Question

Which of the following would be most suitable for (a) job, (b) batch, (c) flow or (d) mass production?

1. A manicure service
2. Fitted kitchen installation
3. Beer manufacture
4. Furniture production
5. Book production
6. A taxi service
7. Motorcycle manufacture
8. Computer manufacture
9. Cardboard box manufacture
10. Tinned food production
11. Gardening

Specialisation

Modern society is based on specialisation. Employees specialise in given occupations. Machines specialise in certain tasks. Regions and countries specialise in producing goods and services.

If people and other resources concentrate on things which they can do relatively well, then everyone usually benefits. Specialisation results in an increase in production.

It pays individuals to concentrate on what they do best. If I can earn £10 an hour from writing this book and it only costs £5 an hour to have someone paint my house, then it will make sense for me to sit and write while the decorator paints. However, things can't just be weighed up in money terms – you also need to consider the satisfaction or dissatisfaction you get from a particular activity.

It also pays groups to let individuals specialise. For example, Jane and Roger can both cook and grow vegetables. However, Roger is twice as good at cooking as Jane, and half as good at growing vegetables. It therefore makes sense for Roger to cook and Jane to grow vegetables.

The principle of specialisation can be applied to trade between areas and between countries. It helps to explain why Scotland might specialise in whisky production and Uganda in growing cotton.

Specialisation is often explained in terms of *comparative advantage*. The principle of comparative advantage is that individuals, groups and nations should concentrate on those activities at which they are better, leaving others to concentrate on things at which they are worse. After all, in the real world everyone will be *relatively* good at something.

Division of labour

The principle of specialisation is easily illustrated in relation to the division of labour (specialisation by job task).

Figures 1.7 to 1.9 illustrate a few of the specialist tasks involved in the production of a tin biscuit box. Each one of the people illustrated is an expert in his own particular field.

In the factory where they work (Huntley, Boorne and Stevens, tin box manufacturers) there are many other specialists including:

1. cleaners
2. printers
3. packers
4. managers
5. lorry drivers
6. office workers

■ Coursework

Study a local manufacturing business.

1. What methods of production are used?
2. Make a list of all the different specialist occupations that contribute to the running of the firm.

There are a number of disadvantages as well as advantages to the division of labour. (The advantages and disadvantages relate to a wide number of individuals and groups including businesses, employees, consumers, etc. What appears to be an advantage to one group may be a disadvantage to another group.)

Advantages of division of labour

1. *Increase in skill.* 'Practice makes perfect', as the saying goes. By doing something over and over again the worker becomes more skilled. This applies to a wide range of skills from cooking to typing.
2. *Time saving.* When a worker changes task regularly then time is wasted in switching from one thing to the next. By specialising, time wasting is cut out. Another advantage is that if people concentrate on the same thing they will need less training.
3. *Specialising in best lines.* Division of labour makes it possible for people to concentrate on the things that they do best. Some people like working with their hands, others enjoy selling things.
4. *Use of machinery.* As tasks become more broken down and specialised it becomes possible to use specialist machinery at each stage. For example, in offices that have to produce thousands of similar letters and documents it pays to use specialist word processing equipment.

Disadvantages of division of labour

1. *Dependency.* Because of specialisation many individuals, groups and processes become dependent on each other. If the person or machine at the previous stage to you is slow, on strike, unreliable, etc., you will suffer.
2. *Unemployment.* Specialisation means that a large number of people have only a limited

Figure 1.7 *The artist prepares some drawings for a new biscuit box design.*
Source: *The International Tin Research Institute.*

Figure 1.8 *The designer makes a mock-up of a tin box.*
Source: *The International Tin Research Institute.*

Figure 1.9 *The production engineer produces tin sheets for production into final boxes.*
Source: *The International Tin Research Institute.*

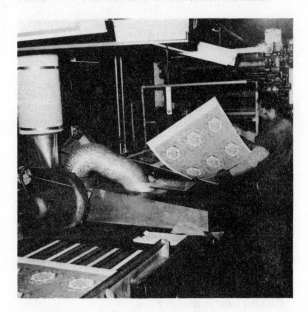

training. If their skill is no longer needed because of change, they might find it difficult to find new work.

3. *Frustration and boredom.* If the work that people have to do is very unimaginative and repetitive they might not enjoy work. Accidents are more likely to occur and people will be less motivated to work hard.

Organisational structures

Every enterprise made up of more than one person will need some form of organisational structure.

An *organisational chart* shows the way in which the chain of command works within the organisation. You must remember however, that what you see on paper is often very different from the way that things work in the real world. An individual with a strong personality can play an important part in the running of an organisation, although he or she might only appear at the bottom of the chart.

The way in which a company is organised can be illustrated by looking at a small packaging company, Mitchell Packability (see Figure 1.10). The company is owned by a small number of shareholders who chose the directors to look after their interests; the directors then chose a group of managers to run the company.

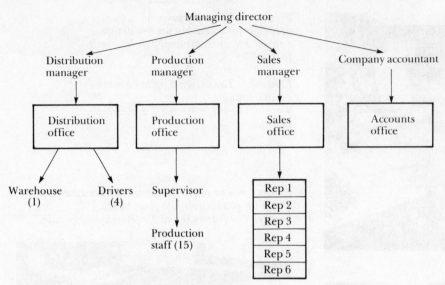

Figure 1.10 The organisational chart of Mitchell Packability.

Managing director

The managing director has the major responsibility for the running of the company, including setting company targets and keeping an eye on all departments.

Distribution manager

The distribution manager is responsible for controlling the movement of goods in and out of the warehouse, supervising drivers and overseeing the transport of goods to and from the firm.

Production manager

The production manager is responsible for keeping a continuous supply of work flowing to all production staff, and also for organising labour to meet the customers' orders.

Sales manager

The sales manager is responsible for making contact with customers and obtaining orders from those contacts.

Company accountant

The accountant controls all the financial dealings of the company.

Communications

Effective communication links are essential if an organisation is to run smoothly. Communications can also be illustrated by reference to Mitchell Packability (see Figure 1.11).

Customer–Sales

The customer will liaise with the sales department to obtain his or her requirements. The types of communication technique used are:

1. Telephone
2. Personal meetings
3. Official written orders

Sales–Production

The sales department reports back to the production department to see if the customer's requirements can be met, and to discuss a reasonable delivery date. The type of communication techniques used are:

1. Official written orders
2. Drawings

Production–Stores

The production department will process the customer's order, instructing the stores department of all the materials required to manufacture the customer's order. The type of communication techniques used are:

1. Official written orders

Stores–Suppliers

The stores department checks the stock of raw materials for manufacturing and then orders any additional materials that may be required to manufacture the customer's order. The type of communication techniques used are:

1. Telephone
2. Written orders

Accounts

The accounts department controls all the money in and out of the company. This includes paying the suppliers and collecting the money from the customers. The type of communication techniques used are:

1. Telephone
2. In person
3. Occasional memos

■ Coursework

Study a local company (manufacturing or service). Draw up an organisational chart and describe the structure of the organisation. Explain how the communication links operate within the organisation.

Outlets for products and services

There are many ways of getting a product to its eventual consumer. Goods and services can either be supplied to consumers direct or through intermediaries (see Figure 1.12).

Selling is an important part of running a successful enterprise. It involves finding customers and keeping them satisfied. (Distribution is dealt with at length in Chapter 8.)

Profits

There are several ways of looking at profits. From a business owner's point of view, the

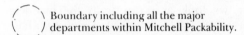

Boundary including all the major departments within Mitchell Packability.

Figure 1.11 Communications between departments at Mitchell Packability.

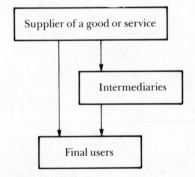

Figure 1.12 Channels of distribution.

financial profit of a business will be the difference between its money costs and money receipts.

However, the owner(s) would need also to consider whether the risks, headaches and problems of running the business made it worthwhile. Of course, on the plus side there would be the non-money benefits such as the satisfaction of working for yourself:

Plus points of running a business	Minus points of running a business
Financial receipts	Financial costs of setting up and running
Satisfaction and other non-money rewards.	Non-money costs (hard work, long hours, etc.)

It is also possible to take a wider view of profit, at how communities profit from a particular activity. For example, on paper it might look as if a local fast-food business is doing well, and the owner might be pleased with the number of customers and money profits. However, local residents may be very unhappy about the litter being left in their gardens and the noise late at night. Their view could be that the business owner should be fined, taxed heavily or made responsible for clearing up the litter.

Here we look at profit from the business organisation's point of view. Later we shall return to alternative views about profit.

Once a business organisation is trading, its profit will provide an important source of finance. This circulation of capital is at the centre

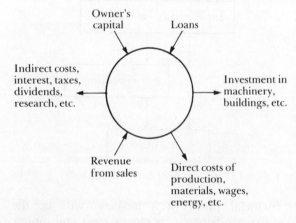

Figure 1.13 The circular flow of capital in a business.

of business activity and is illustrated in Figure 1.13.

The business would start off with an inflow of cash from the owners and from borrowings. Money would then need to be paid out to purchase investment items such as machinery and office equipment. The firm would also need to pay out cash in order to produce a good or service. These are the *direct costs*.

When goods or services are sold, money will enter the flow in the form of sales revenue. The firm will also have to pay out *indirect costs* which are not tied directly to production, e.g. interest on money borrowed and money spent on researching new projects.

Once all the inflows and outflows of cash have been accounted for the firm will be left with a sum of cash available for a fresh circulation. The cash available for the new circulation will be greater than the original stock of cash if sales revenues have been greater than all the outflows of cash.

In order to examine profits in more detail we need to look at costs and receipts.

Costs

Total cost is the cost of all the resources necessary to produce given levels of output. Total cost rises as you produce more. For example, a small boat-yard calculated that to produce one boat in a week would cost £7,000, two boats would cost a total of £12,000 and three boats £15,000.

Total cost is split into two parts: fixed costs and variable costs.

Fixed costs

Fixed costs do not vary with the amount produced. These costs have to be paid whether the business is producing nothing or as much as possible. Fixed costs can be illustrated as in Figure 1.14.

You can see that the firm's fixed costs were £200 a week whether it produced no goods, five goods or 25 goods. The sorts of costs that are fixed depend on the type of business. They often include items such as rent and rates, perhaps wages, and interest on money borrowed.

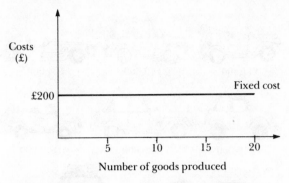

Figure 1.14 Fixed costs of production at different levels of output.

Variable costs

Variable costs vary with output. Variable costs are zero when output is zero and rise directly with output. The variable costs given in Table 1.2 are illustrated in Figure 1.15.

Table 1.2 Variable costs at different levels of output.

Output per week	Variable cost (£)
0	0
5	25
10	40
15	50
20	70

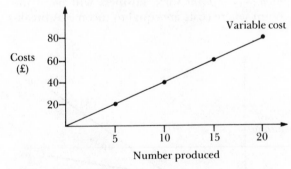

Figure 1.15 Variable costs of production at different levels of output.

Total costs

Total cost can be calculated by adding together the fixed and variable costs at different levels of output. The total, fixed and variable costs given in Table 1.3 are illustrated in Figure 1.16.

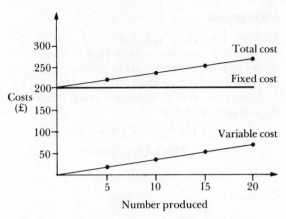

Figure 1.16 Total, fixed and variable costs.

Table 1.3 Total, fixed and variable costs at different levels of output.

Output per week	Fixed cost (£)	Variable cost (£)	Total cost (£)
0	200	0	200
5	200	25	225
10	200	40	240
15	200	50	250
20	200	70	270

■ Activity

A group of students investigating a local insurance firm classified its costs as follows:

Variable costs	Fixed costs
Paper and stationery	Rent
Petrol	Rates
Overtime pay	Insurance cover
Lighting and heating	Basic wages
Postage	Advertising
Telephone charges	Interest on money borrowed
	Canteen costs

What would you expect the fixed and variable costs of the following firms to be?

1. A taxi firm
2. An advertising agency that only works on a 9.00 a.m. to 5.00 p.m. basis
3. A zoo

Why is it that certain items are fixed costs for some firms, yet variable for others?

Average cost

Another important calculation of cost is the *average cost*. Average cost is useful because it shows us how much it costs to produce a unit of output. The average cost can be calculated by dividing the cost of producing a given output by the number produced:

$$\text{Unit cost} = \frac{\text{Total cost of production}}{\text{Quantity produced}}$$

Revenue

Receipts are the sums of money that an enterprise takes in from its activities. *Mark-up* and *turnover* are terms commonly used in relation to sales.

Mark-up

The British Tea Company is a wholesaling business that imports chests of tea from Sri Lanka for £10 each. It then resells the chests to British tea firms for £15 each. Illustrated in Figure 1.17, the *mark-up* is the difference between the buying and the selling price, i.e., £5.

Buying price for British Tea Co.: £10

Selling price from British Tea Co.: £15

Figure 1.17 Marking up chests of tea.

Turnover

The Vintage Garage sells old cars as in Figure 1.18 at an average price of £20,000. In a normal year it sells ten vehicles. Its turnover is therefore £200,000, i.e., Number of sales × Average price of items. *Turnover* is therefore the total value of sales made by a company.

The receipts a business takes in from its trading activities are called its *sales revenue*. Sales revenue will increase directly as sales increase.

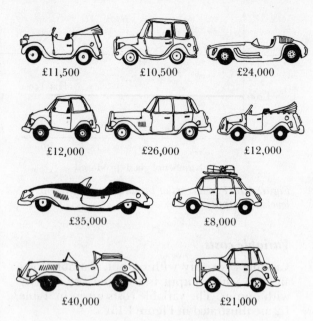

£11,500 £10,500 £24,000

£12,000 £26,000 £12,000

£35,000 £8,000

£40,000 £21,000

Figure 1.18 Sales of vintage cars.

The break-even point

If goods are sold at a constant price then an enterprise's income from sales will rise as a straight line. We have already seen that costs are made up of fixed and variable elements. The *break-even point* for a business will be at the point where costs are equal to income. A break-

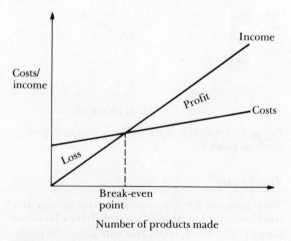

Figure 1.19 A break-even chart.

even chart as illustrated in Figure 1.19 will show how much needs to be produced in a period of time before profits start to be made.

Accounts

Financial transactions are recorded in accounts. There are two types of transaction:

1. *Cash transactions* where goods and services are exchanged and paid for immediately.
2. *Credit transactions* where goods and services are exchanged and paid for later.

Financial transactions are recorded in ledger accounts, sometimes referred to as 'T' accounts because they look like the capital letter T. Ledger accounts all have a debit and a credit side:

Dr (debit)	Name of Account	Cr (credit)
Records money or value received		Records money or value given

To show how an account works imagine that the following details represent your personal transactions in a given week.

Saturday	Received wages from part-time job: £20
	Spent £5 on a record
Tuesday	Bought book: £4.50
Wednesday	Received cash for birthday: £15
Thursday	Spent £20 on clothes
Friday	Spent £3 on haircut

You can then enter these details into your personal cash account, which would look like this:

Dr		Cash Account			Cr
		£			£
Saturday	Wages	20.00	Saturday	Record	5.00
Wednesday	Birthday	15.00	Tuesday	Book	4.50
			Thursday	Clothes	20.00
			Friday	Haircut	3.00

All the above transactions involve your cash account. You will debit the cash account when it receives money or goods. You will credit the account when it pays out money or supplies goods.

Question

Set out a cash account to show the following transactions:

1 March	–	You receive wages of £15, and on the same day you buy £3 worth of magazines.
2 March	–	You buy new clothes costing £8.
3 March	–	You receive a present of £30.
4 March	–	You spend £8 on records and £3 on fish and chips.
6 March	–	You spend £4 on getting into a disco.

The trading account

A *trading account* simply shows the purchases and sales of a business in a given period of time. The difference between sales and purchases is called gross profit. Figure 1.20 shows a simple trading account.

	Any business Ltd Trading Account		
Dr	for the period ending 31 December 19—		Cr
	£		£
Purchases	30,000	Sales	40,000
Gross profit	10,000		
	£40,000		£40,000

Figure 1.20 A simple trading account.

The profit and loss account

Net profit will give you a more accurate picture of how well a business is doing and is calculated from the profit and loss account, an example of which is given in Figure 1.21. To arrive at net

	Any business Ltd Profit and Loss Account		
Dr	for period ending 31 December 19—		Cr
	£		£
Rent	300	Gross profit	10,000
Rates	400		
Insurance	110		
Advertising	90		
Total expenditure	900		
Net profit	9,100		
	£10,000		£10,000

Figure 1.21 A simple profit and loss account.

profit we need to deduct business expenses such as wages, rent and rates – all the costs involved in making sales – from gross profit.

The objectives of running a business

Businesses are set up for many different reasons. Profit may be an important motive but it is certainly not the only one. Many people are prepared to take a cut in money earnings because of the satisfaction and freedom of working for themselves.

Small businesses can have a wide number of possible objectives, including:

1. to make as much profit as possible;
2. to provide a steady income for the owner/s;
3. to provide the freedom for the owner/s to express themselves at the work they enjoy;
4. to grow into larger organisations.

Judging the success of a business

Whether or not a business is seen as successful will depend on how the person looking at the business measures success. A number of questions need to be considered, including:

1. Does success mean that you make a large profit?
2. How big is a 'large profit'?
3. What other aims does the business have?
4. Does it live up to these aims?

Although at times a 'successful' business does not make a money profit, in the long term it might need to do so. This is particularly true when other people have put money into the enterprise. A bank manager or shareholder might not be prepared to invest money in your enterprise if it continues to lose money.

Some people might judge the enterprise to be a success if it continues to expand, employing more people, making more sales, acquiring more equipment or becoming better known.

Other people involved in an organisation may judge its success in other ways. An employee for example might regard a business as successful if the work is interesting, wages are good and employment is secure. On the other hand, cus-

tomers may regard an enterprise as a success if it provides good quality products at reasonable prices.

■ Case Study: The furniture shop

Jane Day opened up a furniture shop selling hand-made designs which she had produced herself. Her furniture was of a high quality and sold for high prices. Jane was proud of her 'quality image'.

However, her starting-up costs had been high because she had spent a lot of money on modern woodworking equipment. She had borrowed £15,000 from the bank and after three months of trading was having difficulty in repaying the interest.

At this time, a wholesaler offered her some cheap imported furniture on credit terms. She could take a delivery of the furniture and pay for it three months later. The furniture sold well and brought a lot of quick money into the business. Jane was able to make a good profit and more than pay back the interest on the loan. It did mean however that Jane had to spend rather a lot of time dealing with buying, storing and selling the imported furniture.

Questions

How might each of the following have judged the success of Jane's enterprise?

1. Jane
2. A rival furniture shop
3. Jane's bank manager
4. Jane's customers

The business balance sheet

A balance sheet summarises a business's financial affairs at a given date, usually at the end of the trading year. It is important to balance the books to show that the accounts have been kept accurately.

The main elements of the balance sheet are as follows and are illustrated in Figure 1.22:

1. *Where the money has come from.* These are

Figure 1.22 A simple example of a balance sheet.

Balance sheet of Dragina Radmilovic as at 31 December 19—			
	£		£
Capital	10,000	Fixed assets:	
Add Net profit	5,000	Land and buildings	20,000
		Motor vehicles	4,000
	15,000		
Less Drawings	500		
		Current assets:	
	14,500	Debtors	2,000
Long-term liabilities:		Stock	1,000
Mortgage	12,000	Bank	500
Current liabilities:	1,000		
	£27,500		£27,500

called the *liabilities* of the business because these sums are owed:

(a) Shareholders' funds;
(b) Loans;
(c) Profits kept in the business;
(d) Current liabilities (short-term debts).

2. *Where the money has gone to.* These are called the *assets,* i.e., the things that the business owns and the sums owed to it:

(a) Fixed assets (money tied up in buildings and equipment);
(b) Current assets (these will be turned into cash in the short term): work-in-progress, debtors, cash.

Items which can be most quickly turned into money are put at the bottom of the balance sheet.

The assets side shows *fixed* and *current assets.* (*Debtors* are customers who have bought goods or services from the business without paying cash.)

The liabilities side shows what the business owes and to whom the debts are owed. This side includes *capital* as the business owes the owners the sum of their original investment; *net profit* which adds to the amount owed to the owners; *drawings* which are moneys taken out of the business by the owners for their own use; and *creditors* who are suppliers to whom the business owes money.

Help for small businesses

There are a large number of organisations that offer help to small businesses. Unfortunately,

one criticism often made by people setting up a business is that they are not made aware of what is available and that agencies do not always work together.

Enterprise agencies have become increasingly important in providing advice and accommodation for new start-up businesses. They are supported financially by large businesses and local government, and are able to offer free advice and help as well as low rental premises.

Businesses setting up in country areas can often get direct help and support from specialist agencies.

The government itself runs a Small Firms Service. Additional help and advice is often given by large companies such as Shell UK which has its own small business unit.

People who have been unemployed for at least 13 weeks and can put up £1,000 of their own capital can apply to join the government-run Enterprise Allowance Scheme. You must first produce a convincing business idea. Once you set up you will receive a weekly sum of money for the first year of your business life.

Prince Charles has set up the Prince's Youth Trust. This is a scheme enabling young people with business ideas to receive grants and loans to get their businesses started.

■ Activity

For the following activity you need to work in three groups. Each task represents an activity related to a project being carried out by a small company producing record sleeves. An organisation chart of the company is given in Figure 1.23.

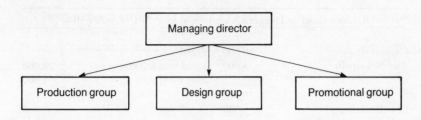

Figure 1.23 Organisational chart of the company.

The company is trying to win a contract to produce sleeves for a large record producer. In order to win the contract the company is planning a presentation to put to the record company. The presentation involves the production and design of an 18 cm sleeve and the production of a short radio jingle to support the record.

You are still at the planning stage of the presentation. You must therefore produce a presentation to be discussed by your own staff.

Before carrying out the group tasks below you must decide on the title of the record and the artist. You must also choose a managing director who has the responsibility of making sure that each group completes its task within 35 minutes.

Task 1: Production group

Your task is to produce two alternative prototypes of a blank 18 cm × 18 cm record sleeve. The sleeve must be easy to mass-produce and will use the minimum amount of materials.

Resources: A1 paper, scissors, glue, example record sleeve (to work from).

Task 2: Design group

Your task is to produce at least two alternative record sleeve designs 18 cm × 18 cm.

Resources: A1 paper, felt-tip pens.

Task 3: Promotional group

Your task is to produce two alternative 30-second radio jingles to publicise the record.

Resources: Tape recorder.

(An alternative way of running this activity is for the class to divide up into six groups (two production, two design, two promotional).)

At the end of the 35 minutes the groups should be brought back together to make presentations. The managing director should comment on whether the work is satisfactory and where further activity needs to take place.

■ Revision

Complete the following sentences using the words below:

market research	loan
cash flow	overdraft
shares	venture capital
hire-purchase	trade credit
prototype	job production
flow production	mass production
division of labour	production department
sales department	fixed costs
variable costs	average costs
balance sheet	trading account

1. The _____ of a business do not alter with output.
2. Under a _____ agreement the hirer of the equipment will not own it until the final payment has been completed.
3. A business's _____ shows its assets and liabilities at a given moment in time.
4. Small firms can often raise _____ direct from larger firms.
5. _____ involves the large-scale production of standardised items.
6. A company can offer _____ to the public if it wishes to expand.
7. _____ increase as the output of a firm increases.
8. _____ can be calculated by dividing total cost by the level of output.
9. A bank might offer a business _____ to a firm to buy a specific item of equipment.
10. Before setting up a business can carry out a

_____ analysis to calculate expected costs, revenues and profits.

11. Interest on an _____ is calculated on a day-to-day basis.

12. The extent of _____ involved in the production of a good will very often depend on the size of the market.

13. _____ will answer several important questions such as what customers are looking for and how much they are prepared to pay.

14. Many businesses offer _____ to each other to ease the problem of payment.

15. The _____ of a firm will try to win orders.

16. A _____ shows the purchases and sales of a business in a given trading period.

17. Producers will often build a _____ of an item in order to test it out.

18. The _____ of a business is responsible for controlling the output of goods.

19. _____ involves the production of single, individual items.

20. With the _____ method, production parts are passed on from one stage of production to another in a regular sequence.

CHAPTER 2
The UK industrial structure

Business activity

Business activity can be conveniently divided up into:

1. extractive (primary)
2. manufacturing (secondary)
3. services (tertiary)

Extractive industries like farming take out things which are already provided by nature, for example:

1. farmers grow crops.
2. miners take out fuel, minerals, etc.

Primary industry sometimes produces raw materials, e.g. iron ore (that goes into making steel) and oil (that makes petrol, plastics, etc.), as well as producing final products like fish and oranges.

Manufacturing and construction industries make, build and assemble products. Manufacturers will use raw materials and parts from other industries. A semi-manufactured good is one that is only part made, and most products involve several stages of production. Examples of manufactures are books, furniture, cars, chocolates and oil rigs.

Service industries are particularly important in modern Britain. Services give value to people but are not physical goods. Examples of services are banks and public transport. Services are sometimes classified as *direct services* (to people), e.g. the police, hairdressing, etc. and *commercial services* (to business), e.g. business insurance, business post, etc. However, this is not a very good classification because most commercial services like banking and the post are as much used by individuals as by business.

■ Question

Set out table headings like those below and then classify the listed activities as primary, secondary or tertiary industries.

Primary industry	Secondary industry	Tertiary industry
Fishing	Shoe-making	Cinema
…	…	…

Coal mining, Laundry, Market gardening, Transport, Key cutting, Road sweeping, Cloth making, Mushroom growing, Book illustration, Road building, Signwriting, Theatre, Window cleaning, Oil refining, Chocolate manufacture, Building, Shoe repair, Advertising, Insurance, Retailing, Civil service, Oil drilling.

In the UK, production is heavily weighted towards the service side. The percentage involved in each sector in 1987 was:

Primary	13%
Secondary	31%
Tertiary	56%

The UK manufacturing sector has been in decline over many years, particularly the so-called 'heavy' industries. Metals, mechanical engineering, motor vehicles and construction are producing less than they were ten years ago while electrical engineering and chemicals are expanding. In the service sector, communications (e.g. British Telecom) and finance (e.g. the banks) are the main growth areas.

The process when manufacturing industry goes into relative decline and the service industries

Table 2.1 Standard Industrial Classification divisions and example groupings within divisions.

Division 0: Agriculture, forestry and fishing
Farming and horticulture
Forestry
Commercial sea and inland fishing

Division 1: Energy and water supply industries
Coal mining and manufacture of solid fuels
Extraction of mineral oil and natural gas
Production and distribution of electricity, gas and other forms of energy

Division 2: Extraction of minerals and ores, manufacture of metals, mineral products and chemicals
Metal manufacture
Extraction of stone, clay, sand and gravel
Manufacture of non-metallic mineral products
Chemical industry (includes paints, varnishes and inks, pharmaceutical products, some perfumes, etc.)

Division 3: Metal goods, engineering and vehicle industries
Foundries
Mechanical engineering
Electrical and electronic engineering
Manufacture of motor vehicles and parts
Instrument engineering

Division 4: Other manufacturing industries
Food, drink and tobacco manufacturing industries
Textile industry
Manufacture of leather and leather goods
Timber and wooden furniture industries
Manufacture of paper and paper products, printing and products
Processing of rubber and plastics

Division 5: Construction
Construction and repairs
Demolition work
Civil engineering

Division 6: Distribution, hotels and catering, repairs
Wholesale distribution
Retail distribution
Hotel and catering (restaurants, cafés and other eating places, public houses, and hotel trade)
Repair of consumer goods and vehicles

Division 7: Transport and communication
Railways and other inland transport
Air and sea transport
Support services to transport
Postal services and telecommunications

Division 8: Banking, finance, insurance, business services and leasing
Banking and finance
Insurance
Business service
Renting of moveables
Owning and dealing in real estate

... continued

Table 2.1 continued

Division 9: Other services
Public administration, national defence and compulsory social security
Sanitary services
Education
Medical and other health services, veterinary services
Other services provided to the general public
Recreational services and other cultural services
Personal services (laundries, hairdressing and beauty parlours)
Domestic services
Diplomatic representation, international organisations, allied armed forces

become more important is often called de-industrial-isation.

Between June 1977 and June 1987 the number of people employed in service industries grew by 14%. Employment in financial and business services (banking, insurance, etc.) has grown a lot, as has leisure and tourism. There are also a lot more people working for themselves setting up small businesses.

For statistical purposes industries are normally grouped together under a major heading or division in what is called the Standard Industrial Classification (SIC). This is outlined in Table 2.1.

■ Questions and coursework suggestions

1. Using the Standard Industrial Classification in Table 2.1 list six groupings that are concerned with: (a) primary, (b) secondary, (c) service industry.

2. As a group, map out a large section of your town (or village) and classify businesses into each of the divisions used in the SIC.

3. The map and charts in Figures 2.1 and 2.2 relate to two adjacent local authority districts -- the city of Lincoln, and the rural area of North Kesteven which only contains one small market town, Sleaford. Lincoln combines a historic cathedral city with a modern shopping and industrial area. North Kesteven is an area of large scale agricultural production, major crops being potatoes and sugar beet. In Lincoln 55,000 people are employed compared with under 10,000 in North Kesteven.

(a) Describe and try to explain the differences you can see in the occupational structures in Lincoln and North Kesteven.

(b) Find out from your local Department of Employment (write a letter) the percentage of the workforce in each of the SIC industrial divisions in your area. Describe and try to explain the pattern that you can see.

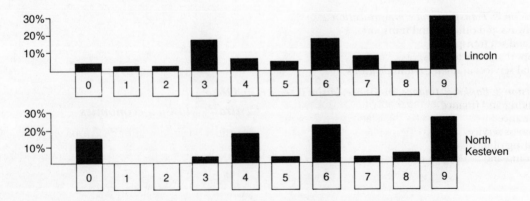

Figure 2.1   Percentage employment by SIC division.

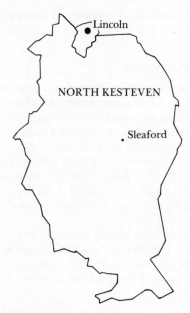

Figure 2.2 *Geographical areas of Lincoln and North Kesteven.*

Types of economy

In any society it is important to decide:

1. What to produce.
2. How to produce.
3. Who to produce for (i.e. who gets the goods).

There are many ways of making these decisions and different societies have different ways of going about things. These decisions need to be made because the resources used to produce goods are scarce.

■ Case Study: Making decisions

A group of 12 people have been washed ashore on a remote island off the West Coast of Scotland. They quickly realise that the empty tin cans which have been left by trippers on the island are a useful source of raw materials. (Tools which will help them to cut and shape the cans are found in a broken down hut.) The group carries out a brainstorming session and thinks of the following items that could be made from the tin cans (figures in brackets indicate the number of tins needed to make the items):

fish hooks (2)	drainpipe (30)
tin roof (50)	dustpan (8)
ear-rings (10)	money (50)
cups (12)	spears (25)
cooking pots (30)	other items (80)
arrows (20)	knives and forks (24)
warning system (20)	

However, there are only 100 cans in total on the island.

Questions

1. Working on your own, write down how you think that the group should decide what to make. When you have done this you should present your suggestions to the rest of the class.
2. When everyone has presented their ideas you should discuss which system would be:
    (a) quickest
    (b) slowest
    (c) most considerate of everyone's views
    (d) most fair
    (e) least fair
    (f) best
3. What is meant by 'fair'? Does everyone agree? Why might some people disagree about what is fair?
4. What does 'best' mean in this particular example?

Traditional economies

In some societies 'what', 'how' and 'for whom' decisions are settled by tradition. In the Andaman Islands, for example, in the recent past, people shared their possessions and fishing, farming, fruit gathering, and hunting were carried out in the same way year after year.

The use of resources is determined by tradition.

Centrally planned economies

In some economies major decisions will be made by a central planning body. The planning authority will collect information about the quantities of resources (e.g. coal, steel, bricks, etc.) that might be available in a given time period (e.g. five years).

They will then ask local planning authorities

to state what quantity of resources they will need and how much they will produce. The central planners will then need to decide how to allocate (give out) resources. The planning authorities will have to give careful thought to how to use resources in order to give best value to society in a given period of time. Plans can be adjusted from time to time to deal with any problems that might arise.

A major danger of this system is that local planners might deliberately overestimate the quantity of resources that they need in order to get projects finished more quickly and so boost their local output (because this makes local officials look good). Resources could be wasted in this way.

The use of resources is determined by central and local planners.

Locally planned economies

In some planned economies there is a lot of decentralisation (allowing decisions to be made in local areas). Local planning can be carried out by very small units such as co-operative farms. This system is most commonly found in countries with vast agricultural areas.

The use of resources is determined by a local plan.

The price system

In many economies, a large number of decisions about what to produce, how to produce and who gets the product are made through the price system. Rising prices of goods can signal to producers that they might be able to profit by producing items for which demand is growing. Falling prices might signal a lack of demand. When prices of some goods rise, this is a signal to consumers to shop around to see if they could spend their money on buying alternatives.

Prices also give information about ways of producing goods. Manufacturers, for example, will weigh up alternative methods of making goods in terms of how much money a project will cost, and how much profit they will make from the project.

People can 'vote' for goods by buying them with their money income.

The use of resources is determined through the price system.

The mixed economy

In most countries today there is a mixture of different ways of making economic decisions. Some decisions are made by central planners, some by local planners, some through prices and even occasionally by tradition.

Your local bus service, for example, might be subsidised by the local council because it believes that certain routes need to be kept open to help people who do not have cars (pensioners, disabled people, etc.).

Your local cinema almost certainly has to pay its own way. Decisions, therefore, about which films to show depend on the cost (price) of hiring particular films and the demand to see that film.

The use of resources is decided by both planning and by prices.

■ Questions

1. In Britain today who would make the following buying decisions, a planning official or a private citizen?
   (a) To go to the cinema
   (b) To buy military aircraft
   (c) To buy pens and paper
   (d) To buy a set of textbooks for a school
   (e) To buy police uniforms
   (f) To have a haircut
   (g) To buy medical syringes
   (h) To buy chocolate
   (i) To buy soya milk
   (j) To buy a typewriter
2. In Britain today who would make the following production decisions, a planning official or a private entrepreneur?
   (a) To build a new motorway
   (b) To build a new hospital
   (c) To build a shop
   (d) To build a town hall
   (e) To build a cinema
   (f) To build a public library
3. Which of the following decisions do you think should be made by (i) private individu-

No power for the people

● To obtain your coal coupon is one thing: you are only half way there. Now, as for actually getting your coal . . .

The night before, you take your place in the square at the gates of the coal depot. You queue all night long only to discover that there isn't enough coal for everyone. The reasons vary: sometimes lorries don't arrive, sometimes people are off sick.

How can it be that in a centralised system, with fixed prices, providing people with adequate supplies of heating fuel is such a complicated procedure? It's been a whole year since our local paper, Krymskaya Pravda, raised the issue — and still no results. Confusion continues.

Another problem: the allocated maximum amount of coal per family — 1.5 ton — is not enough, particularly during severe winters like last year. What's more, all we get is low-grade coal. Only half of it is any good — the rest is dust. As a result, towards the end of winter, people are compelled to buy coal illegally on the black market and to pay the earth for it.

Something should be done about the whole system: people should be able to buy coal at official coal depots without coupons. Not, of course, for 15 to 18 roubles per ton, but twice or even three times as much. And the coal would have to be better quality! — **V. Karienko**, Simferopol

Figure 2.3 Letter to a newspaper looking at the distribution of coal in the Soviet Union.
Source: Monthly Digest of Pravda, *April 1988.*

als, (ii) government officials? Explain your answers.
(a) The building of new roads
(b) The provision of swimming baths
(c) The size of lorries to be allowed on the roads
(d) The programmes to be shown on television

■ Case Study: The distribution of coal

The letter produced in Figure 2.3 appeared in the Russian paper *Pravda*.

Questions

1. How is coal distributed in the Soviet Union according to the letter?
2. List three problems that the letter writer sees arising from this system.

Changing fashions

IT IS not so long ago that people in the trade had to be literally forced to accept goods from the Kaluzhanka clothing factory. Coats, jackets and dresses bearing this trademark were not popular with the public.

During the last two years, however, market studies, improved quality, an updated model range and a wider assortment of output have combined to put this business to rights, resulting in successful sales not only in the Kaluga area, but also in many other areas and republics of the USSR.

Preparations were made for the transfer to self-financing, and new financial management methods came into force in the New Year. Twice as much attention is now given to the state of the market.

Figure 2.4 Newspaper article about a clothing factory in the Soviet Union.
Source: Monthly Digest of Pravda, *April 1988.*

3. Why do you think that coal is distributed by this method in the Soviet Union?
4. How does the writer suggest that the system could be made to work better?

■ Case Study: Changes in taste

The article reproduced in Figure 2.4 also appeared in *Pravda* (1988).

Questions

1. Why do you think that Kaluzhanka clothing might not have been popular in the past?
2. Why do you think that Kaluzhanka was able to

keep producing in spite of its poor reputation?
3. How has Kaluzhanka been able to change its image in the last two years?
4. What do you think is meant by 'self-financing' in this example? Why might this have helped to force change on practices at the factory?

■ Case Study: Competitive tendering 'threatens research'

Tendering is when individuals or companies put in a written bid to carry out a project. The lowest bid wins.

Figure 2.5 is an extract from an article appearing in a newspaper in April 1988.

> British archaeologists fear that American style competitive tendering could threaten the quality of important archaeological research in this country.
>
> A distinguished professor said that if American experience was anything to go by tendering would inevitably be on the grounds of price rather than quality.
>
> Archaeologists believe that government bodies will increasingly follow the American practice and invite archaeological units to compete by competitive tender to excavate sites.

Figure 2.5 Tendering to excavate archaeological sites (April 1988).

Questions

1. List five possible advantages and disadvantages of allowing competitive tendering for archaeological excavations.
2. Do you think that this sort of work should be allocated according to price? What alternative ways of allocating the work can you think of? Would these be better/worse? Explain your answer.

Public, private and mixed sectors of the economy

The public sector of an economy is the part that is run by the government. The government in Britain is responsible for almost half of all spending, much of which goes on pay to government employees and on running costs. The government is the major employer of labour in this country and its employees include civil servants, teachers and road-sweepers. The public sector also includes the public corporations which are industries and businesses that are government-owned.

The private sector of the economy includes a wide range of different types of business organisations which are owned by private individuals and groups. This sector includes giant companies like Shell and Mars as well as your local newsagent and hairdresser.

The mixed sector includes businesses and concerns which are partly government-funded and owned and partly in private hands. The local bus company may be part-owned by the local council, and the government from time to time has shareholdings in large companies such as British Petroleum.

The changing structure of business activity

It is felt that as a country's economy grows older it moves through three stages. First, it is agriculture-based. Then, as the country learns to feed itself better and begins to develop industry, labour moves from agriculture into manufacturing. The third stage is when labour moves out of manufacturing into services.

Between 1981 and 1986 the numbers employed in manufacturing in the UK fell by 18% and Britain is well into the third stage. Many people feel that this 'third wave' economy is cleaner, less noisy and more 'advanced'.

■ Case Study: Service sector employment

Table 2.2 Service sector employment in the UK.

	Numbers employed in service sector (000s)	Numbers employed in all industries (000s)
March 1984	13,340	20,745
June 1984	13,380	20,760
September 1984	13,435	20,810
December 1984	13,540	20,915
March 1985	13,600	20,950
June 1985	13,650	20,985
September 1985	13,700	21,000
December 1985	13,815	21,085

Questions

1. What has been happening to the number of people employed in the service sector?
2. In which month was there the biggest change?
3. How has the percentage of people employed in the service sector changed during 1984–85?
4. List four growing areas of service employment.

■ Case Study: Does an economy need a manufacturing base?

The following article was written by Akio Morita, Chairman of the Japanese corporation Sony.

'In the long run, an economy which has lost its manufacturing base has lost its vital centre. This is because it is only manufacturing that creates something new, which takes raw materials and fashions them into products that are of more value than the raw materials they are made from. Services depend on manufacturing. When manufacturing prospers, all industries connected with it prosper – not only are more components, parts and salesmen needed, but also more accountants, more dentists, more petrol stations, more supermarkets and more schools.

'When the manufacturing engine of an economy stalls, all these things are in less demand. You do not build dentists' offices or department stores unless you have a population with the resources to take advantage of them – and these resources can only come from jobs that add real value to goods – that is, manufacturing jobs.'

Questions

1. Do you agree with Akio Morita that manufacturing is the engine of the economy? Explain.
2. Do you agree with Akio Morita that 'these resources can only come from jobs that add real value to goods – that is, manufacturing jobs'?
3. Rewrite the above article to argue that services are the engine of the economy.
4. What dangers are there from having too large a service sector?
5. What dangers are there in having too small a service sector?

Women in industry

Women have won the vote and the right to sit in both Houses of Parliament. Britain has a woman prime minister, Margaret Thatcher. Women have gained entry to professions once closed to them, such as medicine, the law, banking and accountancy. There are women professors, women judges as well as senior women in advertising and the media. And yet there are hardly any women in the boardrooms of industry. Women managers in industry tend to be in personnel or in public relations. A study in 1987 showed that women held 5.5% of the managerial positions in industry but these tended to be at a very junior level.

There are a wide number of reasons why women have as yet not moved into managerial positions in industry on a large scale. These include:

1. Opposition to the idea from those with power to make appointments.
2. Low expectations on the part of girls. The home, school and media have tended to put over the image that girls should be lively, attractive and caring, that their jobs should either be glamorous ones like advertising or noble ones like nursing, but that these jobs will come second to marriage and the family.

Today some of these attitudes are changing. It is in the new, expanding service industries that women are being treated more as equals and enlightened parents and teachers are tackling the problems of low expectations by encouraging equal opportunities.

Many of the new jobs being created today are

taken by women. However, most of these jobs are part-time ones. In 1987 women made up 45% of the labour force but about half worked part-time.

Part-time work tends to offer pay and conditions that compare unfavourably with those of full-time workers doing similar work. Pension rights, job security, holidays and training are often less favourable. Part-time workers have fewer prospects for promotion because, in the kind of work they do, there are few opportunities. Women workers tend to be concentrated in the three C's: cleaning, catering and clerical.

■ Case Study: Women's employment in Lincolnshire

Questions

1. Examine Table 2.3. In which industrial group do you find the greatest number of men in Lincolnshire?
2. In which industrial group do you find the greatest number of women in Lincolnshire?
3. In which four industrial groups do you find the greatest concentration of women (i.e. biggest percentage)? How would you explain this?
4. In which industrial groups do you find the smallest concentration of women? How would you explain this?
5. Draw a bar chart showing the percentage of women concentrated in primary, secondary and tertiary occupations. Compare this with a bar chart showing male employment.

The growth of small firms

In 1987 there were about 1.6 million small firms in the UK employing 200 or fewer people. They have created around six million jobs. Without them, Britain's unemployment problem would be a lot worse.

In recent years the government have produced a range of measures to encourage small businesses. Big firms have also been taking an interest in small firms. Shell UK, for example, has its own small firms unit offering free advice, and the Shell Enterprise Fund grants loans of up to £5,000 to small enterprises with worthwhile projects. Shell also runs 'Livewire', a business competition for young people.

Many big firms have always been heavily dependent upon small firms. Tobacco and newspaper manufacturers and wholesalers and other trades that sell a large proportion of their output through thousands of small retail outlets are obvious examples. Others are the oil companies, the brewers, confectionery, publishing and insurance companies.

As small firms play an increasingly important part in the economy the banks have been competing strongly to pick up their accounts, by offering advice, easy to pay back loans and other incentives.

Table 2.3 Employees in employment (by SIC industry and sex) in Lincolnshire.

Industrial group	Male	Female	Total	Females as % of total
9 Other services	17,108	29,552	46,660	63
6 Distribution/hotel and catering/repairs	19,108	20,288	39,468	51
4 Other manufacturing	12,081	9,592	21,673	44
3 Metal goods/vehicle	18,373	3,211	21,584	15
0 Agriculture/forestry/fishery	11,691	5,514	17,205	32
7 Transport/communications	7,674	1,790	9,464	19
8 Bank/finance/insurance	4,735	4,619	9,354	49
5 Construction	8,150	854	9,004	9
2 Extractive minerals	2,309	507	2,816	18
1 Energy/water	2,124	399	2,523	16
Total	103,425	76,326	179,751	42

Causes of the changing structure of business activity

As new economies such as Korea and Taiwan have increasingly taken a larger share of world manufacturing, countries like the United Kingdom have become more service based. The increasing use of automatic machinery has meant that a large number of manufacturing jobs have disappeared.

Automation is the process by which machines are programmed to control themselves, e.g. in an automatic car gear-changing and other operations do not involve the driver.

Large business organisations have become increasingly less labour intensive (i.e. the amount of labour relative to machinery and other inputs is falling). Large organisations with spare capital have been in the best positions to automate and use bigger, faster, more accurate and more versatile machinery.

■ Revision

Complete the sentences opposite using the words below:

primary	tertiary
mixed economy	Standard Industrial
central planning	Classification
prices	traditional economy
public sector	part-time
private sector	cleaning, catering and
mixed sector	clerical
automation	labour intensive
local plan	extractive industry
local council	resources
secondary	local cinema

1. The _____ is an example of an organisation in the private sector of the economy.
2. Fishing, mining and agriculture are all examples of _____ industries.
3. An _____ takes out natural resources.
4. In a _____ decisions are made in the same way generation after generation.
5. _____ indicate to producers the wishes of consumers in a free enterprise economy.
6. _____ employment is a typical feature of working life for many women.
7. _____ is a common form of economic organisation in Eastern European countries.
8. Land, labour and capital are all examples of productive _____.
9. The fastest growing sector of the UK economy is made up of _____ industries.
10. The _____ is used to catgorise employment.
11. Manufacturing jobs are classified as _____ industries.
12. The _____ of the economy is government-owned.
13. The _____ is responsible for supervising local government services.
14. _____ are the three occupations with the highest concentration of part-time female labour.
15. The _____ of the economy includes government and privately owned firms.
16. Newsagents are all in the _____ of the economy.
17. A _____ industry would have a low capital/labour ratio.
18. A _____ is a feature of a decentralised state-planned economy.
19. A _____ combines the price system with a government-owned sector.
20. _____ involves the control of machines by machines.

CHAPTER 3
Business enterprise

Main types in the private sector

The main types of business organisation in the private sector are shown in Table 3.1.

Shareholders in companies and co-operatives have the legal protection of limited liability. Sole traders and ordinary partners cannot have limited liability.

Limited liability means that, if the business goes bankrupt because it is unable to meet its debts, the shareholders/owners will not be liable (responsible by law) to lose their possessions to pay the money that is owed. The maximum amount that they could lose is the amount that they have put into their shares.

The sole trader

The sole trader is the most common form of business ownership and is found in a wide range of activities (e.g. graphic designers, signwriters, jewellers, window cleaners, market traders, etc.).

No complicated paperwork is required to set the business up, decisions can be made quickly and close contact can be kept with customers and employees. All profits go to sole traders, who also have the satisfaction of building up their own businesses.

Disadvantages of being a sole trader are that you have to make all the decisions yourself, you may have to work long hours (what do you do if you are ill or want a holiday?), you do not have limited liability, and you have to provide all the finance for yourself. As a sole trader you need to

Table 3.1 Types of business organisation in the private sector.

Type of enterprise	Who owns the enterprise?	Who controls the enterprise?	Usual sources of finance
Sole trader	1 person	1 person controls	Owners' savings, bank loans and overdrafts, profits.
Partnership	2–20 partners	Partners control	Partners' savings, bank loans and overdrafts, profits.
Company	2 to any number of shareholders	Major decisions and day-to-day running by directors.	Shares, bank loans and overdrafts, venture capital and profits.
Co-operative	2 to any number	Decisions jointly made by managers and other co-operators.	Shares, bank loans and overdrafts, profits.

Figure 3.1 Maggie Rainsthorpe – sole trader.

be a jack-of-all-trades – just because you are a good hairdresser does not necessarily mean you have a head for business!

■ Case Study: The sole trader

Maggie Rainthorpe opened up Magpie Fashions in Grantham when she was 21. Maggie had been interested in design and dressmaking for as long as she could remember. Before setting up her own business she had worked for a firm of specialist dressmakers.

Setting up was a big gamble. She had first of all interviewed a few people to see what they felt about the range of clothes on offer in Grantham. She found that there appeared to be a gap in the market for good quality interesting clothes and for ballgowns to hire.

Maggie worked out how much it would cost her to make her own clothes and how much she could sell them for. The figures suggested that if she could find a shop site in a good position with low property costs then she would be able to make a living from doing something that she enjoyed.

A number of shop sites became available. Maggie was particularly interested in one at the junction of three major roads running through Grantham (see Figure 3.2). Most people in the town pass this way

at some time during the week and the junction is a bottleneck for traffic. People sit in their cars looking in the shop windows. The shop had a low rental charge and seemed an ideal location.

Maggie took the plunge, and set up in business in 1987. She divided the shop into two sections. The back section is used as a workshop to make new

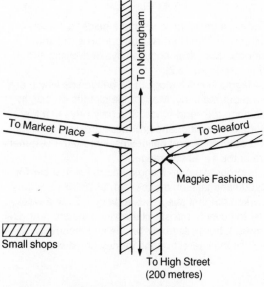

Figure 3.2 Location of Magpie Fashions.

Figure 3.3 Magpie Fashions shop-front.

Questions

1. List eight different jobs that Maggie might have to do to run her business.
2. Why might it be a problem to have to be a 'jack-of-all-trades'?
3. What do you think was the most important decision that Maggie had to make in setting up her business? Explain your answer.
4. List three advantages to Maggie of being a sole trader.
5. List three disadvantages to Maggie of being a sole trader.
6. As a sole trader Maggie would not have limited liability. Explain how this could cause her worry.
7. Do you think that Maggie chose a good location? Explain your answer. What further information would you want to know to give a better answer?
8. What market research did Maggie do before setting up? What else did she do before making the decision to set up?
9. Describe two sacrifices that Maggie made in setting up in business.

The partnership

An ordinary partnership can have between two and twenty partners. They are often found in businesses where people can share skills, share the workload, and when more capital is needed than can be raised by a single owner.

For example, a group of vets is able to pool knowledge of different diseases and groups of animals. By having at least two or three vets working together they are also able to operate a 24-hour service. When one of the vets is ill or goes on holiday, the business can cope.

Partnerships are usually set up by writing out a 'deed of partnership' which is witnessed by a solicitor. This sets out important details such as how much each partner should put into the business, how the profits and losses will be shared, and the responsibilities of each partner.

Partnerships are particularly common in professional services such as doctors' practices, solicitors' and accountants'. Small businesses such as corner-shops may take the form of a husband and wife partnership. Builders, plumbers and other household services also frequently take this form of organisation.

clothes, a dressing room and a place to display the ballgowns. The front section contains the shop window, cash desk and displays of dresses and tops (see Figure 3.3).

Maggie keeps a stock of 25 ballgowns which are hired out regularly. Most of the clothes on sale in the shop are hand-made. She only buys in a few clothes for resale. She produces dresses, T-shirts and other tops, and ballgowns. Her main customers are in the 17–40 age range.

In order to set up Maggie had to sell her car for £3,000 and take on a bank loan of £8,000. She has worked out that she needs to take in £124 a week just to cover her costs. Her main costs are rent (£54 a week), business taxes, phone and electricity, as well as the interest on the money borrowed.

The main disadvantages of partnerships are that: people can fall out (she doesn't work as hard as me!), ordinary partnerships do not have limited liability, and partnerships can rarely borrow or raise large amounts of capital. Business decisions may be more difficult to make (and slower) because of the need to consult partners. There may be disagreements about how things should be done. A further disadvantage is that profits will be shared.

There is also a special form of partnership called a *limited partnership*. Limited partners (sometimes called sleeping partners) can put money into a partnership and have the protection of limited liability. However, they play no part in the running of the business. The business will be run by at least one non-limited partner.

■ Case study: Poise

At school Lesley Mensah enjoyed designing and making her own clothes. Lesley's mother had often had a circle of friends sewing and making garments at home.

After leaving university Lesley had first of all gone into a science-based career. However, she had continued with her clothes designing in her spare time. A number of people showed an interest in her designs and in 1986 she was offered a stand at the London Fashion Show. Her clothes were a big hit and C & A asked her to make a range of outfits for them. She decided to go into fashion design on a full-time basis. She was now designing, manufacturing and selling clothes. This involved going round to boutiques to pick up orders before actually making the clothes. She soon found out that it was too much work to be done by one person.

Lesley asked at the London School of Fashion to see if there was another young designer who would be prepared to join her. Carol Sewell had just graduated from the London School of Fashion when she agreed to set up a partnership with Lesley. Carol had done a wide range of fashion design and production jobs before joining Lesley and had already worked for a number of top designers.

The business which they run is called Poise and today it has a national and international reputation. Their clothes have appeared in all the major fashion

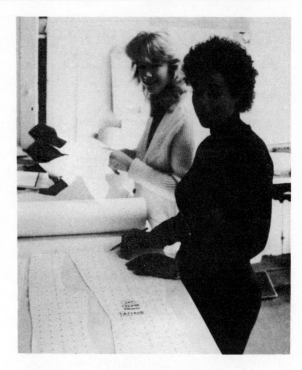

Figure 3.4 Lesley Mensah and Carol Sewell.

magazines and at some of the best fashion shows in Europe. Carol tends to concentrate on the design and manufacture side of the business. Lesley handles some of the design work, the selling and the general administration.

Questions

1. Why did Lesley Mensah find it necessary to form a partnership with Carol?
2. What advantages were there to be gained by forming a partnership?
3. What possible disadvantages might there be to such a partnership?
4. What do you think the success of the partnership would depend upon?
5. Would Lesley have been able to survive as a sole trader? Explain your answer.

■ Coursework suggestion

What are the main problems of setting up a small business and how can these problems be tackled?

Figure 3.5 Advertisement for the Carousel
Dress Agency

A group of students investigated a small business called Carousel. It is a second-hand dress agency, an advertisement for which is given in Figure 3.5. They set out to find out some typical problems faced by a small business. They wanted to evaluate how successful the owner had been in tackling these problems and to come up with some alternative strategies.

First of all they discussed the sorts of problems that they would expect a typical small business to have. They then put together sets of related questions about location, marketing, finance, etc. When they had chosen some questions they then evaluated them in terms of how useful they would be to tackle the main question.

They then wrote up their work individually. This involved explaining what they considered to be the major problems and how the owner, Margaret Greaves, had gone about tackling these problems. They then looked at alternative strategies. For example, raising capital could have been done through savings, a bank business loan, a bank overdraft, borrowing from friends and relatives, etc.

They examined the alternative marketing strategies that Margaret could have used. They considered questions like should Margaret have done more market research, and could she have chosen a better location? They concluded by considering whether Margaret had made a success of tackling her problems. Finally, they thought about whether Margaret's problems were unique or common to other small businesses.

Set about your own investigation of a small local business.

Companies

A company is set up to run a business. It has to be registered before it can start to operate, but once all the paperwork is filled in and approved the company becomes recognised as a legal body.

The owners of a company are its shareholders. However, other individuals and businesses do not deal with the shareholders – they deal with 'the company'.

Shareholders put funds into a company by buying shares. New shares are often sold in face values of £1 per share, but this is only a general rule. Some shareholders will only have a few hundred pounds worth of shares, whereas large shareholders may have millions of pounds worth. This is illustrated in Figure 3.6.

There are two main types of companies:

1. Private limited companies
2. Public limited companies

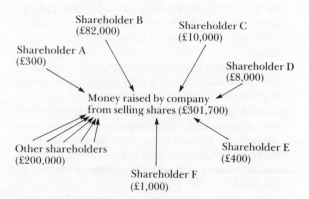

Figure 3.6 Shareholdings in a company.

Private companies

Private companies tend to be smaller than public ones and are often found in family businesses. There must be at least two shareholders but there is no maximum number. Shares in private companies cannot be bought on the Stock Exchange and often shares can only be bought with the permission of the board of directors.

The board of directors is a committee set up to protect shareholders. The members of the board choose the managing director, who is responsible for the day-to-day running of the business. The rules of the business set out when shareholders' meetings will take place and the rights of shareholders.

Private companies can raise more cash (by selling shares) than unlimited businesses. The shareholders also have the protection of limited liability. Private companies are also usually big enough to have specialist managers.

The disadvantages compared with unlimited businesses are that they have to share out profits among shareholders, they cannot make decisions so quickly and they cost more to set up as well as involving a lot more paperwork.

Public companies

A public company has its shares sold on the Stock Exchange. Today, companies can go to the expense of having a full quotation on the Stock Exchange so that their share prices will appear on the dealers' visual display screens at the Stock Exchange. Alternatively they might choose to enter the Unlisted Securities Market or what is known as the third market whereby they only trade a small proportion of their shares on the Stock Market and prices are not quoted in the financial press.

The advantage of selling shares through the Stock Exchange is that millions of pounds can be raised very quickly. Disadvantages are that businesses can be bought and sold by takeover bids which are beyond the control of the original owners. It is also very costly to have your shares quoted on the Stock Exchange.

In order to become a public company you must apply to the Stock Exchange Council which will carefully check your books. A business wanting to go public will then arrange for a merchant bank, e.g. Rothschild's, Schroder's, Baring's, etc., to handle the paperwork.

Selling new shares is quite a risky business. The Stock Exchange has 'good days' (when a lot of people want to buy shares) and 'bad days' (when a lot of people want to sell). If the issue of new shares coincides with a bad day a company can lose millions of pounds. For example, if a company hopes to sell a million new shares at £1 each and all goes well, it will raise £1 million. However, on a bad day the company might only be able to sell half of its shares at this price – it then stands to lose a lot of money.

The way round this problem is to arrange a 'placing' with a merchant bank. The merchant bank will recommend your shares to some of the share-buying institutions that it deals with, e.g. pension funds and insurance companies, who may then agree to buy, say, one-tenth of the new shares. In this way the merchant bank makes sure that the shares are placed with large investors before the actual date of issue comes round. Then, even if it is a bad day on the Stock Exchange when the shares are issued, the company's money is secure.

Another common method by which public companies raise share capital is by offering new shares for sale to the general public. The company's shares will be advertised in leading newspapers, and the public will be invited to apply for shares.

When companies are up and running a cheap way of selling extra shares is to write to existing shareholders inviting them to buy new shares. This is known as a *rights issue*.

■ Case study: The growth of Angus Brown

In 1907, Dorothy Angus set up her own dressmaking shop in Edinburgh. She employed two seamstresses to work on the patterns she produced. The business flourished and was soon producing dresses for a number of shops in Edinburgh. Dorothy then joined up with Moira Brown who up to that time had been involved in making bridal wear. The partnership they formed concentrated on 'bridal wear and better quality garments'. The partnership deed set out that each would put £1,000 into the business, share the work and profits. They would be entitled to two weeks' holiday a year. Dorothy would concentrate on design and production, whilst Moira would deal with selling. They then had a workforce of 15 full-time employees, including a bookkeeper.

Between the wars, Moira was taken ill and could no longer help in running the business. The deed of partnership was altered: Moira left her money in the business and became a sleeping partner whilst the profits were to be divided 75 : 25 in Dorothy's favour.

In 1952 Dorothy also decided to retire from the day-to-day running of the business. Sarah McPhee became the managing director of the newly formed private company Angus Brown Ltd. Shares were issued in the new company at £2.00 each.

There were now four shareholders: Dorothy Angus (5,000 shares), Moira Brown (4,000 shares), Sarah McPhee (2,000 shares), Elizabeth Angus (2,000 shares). Elizabeth was Dorothy's niece and she was able to bring her accountancy skills to the business. Dorothy and Moira were still the main owners of the business, but the major day-to-day policy decisions were to be made by Sarah.

During the 1970s it was decided to buy up a chain of small shops in several major cities. The finance was raised by a sale of shares to the general public. Today, Dorothy and Moira's shares only account for 15% of the total share capital of the company. Elizabeth Angus is now the managing director and shareholders meet once a year to discuss company policy at the annual general meeting. The business now has plc after its name.

Questions

1. Who originally owned and controlled the business?
2. Who now:
   (a) owns the business?
   (b) controls the business?
3. How has Dorothy Angus's power to influence the running of the business altered over the years?
4. What have been the four main organisational structures that the business has had over the years?
5. At what stage would Dorothy Angus have acquired limited liability?
6. What benefits would Angus Brown have gained when it became a private company?

7. What benefits would Angus Brown have gained when it became a public company?

■ Case study: Takeover bid for Rowntree

Figure 3.7 reproduces an extract from a newspaper article from April 1988 looking at Suchard's proposed takeover bid of Rowntree.
(*Note:* In June 1988 the board of Rowntrees accepted an increased bid from another Swiss multinational, Nestlé.)

Questions

1. What major problem of being a public company is illustrated by the newspaper article in Figure 3.7?
2. How were Suchard's trying to take over Rowntree?
3. List three major motives behind the takeover.
4. What is meant by a global market?
5. Why might the control of global markets be of particular use to chocolate manufacturers?
6. Which individuals and groups might possibly have lost out if this takeover had succeeded?

Co-operatives

Co-operatives have become increasingly popular as a means of business organisation in recent years. At one time they were only to be found in agriculture and retailing. In recent years the biggest growth areas have been in service occupations as well as in small-scale manufacturing.

The basic idea behind a co-operative is that people join together to make decisions, work and share profits.

There are many different types of co-operative. Three which are most commonly found in business are:

1. retail co-operatives
2. producers' co-operatives
3. marketing co-operatives

Retail co-operatives

The first successful co-operative in this country was set up in the northern town of Rochdale in the last century. Twenty-eight weavers clubbed

Suchard poised for Rowntree bid

The takeover bid which Rowntree has long feared emerged yesterday. In a dawn raid on the stock market, the Swiss coffee and chocolate group, Jacobs Suchard, bought 14.9% of the shares.

It plans to buy a further ten per cent in a week's time to put its holding up to 25%.

Rowntree's chairman, described the development as 'wholly unwelcome' and not in the interests of shareholders or employees, pointing out that the Swiss group had a much narrower range of brands.

The attraction is the world market for famous brands. Confectionery, like car manufacturing, has gone global, and Suchard's are a firm believer in global selling. The main brand of Suchard is Toblerone.

Suchard is in the top four in confectionery, with Mars the world market leader by far. Behind it, Suchard, Rowntree and Nestlé are all of much the same size, each with about six per cent of the world market.

Jacobs Suchard was formed by the joining together of three famous firms, Suchard founded in 1825, Tobler founded in 1867, and Jacobs, mainly a coffee business, founded in 1895. Jacobs joined the other two only as recently as 1982.

When Mr Jacobs took charge of Suchard in 1982, he had a clear image of what had to happen based on the information that Europe's trade barriers would be removed and his group's strong position in Central Europe could be extended to cover the whole continent.

Suchard is looking well beyond Europe. It is about to raise £200m with a rights issue to expand in the Far East, It has recently bought out smaller companies in America and Belgium.

A key attraction of taking over Rowntree is its skill in handling filled chocolate bars that are sold in supermarkets, whereas Suchard's main strength is in block chocolate.

Rowntree is currently the leading seller of boxed chocolate in Germany, the joint market leader in chocolate in France, and second biggest in Holland, while Sweden eats more After Eight mints per head of population than anywhere else in the world. Rowntree's best known brand on a world scale is Kit-Kat.

Figure 3.7 Extract from a newspaper article about a proposed takeover bid.

together to set up their own retail shop, selling a few basic grocery items. The profits of the business were to be shared according to the amount spent, and everyone would have an equal say in how the shop should be run.

The basic ideas started in Rochdale continue in today's co-ops. By buying a £1 share in the co-op you are entitled to go along to the annual general meeting to discuss policy (see Figure 3.8). Profits are still shared out among the 'co-operators' (shoppers).

Producers' co-operatives

There are many types of producers' co-operative. A workers' co-operative, for example, is one that employs all or most of its members. In a workers' co-operative members will:

1. share responsibility for the success or failure of the business;
2. work together;
3. take decisions together;
4. share profits amongst the co-operators.

Other examples of producers' co-ops include:

1. a growers' co-operative producing tomatoes
2. a carpentry co-operative making furniture
3. a sewing co-operative making clothes
4. a child-minding co-operative
5. a laundry

The main problems that such co-operatives face are those of finance and organisation. Co-operators sometimes find it difficult to raise capital from banks and other bodies because they are not profit-making organisations. A number of co-operatives in recent years have, however, been able to raise finance by selling shares. Some larger co-operatives have also found that it is necessary to set up a management structure in order to get decisions made.

■ Case study: Paperback Ltd

Figure 3.9 reproduces a newspaper article about Paperback Ltd, a small co-operative attempting to raise finance by selling shares.

Figure 3.8 Advertisement for the AGM of the Greater Nottingham Co-operative Society.

Marketing co-operatives

Marketing co-operatives are most frequently found in farming areas. The farmers set up a marketing board to be responsible for, among other things, grading, packaging, distributing, advertising and selling the farmers' products.

Main types in the public sector

The government has a shareholding in some enterprises and direct ownership of a number of major firms and industries. Local government also has a stake in some enterprises.

Local government enterprises

Municipal enterprises

The local council often runs business activities of its own. For example, in municipal car parks, attendants may be paid to collect parking charges from people using the car park and to check that no one is using the car park without paying. There is a wide range of other services which may be run by the local council, including swimming pools, day nurseries, bus services, parks and leisure centres.

Finance to run municipal enterprises usually comes from local taxes and from charges for using the services.

Council-backed enterprise schemes

The local council might also sponsor job creation schemes. For example, it might set up enterprise workshops where people can start up a business in premises with a very low rental charge.

Central government enterprises

There are three main ways of setting up public ownership of business which have been used in Britain:

1. an activity may be run by a government department;
2. an activity may be run by a public company in which the government has a shareholding;
3. an activity may be run by a public corporation.

Activities controlled by a government department

When an activity is run by a government department a government minister will be in overall charge. The department will then be staffed and run by civil servants. A typical example of this would be the Department of Inland Revenue which deals with the collection of some taxes.

There are a number of criticisms of such an organisation from a business point of view including:

Recycled paper co-op to raise £50,000

A SMALL East London co-operative is joining the swelling ranks of non profit-motivated companies attempting to raise money with loan or equity issues to the public. Paperback Ltd, a fast-growing supplier of recycled paper, has launched a £50,000 loan stock issue.

Jan Kuiper, one of the founders of Paperback, says normal borrowing is more difficult for a co-operative than for a conventionally structured company. Hence the loan stock, which is being marketed in parcels of £100 to sympathetic investors interested in saving trees.

The cost, including printing the prospectus, consultancy, postage, direct mailshots and advertising, is more than £4,000. Investors are offered a minimum 5 per cent interest rate. So far Paperback have had 60 requests for the prospectus and £1,500 has been pledged.

According to Peter Webster of the Ethical Investment Research Service, small businesses are increasingly tapping investors who want to back ventures with some social value.

Last year Tradecraft, a Christian-based importer of products from the Third World, raised £1m through a share issue with a maximum 6 per cent dividend. The Industrial Common Ownership Fund recently collected £500,000 with a share issue.

Figure 3.9 Newspaper article regarding a co-operative raising money by selling shares.
Source: The Independent, *Thursday 31 March 1988.*

1. decisions are made slowly because there are many links in the chain of command;
2. the organisation does not have to be efficient because there is no competition;
3. there is nobody to protect the public's interest by checking on how the department runs.

Activities controlled by companies in which the government has a shareholding

Over the years the government has had shareholdings in a number of public companies, including BP and Rolls-Royce. The shareholding has often been a form of subsidy to the company to help it carry out research, compete with overseas companies, or to prevent unemployment. In recent years the government has been selling off these shareholdings in the belief that companies should stand on their own feet.

Activities controlled by public corporations

The main form of direct government involvement in business ownership has been in the form of public corporations. These are owned by the government on behalf of the people, and are felt to be a suitable form of public ownership because, although the government owns the corporation, the controllers of the corporation are given a lot of freedom to make their own decisions.

A public corporation is set up by an Act of Parliament, and a government minister is made responsible for the industry concerned, e.g., the Minister of Transport is responsible for British Rail. However, the minister must choose a chairperson to run the industry on a day-to-day basis.

The government sets yearly targets for the particular industry to meet. The chairperson and other managers must then decide on the best way to meet these targets. For example, the government might set British Rail a target of making a 15% profit in 1995. The corporation must then decide which lines to concentrate on, which to cut back on, how much to allow in wages, what prices to charge, etc., to meet this target. The corporation is supposed to have the freedom to make these 'day-to-day' decisions and there is a lot of heated debate in the press and parliament if the government tries to interfere.

Up to 1979 many public corporations were given large financial subsidies by the government. There were two main reasons for this:

1. to try to maintain jobs in declining industries (e.g. coal, steel);
2. to encourage the corporations to run services which, although not financially profitable, were of great benefit to certain individuals, groups and communities. Examples would be the provision of electricity and postal services to out-of-the-way places.

Since 1979 public corporations have been encouraged to concentrate more on meeting financial targets, and to be more profit conscious (profit meaning money in the bank).

Members of the public do have some control over the running of a public corporation:

1. They can make complaints to their local MP who can then ask questions in Parliament when the public corporation is being discussed.
2. A committee of MPs has the job of keeping an eye on each of the public corporations.
3. Each public corporation has a consumers' council to which complaints can be made.

Public corporations are sometimes called nationalised industries. Examples of public corporations in 1988 were British Coal, British Rail and the BBC.

Privatisation

One of the major policies of the Conservative government of the 1980s has been that of privatisation. This means putting public sector businesses into private hands (see Figure 3.10). Examples of industries that have been privatised

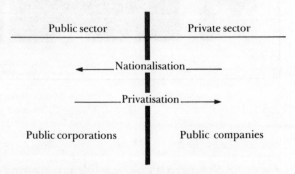

Figure 3.10 Privatisation and nationalisation.

have been British Gas, British Telecom and British Airways.

A number of reasons have been given for privatisation:

1. *To create wider share ownership.* The idea here is that by owning shares in public services like the telephones, electricity, water, gas, etc., people will feel more involved.
2. *To make these industries more competitive.* It is felt that if some of these industries are encouraged to compete more they will produce a better service. In the past losses were made up by taxes. Losses today could lead to bankruptcy.
3. *To raise money* from the sale of the industries so that the government can lower taxes.

There are many opponents of privatisation. They say that the public already owned these industries and that they have lost the ownership to a few million shareholders. Opponents also say that by competing to make financial profits these industries will be cutting services which are a real benefit to certain individuals, groups and communities, and that the money raised from the sale is only helping to cut the taxes of the better off.

■ Case study: Privatisation in China

Privatisation is a world-wide phenomenon. Figure 3.11 reproduces a newspaper article describing the effects of privatisation on health care in China.

Health care begins to go private in China

By Jonathan Mirsky

MARKET FORCES have hit the Chinese health service. Large areas of medicine in the world's largest Communist country are being privatised. This marks another step in the reforms associated with Deng Xiaoping, which dictate that the profit motive is a great spur to action, and that if consumers are willing to pay for something it should be provided.

Medical care in China is rarely free, but until recently charges were modest. However, the idea that health care is an absolute right for which the state should bear the burden is changing. It is "unreasonable" that hospitals are running at a loss, the Vice-Minister of Public Health, He Jiesheng, told a recent meeting in Peking. He claimed that fees cover only one-third of costs.

Chinese medical workers have been informally charging for special care for some time; there are already 133,000 private practitioners, 9 per cent of the national total, and 44,700 collectively-owned — virtually private — medical centres provide 22 per cent of China's health care. Almost one million Chinese already pay for private medicine.

All this is to be expanded. The Ministry of Health will now permit "mismanaged hospitals" to be leased out, and medical centres are to charge government institutions for rat- and insect-extermination, and for monitoring the environment, especially in factories.

Doctors and nurses, whose incomes are low in China, will be encouraged to charge for care in their free time, and hospitals will raise money for new equipment in the community or by issuing shares among medical staff.

According to the Minister of Health, Chen Minzhang, "China's medical facilities are now working under a system of diversified ownership, with public ownership as the centre, and compensation based on performance has aroused enthusiasm on all fronts".

Figure 3.11 Newspaper article about the privatisation of health care in China.

Questions

1. What evidence is shown by this article that the existing system of health care in China is not working effectively?
2. What reforms is China introducing to deal with this problem?
3. How are they expected to make health care more effective?
4. How might individuals and organisations benefit from the new system?
5. How might individuals and organisations lose out from the new system?
6. Do you think that the new system will be fairer than the old one?
7. What do you mean by fairer?

■ Revision

Complete the following sentences using the words below:

sole trader	partnership
private	public
limited liability	shareholders
placing	deed of partnership
offer for sale	rights issue
retail co-operative	marketing co-operative
municipal enterprise	British Rail
British Gas	Act of Parliament
nationalisation	privatisation
consumers' council	wider share ownership

1. A cheap way of raising share capital is by offering a _____ to existing shareholders.
2. Shareholders in a company have the protection of _____.
3. _____ involves the transfer of private companies to the public sector.
4. One of the arguments put forward for privatisation is that it would create _____.
5. A _____ is a person who owns a business by him or herself.
6. A public corporation will be set up by an _____.
7. A _____ can have between two and twenty owners.
8. _____ is an example of a public corporation.
9. _____ is an example of an industry that has been privatised.
10. A _____ company can have its shares quoted on the Stock Exchange.
11. A _____ company is often a family business.
12. In a _____ the profits will be shared by the shoppers.
13. Consumers' interests will be protected in a public corporation by a _____.
14. _____ involves the transfer of public corporations to the private sector.
15. New companies might find that it is safer to have new shares issued by a _____ with financial institutions.
16. It is important in setting up a partnership to have the _____ witnessed by a solicitor.
17. A public company is owned by its _____.
18. An _____ of shares by a public company is usually advertised in national newspapers.
19. A _____ is often used to dispose of agricultural produce.
20. A local government enterprise often takes the form of a _____.

CHAPTER 4
Business expansion

How do firms grow?

■ Case study: *Agritrader*

Chris Davies produces an agricultural advertising magazine that is posted to every farmer in Dyfed. Chris readily admits that he took a gamble when he launched the magazine: the first copy was put together on the kitchen table of the caravan which was the Davies' home at the time.

Chris had very little capital to set the business up with. He persuaded a firm to let him hire a photocopier on credit, and then had to persuade local farm suppliers to buy advertising space in the magazine. Fortunately, his first customers were prepared to pay cash immediately and Chris was able to arrange a postage discount with the Post Office.

The sale of the advertising space in the first copy of the magazine brought in much-needed cash. The gamble had paid off, and *Agritrader* – as the magazine is called – has since gone from strength to strength.

For the next nine months, *Agritrader* was printed by a local printing firm. Chris then bought his own press and as this has proved successful is thinking of buying a larger press and taking in other printing jobs.

Chris was able to buy the mailing list of Dyfed farmers from a firm called Business Data Base which does the research for *Yellow Pages*. The magazine advertises all sorts of agricultural machinery and products and is mailed to 7,000 farmers.

The cost of producing a 20-page magazine is very little more than the cost of producing 16 pages, but the revenue is substantially more. Chris estimates that he breaks even if he produces 16 pages.

Agritrader comes out once a month but only needs three days of printing press time to put it together. Chris is currently hoping to take on other printing jobs for businesses and organisations in the area. He is also hoping to sell franchises to people in other parts of the country to produce *Agritrader*. The franchisees will have their local *Agritrader* magazines printed at Llandyssul.

Questions

1. Set out a flowchart setting out the steps in the growth of *Agritrader*.

   e.g. Step 1 – Chris rents a photocopier.
       Step 2 –

2. What measures could we use to chart the growth of *Agritrader* over a period of time, e.g. level of profits, etc.?
3. What motives might *Agritrader* have for wanting to expand?
4. Who do you think will have benefited from the growth of *Agritrader* up to the point at which it purchased its first printing press?
5. Who do you think might have lost out as a result of the growth of *Agritrader* up to this point? Explain your reasoning.
6. Why is *Agritrader* more profitable with 20 pages rather than 16?
7. What would you expect to happen to the costs and revenue of the business if it started to sell franchises? Explain your answer.
8. Working in groups you should study a local business to find out:
   (a) How it has expanded.
   (b) Why it has expanded.
   Each group should present their findings to the

class. The class should then try to set out some general notes on how and why firms grow in size.

■ Case study: Shell

Shell had its origins in a small shop started by Marcus Samuel in the East End of London. Samuel dealt in antiques and curiosity items, such as shells from the Orient which were very popular as display items in Victorian houses. The trade in shells became so popular that Samuel arranged for regular shipments to be brought in from the Far East.

In 1870, Marcus Samuel Senior died and his sons Marcus Samuel and Samuel Samuel took over the business as a partnership. In 1878 they developed the business into private companies operating in London and Japan. By the middle of the 1880s Marcus Samuel became involved in the transport of paraffin (a form of liquid fuel) from Russia to the Far East. He had a fleet of tankers built to transport the kerosene on the sea voyage.

The Samuels' main rival in the Far East market was the Royal Dutch Petroleum Company which had opened up an oilfield in the East Indies. For many years the two companies battled it out to win the biggest share of the market. In 1907 the two companies came together in a merger, adopting the original name Shell.

Today Shell is a household name and operates in nearly every country in the world. Shell is a major employer, the producer of a wide number of products, and an organisation that believes in helping smaller businesses grow to become part of a wider community. Figure 4.1 illustrates the growth of Shell from Marcus Samuel's small antique shop to today's giant multinational.

Questions

1. What measures could we use to chart the growth of Shell over a period of time, e.g., range of activities etc.?
2. What motives might the Samuels have had for wanting to expand in the early days?
3. What motives might the Samuels have had for merging with the Royal Dutch Company?
4. Who would have benefited from the merger? Explain how they would have benefited.

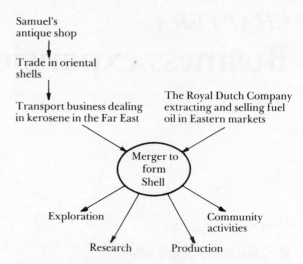

Figure 4.1 Growth of Shell.

5. Who might have lost out as a result of the merger? Explain why.
6. Do the present activities of Shell (exploration, research, etc.) complement each other? Explain your reasoning.

■ Case study: In-Style Clothing

Lesley Cartledge and her friends always found it frustrating not being able to buy the fashion clothes that they liked in their home town of Bakewell. Lesley says that young people in Bakewell are quite 'with it' and fashionable so that it is frustrating having to travel twenty miles into Sheffield to buy decent clothes.

After leaving school Lesley studied bookkeeping and went on to set up a small bookkeeping service for local firms. Lesley had always had an interest in clothes and with her business knowledge it seemed a natural step to set up a boutique in Bakewell at the end of 1987.

She was fortunate to be able to lease one of the most attractive shop sites in Bakewell in a courtyard close to the town centre. She called the business In-Style Clothing to project the modern image of her clothes. Lesley is 21 and In-Style's target market is the 18–35 year old age group, looking for smart, well-made clothes.

The main costs of setting up in business were:

1. Stock of clothing £3,000

2. Rent and rates (quarterly outlay) £1,300
3. Solicitor's fees, decoration and other starting costs £1,000

On top of this she has to pay electricity and phone bills each quarter as well as other minor expenses such as window cleaning.

In the first month that she was open, she managed to sell £1,000 of clothes. This took in the Christmas period and so was a very good month. Because Bakewell is a tourist attraction summer sales figures were also expected to be very good.

Lesley worked out her cash flow and expected to sell £60,000 worth of goods in her first year. She would be able to do this because of high demand and lack of competition.

Lesley felt that In-Style had been able to benefit from a real gap in the market in Bakewell. Clothes shops can make a good profit if sales can be kept high since most clothes are marked up by between 100 and 200%. She is now thinking of starting up a men's fashion shop in Bakewell because of the lack of a clothes shop for men in the 18–35 year old age group. By running both a men's and a women's shop she will be able to get bigger discounts from her suppliers.

Questions

Lesley Cartledge has considered alternative ways of carrying out the expansion. Consider each of the following alternatives below before answering the questions. (This task is best tackled by small groups.)

(a) She could employ somebody to manage the men's shop on a day-to-day basis whilst continuing to do all the administration and bookwork herself.
(b) She could employ a manager to take complete responsibility for all the details of running the men's shop.
(c) She could take on a partner. They would be joint owners of the two businesses and share the responsibility of running the two shops.
(d) She could continue with just the one shop and put all her efforts into the women's clothes side.

1. What other alternatives can you think of to the four outlined above?
2. What do you think is the best solution for Lesley? Explain your answer.
3. Why do you think that the alternatives that you have rejected are unsuitable?
4. What groups and industries in Bakewell have (a) benefited, (b) lost out, as a result of the growth of In-Style Clothing? Explain your answer.

The activities that you have just looked at show some of the many ways in which firms can grow. There are a variety of reasons why firms choose to grow including:

1. to make more profits;
2. to provide a better service;
3. to provide a wider range of goods and services;
4. to sell more goods and/or services;
5. to make a bigger name for the owners/ managers;
6. to take a bigger share of the market;
7. to create more jobs;
8. to make a bigger contribution to the local community.

What other reasons might firms have for wanting to grow? Taking each of the reasons why firms may wish to expand, try to explain them in more depth, e.g. why might firms wish to provide a better service?

There are several ways in which firms can grow, including the following:

1. A change in business organisation
2. A change in finance
3. A process of integration.

A change in organisation

We have already seen that the sole trader is the smallest form of business organisation in this country. The sole trader can expand by joining with partners or co-operators. Alternatively, it is possible to form a company by selling shares. The main advantage of expanding in these ways is that more capital and skill are brought into the business. The main disadvantage is that control over the business has to be shared.

A change in finance

The small business gets its finance from owners' savings and borrowings. As a business expands it might borrow from a wider range of sources including business loans and overdrafts. Share capital and debentures may be sold to a wide range of people.

A process of integration

To integrate means to join together. In order to expand, many firms will look to merge or take over others. Businesses can grow quickly in this way and there are many advantages to be gained from different types of integration. (These are discussed more fully below.)

Taking over another business would involve buying up at least 51% of the shares in that business. A merger occurs when two firms jointly agree to form a single enterprise.

Integration

Firms may join together with others at the same stage of production (*horizontal integration*). Alternatively they may join together with others at an earlier or later stage in a given production process (*vertical integration*). Another form of integration is to join together with others where there is common ground, e.g. a shared channel of distribution (*lateral integration*). Finally, firms may diversify to buy into an unrelated product (*conglomerate integration*).

Horizontal integration

This involves firms at the same stage of production joining together. An example of this would be the joining together of brewers. In the period 1948–71, for example, Whitbread merged with 27 other brewery companies. As a result Whitbread vastly increased the number of public houses that it owned as well as the number of breweries.

■ Questions

1. Why do you think that Whitbread might have wanted to integrate in this way? Try to list at least five motives.
2. Who would have benefited from this integration?
3. Who might have lost out as a result of this integration? Explain your answer.

Vertical integration

Forward vertical integration involves taking over firms at a later stage of production, e.g. a paper manufacturer taking over a book publisher. *Backward* vertical integration involves taking over firms at an earlier stage of production, e.g. a paper manufacturer buying a tree plantation.

In the 1970s and 1980s Whitbread's bought out Beefeater Restaurants and Threshers off-licences.

■ Questions

1. Why do you think that Whitbread may have wanted to integrate in this way? Try to list at least five motives.
2. What would you expect to be the main costs and benefits to people living close to a Threshers off-licence?

Lateral integration

Lateral integration involves joining together with other firms which, although they are different in terms of product, share common characteristics such as distribution patterns. For example, toothpaste and soap are both distributed through supermarkets and chemists.

In recent years Whitbread has acquired European wine companies, like Langebach in Germany and Calvet in France. In 1976 Whitbread took over Long John International, the Scotch whisky and gin company.

■ Questions

1. What motives might Whitbread have for such integration?
2. Can you think of other examples of lateral integration?

Conglomerate integration

A company can spread its risks by buying a range of other business interests with no real relationship to each other. In this way the business will be operating in several major markets at the same time. We talk about a company *diversifying its interests* as in Figure 4.2.

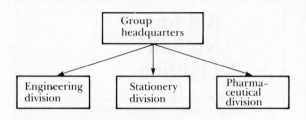

Figure 4.2 *Divisions of a diversified company.*

■ Questions

1. What would be the main advantages to a company of producing a wide range of products?
2. What would be the main disadvantages of producing a wide range of products?

International integration

Companies can also spread their interests by buying overseas companies. There is a wide range of possible motives for wanting to do this:

1. *To sell to a wider market.* In this way firms can benefit from being able to produce and sell more goods. They may also be able to benefit from the weakness of competition in overseas markets.
2. *To penetrate foreign markets.* Buying up a foreign company may be one way of getting round the import taxes which make it difficult to sell overseas.
3. *To have more control over a supplier.* The Co-op for example owns tea estates in India. This enables it to control the quality of the tea that it sells.
4. *To have more control over a later stage of production.* For example, if a clothes manufacturer buys up some overseas clothes shops then it can control the way in which they are sold, e.g. shop layout, display, advertising, etc.

International integration is often simply an extension of one of the other types of integration. The fundamental difference is when the purpose of the integration is to get round some of the laws discriminating against overseas businesses.

■ Case study: *W H Smith*

On the high street, WHS aims to dominate in four areas: books, stationery, magazines and 'sight and sound' (i.e. records, cassettes and videos). The 448-strong WHS chain is in itself insufficient to achieve this. Different kinds of retail outlets have had to be developed.

Currently, there are 42 Sherratt & Hughes stores, appealing to the 20% of book buyers who consider WHS too downmarket. Then there are 172 Our Price record stores, attracting a younger age group. The latest development is the card, gift and stationery concept, Paperchase, and the fifth element of the high-street mix is a growing chain of travel shops.

Another area of W H Smith's activities is its one out-of-town operation, the DIY retailer Do It All. Do It All currently controls 8% of the DIY market. Do It All aims to appeal to the upmarket customer with an interest in decoration rather than to the 'budding builder's merchant'.

W H Smith is also a major wholesale distributor in the UK magazine and newspaper market.

WHS runs over 250 gift shops in the USA and claims to be Canada's biggest bookseller. Just to show its interests are not confined to the printed word plus a few records, WHS bought Television Services International in 1987 to gain an entry into the world of cable programming and production.

Questions

1. Set out a diagram which you think illustrates WHS's range of interests.
2. Why do you think that WHS feels that it is important to dominate the high street in books, stationery, magazines and 'sight and sound'?
3. What strategies would you employ to dominate these product areas?
4. What are the advantages to a consumer of having one firm dominating a particular product area?
5. What are the disadvantages to consumers of having one firm dominating a particular product area?
6. What are the advantages to W H Smith of concentrating on the high street?
7. What are the disadvantages of concentrating on the high street?

8. What are the advantages and disadvantages of 'out of town' retailing?
9. What is meant in the text by an 'upmarket customer'?
10. What is meant by 'the high-street mix'?
11. Why do you think that WHS has a range of interests in the UK?
12. Why do you think that WHS operates in an international setting?
13. Carry out an investigation to find out what contribution WHS makes to your town. This would focus on the range of activities, and the costs and benefits of WHS for your local town. You would need to look at such things as the employment created by Smiths, the volume and value of goods sold, the effect it has on competition, the service it offers, other links with the community and any problems caused by Smiths. Your conclusion should weigh up alternative ways of looking at the good and bad things about the company's activities in your area.

■ Case study: Electrocomponents

Figure 4.3 reproduces a newspaper article covering the acquisition of one company by another.

Questions

1. What do you think is meant by 'low volume, fast turnround ... distribution'?
2. What form of integration would be involved if Electrocomponents took over Nuthall?
3. What would be the main motives behind this integration?
4. What possible disadvantages might there be to Electrocomponents caused by the takeover?

Disintegration

So far we have been looking at the growth of businesses through a process of integration. Firms also frequently *dis*integrate by selling off plant and divisions. There are a number of possible reasons, including selling off loss-making areas and the desire to concentrate on what a business does best.

Bid for Nuthall Lighting

Electrocomponents, the fast-moving business which made its name in low volume, fast turn-round electronic components distribution, is paying up to £7.7m for Nuthall Lighting, a privately owned Midlands group of companies making decorative lighting.

The acquisition marks Electrocomponents' first important step into the manufacturing field and will strengthen its presence in the lighting market, where it is already a major supplier to the do-it-yourself retail chains.

John Robinson, Electrocomponents' managing director, said the deal would give the group more control over its growing supplies to the retail sector.

Figure 4.3 Newspaper article looking at the growth of a company.
Source: based on an article in The Independent, *15 March 1988.*

■ Case study: Rowntree

Figure 4.4 reproduces a newspaper article covering a company's decision to sell one of its divisions.

Questions

1. What do you think are the main reasons why Rowntree is selling its snacks business?
2. What do you think will be the main advantage to Rowntree of this policy?
3. Why do you think that other buyers are interested in taking over Rowntree's snack food division?
4. Why do you think that Rowntree was prepared to buy Tom's Foods in 1983?
5. How might each of the following benefit from the selling off by Rowntree of its snack food division:
   (a) a shareholder in Rowntree?
   (b) an employee in the snack food division in Texas?

Rowntree puts snacks side up for sale

Rowntree, the York-based confectioner, has put its snacks business up for sale in a sudden switch of policy.

Within hours of making the announcement yesterday, Rowntree had received half a dozen calls from possible buyers including most of the major crisp manufacturers.

Rowntree wants to invest the money it gets from the sale in its branded sweets and chocolates and in specialist shops.

Rowntree entered the snacks business only six years ago when it bought its UK snacks business then called RPC. In 1983 it bought Tom's Foods, a US crispmaker.

Neither business has well-known brands and both are suffering from increasing competition.

The UK business, which is based in Scunthorpe, makes Riley's and Murphy's crisps, Wheat Crunchies and Nik Naks. It employs 1,500 people.

Tom's makes 350 different snacks, with crisps making up half the output. It has factories in Georgia, Tennessee, Florida, West Virginia, Texas and California.

Figure 4.4 Newspaper article looking at the process of disintegration.
Source: based on an article in The Independent, *17 March 1988.*

(c) a shareholder in a business buying up the Rowntree snack food division?
(d) a consumer of crisps?
6. How might each of the following lose out from the selling off by Rowntree of its snack food division:
   (a) a shareholder in Rowntree?
   (b) an employee in the snack food division in Texas?
   (c) a shareholder in a business buying up the Rowntree snack food division?
   (d) a consumer of crisps?

Economies of scale

There are many advantages to producing on a large scale rather than a small scale.

■ Case study: Keith Samuels' iced buns

Keith Samuels has been asked to make some iced buns to sell at the village fete. He is not sure how big the demand will be but has worked out that the most effective way of using up all the materials he buys is to produce either 4 dozen or 8 dozen buns.

Materials required to produce 4 dozen buns:		Materials required to produce 8 dozen buns:	
250 g tub margarine	30p	500 g tub margarine	55p
250 g castor sugar	30p	500 g castor sugar	55p
6 size 2 eggs	60p	1 dozen size 2 eggs	£1.10
250 g self-raising flour	30p	500 g self-raising flour	60p
500 g icing sugar	40p	1 kg icing sugar	75p
50 paper cases	30p	100 paper cases	55p

It would take 35 minutes to prepare and cook 4 dozen buns and 40 minutes for 8 dozen buns. He has costed out the use of electricity at £1, however many buns he produces. He is looking forward to making the buns and is not going to count his labour time as part of the costing.

Questions

1. What would be the cost per bun (to the nearest penny) of producing:
   (a) 4 dozen buns?
   (b) 8 dozen buns?
2. How would you explain this difference in cost per unit? (Think of as many reasons as possible.)
3. Will the unit cost of producing more items always be lower than that of producing less?
4. What pitfalls might there be to producing 8 dozen rather than 4 dozen buns?
5. How might the cost advantage of producing 8 dozen buns help Keith to sell more buns and still make more profit than if he sold 4 dozen?
6. What conditions would be necessary to make it worth while to produce 8 dozen buns?

■ Case study: The Prudential chain of estate agents

One way of setting up a business is to start from scratch. Another way is to take over existing outlets.

The Prudential, until recently, was largely associated with life insurance. In the late 1980s it rapidly developed a range of new interests including estate agency. Market research carried out by the Prudential showed that customers were less than happy with existing services. There was room for improvement by cutting costs, extending opening hours (to include evenings and weekends) and developing a national chain.

The Prudential therefore set out to create a national chain with a standard range of charges and services. Prudential were able to market themselves through a well-known national logo and a standard Prudential service. By using new technology it became possible to join up the chain into a national network. The Prudential was able to expand quickly by buying up many small estate agencies (there are over 1,000 in the UK). People buying and selling properties are often more confident in dealing with well-known names.

A further advantage to the Prudential has been that it is able to sell some of its other financial products such as insurance through its estate agencies.

Questions

1. Why do you think that the Prudential bought into estate agencies?
2. Why was Prudential able to move quickly into this market?
3. What advantages are there to the Prudential from moving into a new product line?
4. What possible disadvantages might have resulted from the move into estate agencies?
5. What advantages are there for house buyers resulting from the Prudential's move into the estate agency market?
6. Which groups might lose out from the Prudential's action?

Business can benefit from two main types of economies of scale:

1. *Internal economies* are the advantages which a firm gets from its own growth.

2. *External economies* are the advantages which a firm gets from the growth and improvement of its industry and locality.

Internal economies of scale

Being big can bring a lot of financial benefits to a company. The most obvious one is that large firms can produce goods and services more cheaply per unit. There are a number of major internal economies.

Technical advantages

Large firms can often benefit from superior techniques of production. Automated plant and equipment (e.g. in car manufacture, cigarette manufacture, beer production, etc.) may be so expensive to install that only large companies can afford it. A large oil and chemical company like Shell can join its forces together and organise a whole range of activities, from the drilling of oil to its final sale as petrol to the consumer.

■ Case study: Large-scale production at Shell
Question

Study the pictures in Figure 4.5 which show the production and distribution of petrol. Describe the stages involved and then list 10 advantages of large-scale production which are apparent in the photographs, making possible production at low unit cost.

Expensive equipment may only be a good buy if it is used to the full. A large sweet manufacturer producing bars of chocolate may, for example, be able to work its computer controlled production line 24 hours a day using three shifts of employees. Large units of equipment, e.g. storage tanks, may be cheaper to install, produce and maintain than smaller ones in relation to the quantity of liquid that can be stored in them.

Financial advantages

Large firms usually find it easier and cheaper to borrow money than small ones. For example, a

Figure 4.5 Operations at Shell.

bank manager has the discretion to charge different rates of interest to different customers. Because the bank manager will be more interested in keeping British Telecom's account than yours or mine, British Telecom is likely to be offered overdraft facilities at a lower interest rate.

Raising money through the Stock Exchange is also cheaper for a larger company than for a smaller one. For example, the fee that a merchant bank charges for issuing £5 million worth of shares will be nowhere near ten times more than if it was offering £½ million worth of shares for sale.

Managerial advantages

Administrative and managerial economies arise because a large manufacturer can employ specialist staff to manage and supervise production. The costs of hiring these specialists are then spread over a larger quantity of goods. Large firms can also afford to use expensive administrative machinery such as computer systems.

Commercial advantages

Large firms are able to buy and sell in bulk. They are able to obtain discounts on their purchases, and the cost of transport per unit is much lower with bulk loads.

Selling costs such as advertising do not rise in proportion to the quantity sold.

Risk spreading advantages

Large firms will carry out a range of activities rather than putting all their eggs in one basket. There are a number of ways in which they can diversify (spread out their interests):

1. *Product diversification.* A company may produce a number of products so that if some do badly others will ride the storm, e.g., sweet manufacturers produce a range of sweets.
2. *Market diversification.* A firm might produce and sell in different countries in case problems arise in one area (e.g. a new competitor enters the French market).

3. *Supplier diversification.* A large producer might buy its raw materials and parts from several suppliers just in case one has problems, e.g., its workforce are out on strike.

4. *Production diversification.* Large firms may have several plants or production lines producing the same product in case it has problems with one line.

Internal diseconomies of scale

There are also *disadvantages* from the growth of an enterprise. The most common disadvantages arise from:

1. *Managerial diseconomies.* Management cannot cope with too large an operation. An example of this would be the growth of a school to such a size that senior teachers lose control of what is going on.

2. *Technical diseconomies.* There are so many processes and activities taking place that once things start to go wrong the problems start to pile up.

3. *Marketing diseconomies.* If an enterprise is producing more than it can sell, advertising costs might become an increasing part of costs.

4. *Risk spreading diseconomies.* The enterprise may be running so many products and lines that when a number of them go wrong at the same time the more profitable ones are dragged down by lack of research and other necessary expenditures.

External economies of scale

External economies arise from the growth of the industry rather than the firm. As the environment in which the industry operates improves then all firms in the industry stand to benefit.

There are a wide number of possible reasons why the environment in which an industry operates may improve, including:

1. Communications and transport links to an area improve, reducing costs of distribution.

2. Educational facilities develop in an area, reducing the costs of training (e.g. the development of information technology courses at the local college).

3. The government sponsors a research project at the local university which specialises in a subject with applications for local industry. This helps to reduce the costs of research.

4. Suppliers for the industry emerge – specialist firms that produce or service machinery or supply parts. Production costs are lowered because firms do not have to produce these parts themselves but buy in from the specialist producers.

5. Housing and recreational facilities improve in the area reducing recruitment and training costs as the labour force becomes more stable.

6. Banking and financial services improve in an area making it easier and cheaper to raise finance.

External diseconomies of scale

Problems also arise from the growth of an industry. Labour and other costs might rise as more competition arises to hire more labour, buy more land and machinery, etc. Congestion and pollution might arise from an over-concentration of industry.

The Stock Exchange

The Stock Exchange makes it possible for large companies to raise finance. Most people in the UK are involved in investing in one way or another.

An increasing number of people have shares of their own. As well as these direct shareholdings we nearly all have indirect holdings – if you put money into an insurance company, pension fund or trade union it is very likely that some of the spare cash will be invested on the Stock Exchange.

How the Stock Exchange works

At the heart of the Stock Exchange system are the market makers who belong to firms that buy and sell shares first-hand. Market makers are in contact with each other by telephone and through screens of viewdata. The screens show the prices at which other market makers are prepared to buy and sell shares.

There are many market makers competing in the London market, but it is easiest to explain if we assume that there is just one. The market maker quotes two prices: a higher one at which he will sell and a lower one at which he will buy. If Shell UK shares are quoted at 100–102 by a particular market maker, it means investors can sell them to the market maker at 100p and buy them at 102p. The difference between the two prices is the 'spread'.

Most newspapers quote a middle price for simplicity – in this instance. Shell UK would be shown at 101p. In fact, the price quoted in newspapers is the price as it stood when the stock market closed on the previous day.

Why do prices go up and down? It depends on the balance between buyers and sellers in the market. If there are more buyers than sellers the price is likely to go up, and vice versa. How does this happen? Suppose that at 101p (middle price) there are seven people who want to buy one Shell UK share and only two who want to sell one share. Not all the would-be buyers can get the share they want and prices are pushed up.

In the London market, investors wanting to sell do not have to seek out other investors wanting to buy. Instead, they sell the shares to the market maker. The market makers buy and sell shares for their own self-interest. They hope to make a profit on the difference between the prices at which they sell and buy.

Buying and selling shares

Buying and selling shares has become easier since the reorganisation of the Stock Exchange in 1986 known as 'Big Bang'. There are a number of ways:

1. You can deal with a market maker direct. This is commonly done by large share buying institutions, e.g., pension funds, unit trusts.
2. You can deal with a local broker/dealer who will then deal on your behalf.
3. You can buy from a share shop which deals directly in stocks and shares. Some major department stores have departments specialising in stocks and shares.

'Big Bang' was intended to make the Stock Exchange more competitive. Up to that time dealers in stocks and shares charged the public at a fixed rate of commission for sales and purchases. Dealers are now able to compete by

undercutting each other. The changes also made it possible for the public to deal directly with market makers without having to go through a middle broker.

Until they have had it explained to them people can be confused by the share pages of a major newspaper. In fact, it is very easy to read the important details on a share page. Consider the following which shows the main columns:

Class of share	Price	±	High	Low
Breweries				
Allied	88	+2	94	80
Whitbread	74	–1	75	70
Oil				
BP	384		384	360
Shell	422	+1	422	416

The price column shows yesterday's closing price, the + or – shows the change from the day before's closing, the high shows the highest price the share has been this year, and the low shows the lowest. We can see from the above information that Whitbread shares can be bought at 74p. They had fallen by 1p since the previous day. The highest price they have been this year is 75p and 70p is the lowest.

■ Case study: Reading share prices

Class of share	Price	±	High	Low
Entertainment				
Tottenham Hotspurs	88	–1	103	88
Ladbroke	233	+2	233	201
Oils				
Atlantic	643	+85	643	500
BP	426	+5	441	418

Questions

1. Which share has experienced the most dramatic rise since the previous day? Can you give a likely explanation of this rise?
2. What has been the cheapest price of BP shares in the financial year?
3. When Tottenham Hotspurs' shares were originally sold it was at 100p each. How much

were they selling at when the information above was printed?

4. What are the two main ways in which you can earn money from holding shares?

■ Coursework activity

Here is a list of 18 well-known shares and their prices (in pence) on 21 January 1984. Choose two of these shares and imagine that you had bought £100 worth of each. How much are they worth today? (If the shares you have chosen do not appear in the newspaper you consult, choose two more.)

Breweries:
Guinness   142
Food:
Tesco   174
Chemicals:
ICI   634
Rentokil   139
Engineering:
Hawker   394
Vickers   134

Entertainment:
Tottenham Hotspurs   88
Industrials:
Boots   184
Bowater   295
Dunhill   523
Dunlop   56
Metal Box   330
Rank   206
Motors:
Honda   326
Lucas   281
Oils:
BP   426
Stores:
Debenhams   153
Woolworth   361

Questions

These questions should be tackled as a group activity:

1. What has happened to share prices in general between these two dates? How would you explain these changes?

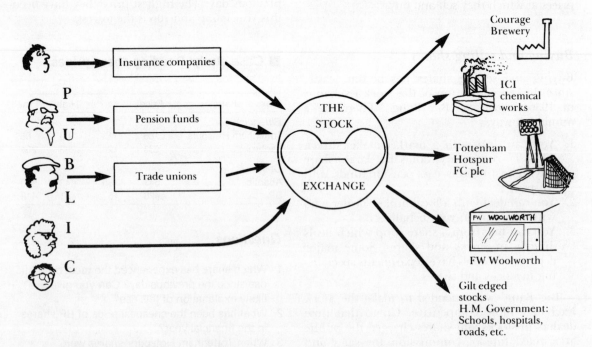

Figure 4.6 The Stock Exchange as intermediary.

Figure 4.7 The annual general meeting.

...ALL THOSE IN
FAVOUR OF REAPPOINTING
MR SHARKY...

2. Find out which sectors have seen the biggest increases. Try to explain why.
3. Which sectors have seen the smallest change? Why?
4. Are there any companies that have done particularly well/badly? Why?

How the Stock Exchange helps industry, commerce and government

The Stock Exchange is a market for money. At the Stock Exchange people's money can be invested in stocks and shares as in Figure 4.6.

The money from citizens' savings can be transferred to public companies and to the Government. By buying 10,000 shares in Miss World Enterprises, Mrs Investor becomes a part owner of the company. She can go to the annual general meeting of the company every year and listen to the company report. If the shareholders are not happy with the way the company is being run they can vote out the board of directors (see Figure 4.7).

As a shareholder, Mrs Investor can gain in two ways from holding shares in the Dynamic Micro Company. First of all she is entitled to a share of the profits every year in the form of a *dividend*. The company pays out a dividend to its shareholders every 31 March. Sometimes it also gives out an *interim* (half yearly) dividend on 30 September.

When the shares were first sold on 31 March

1980 they were priced at *100p* each. Every year the company announces a dividend as a percentage. In 1981 it was 9%. In 1982 it was 14%. In 1983 it was 15% and in 1984 16%. So for every share Mrs Investor holds in the company she received 16p in 1984.

Because the company does so well many people want to buy shares in it, so the price of these shares have gone up. In 1980 they were 100p. In 1981 they rose to 104p. In 1982 they rose to 112p. In 1983 they rose to 120p and in 1984 to 130p (see Figure 4.8).

We can see from Figure 4.8 the second way in which Mrs Investor can gain. She bought the

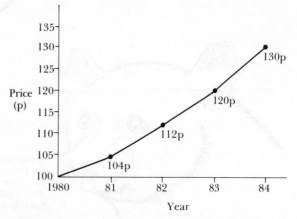

Figure 4.8 Price of shares in Dynamic Micro Company.

shares for 100p each and if she sells them now she could get 184p each.

Bulls, bears and stags

A *speculator* is a person who buys and sells shares on the Stock Exchange hoping to make a profit. Figure 4.9 shows the types of speculator to be found in the Stock Exchange.

■ Question

When the government sold shares in British Telecom Geoff Davies asked his broker to buy him 10,000 of these brand new shares because he expected their price to rise immediately.

Six months later Martin Angus bought 5,000 of them because he thought the price was just about to rise.

However, Claire Short who worked on the Stock Exchange felt that their price was just about to fall so she sold 5,000 hoping to buy them back when they were cheaper.

Who was the *bear*, who was the *stag*, and who the *bull*?

Government stock

If the government wants money it can raise it by taxes, by printing money or by borrowing it. One of the ways in which the government can borrow money for long periods is by selling gilt-edged stock through the Stock Exchange.

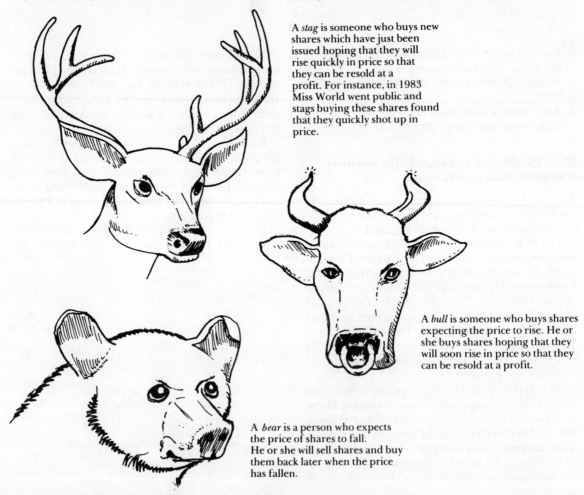

A *stag* is someone who buys new shares which have just been issued hoping that they will rise quickly in price so that they can be resold at a profit. For instance, in 1983 Miss World went public and stags buying these shares found that they quickly shot up in price.

A *bull* is someone who buys shares expecting the price to rise. He or she buys shares hoping that they will soon rise in price so that they can be resold at a profit.

A *bear* is a person who expects the price of shares to fall. He or she will sell shares and buy them back later when the price has fallen.

Figure 4.9 The Stock Exchange zoo.

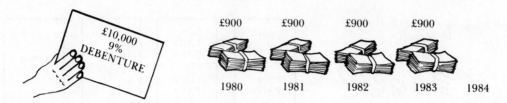

Figure 4.10 Returns on debentures.

Of course, government stock are not really gilt-edged but are said to be so because we know that they are a safe investment. The government can always raise the money to pay back its debts when they mature.

Government gilt-edged stock have a fixed date of maturity, e.g. 1994, and investors are paid a fixed rate of interest which must be as good as they can get from any similar investment.

Loans to and investments in companies

Suppose Gloria Smith wants to invest some money in Superstores which is her employer. Her bank manager tells here that there are a number of ways of investing her money depending on how big a risk she is willing to take and how much return she wants. The four main ways are:

1. debentures
2. preference shares
3. cumulative preference shares
4. ordinary shares (also known as equities)

Debentures

Debenture holders are not part-owners of a company. They have simply lent the company money and do not have shares. A debenture is a safe way of putting money into Superstores. Superstores must pay debenture holders *first*. Debentures have a fixed rate of interest – in this case 9%. If Gloria buys £10,000 worth of Superstore debentures when they are first issued she is entitled to £900 in interest every year, as illustrated in Figure 4.10. If they can't pay her they will be bankrupt.

Preference shares

Gloria's bank manager advises her that if she wants to take a higher risk she could become a shareholder and get a higher rate of return. After the company has paid back its debenture holders it will pay back *preference* shareholders. She could invest her £10,000 in Superstore preference shares which pay out a dividend of 10%, as in Figure 4.11.

The danger is, of course, that if the company does badly it might not be able to pay the preference shareholders.

Cumulative preference shares

Gloria's bank manager advises her that *cumulative preference shares* are a safer investment than plain preference shares. If the company cannot pay a cumulative preference shareholder all the dividend it owes in one year, the debt is carried over to the following year. For instance, suppose Gloria buys £10,000 worth of 10% cumulative preference shares in Superstores in 1980. At the end of the year the company owes her a dividend of £1,000. However, it does not have all the money available and it can only pay her £500.

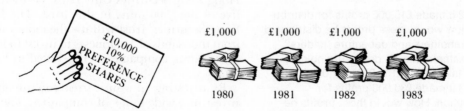

Figure 4.11 Returns on preference shares.

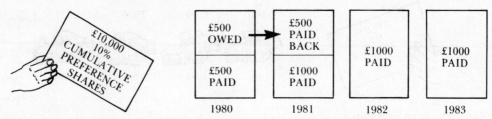

Figure 4.12 Returns on cumulative preference shares.

Therefore, at the end of 1981 the company will owe her £500 for 1980 and £1,000 for 1981. This process is illustrated in Figure 4.12.

Ordinary shares (equities)

Companies like to raise a lot of their money by selling *equities* because they are not tied down to making fixed payments every year. An ordinary shareholder is the last to be paid out of a company's profits. In a bad year he or she will get very little dividend, but in a good year a very good dividend may be possible.

An ordinary shareholder, therefore, carries a lot of the risk taken by a company. Let us imagine that a company's debenture holders are entitled to half a million pounds a year, and preference shareholders one quarter of a million pounds. We can see then that the company must distribute more than three-quarters of a million pounds before ordinary shareholders get anything at all. Of course, if profits are very high ordinary shareholders can get a very big dividend.

■ Questions

1.   The Baked Biscuit company has issued:
     (i)   100,000 £1 debentures at 7%
     (ii) 100,000 £1 preference shares at 8%
     (iii) 100,000 £1 ordinary shares.

   (a) In 1982 it made £15,000 profits for distribution. How would these profits be distributed to shareholders and debenture holders? (For example, the 7% debenture holders would take 7% of £100,000 = £7,000.)
   (b) In 1983 it made £30,000 profits for distribution. How would these profits be distributed to shareholders and debenture holders? What would the percentage rate

of return be for ordinary shareholders?
   (c) List two disadvantages of being an ordinary shareholder.

2.   Multimillion Incorporated has issued:
     (i)   1,000,000 £1 debentures at 7½%
     (ii) 1,000,000 £1 cumulative preference shares at 8%
     (iii) 1,000,000 ordinary shares.

   (a) In 1982 it made £100,000 profits for distribution. How would these profits be distributed to shareholders and debenture holders?
   (b) In 1983 it made £200,000 profits for distribution, and in 1984 £500,000. Show how these profits would be distributed.
   (c) Explain the statement that 'Ordinary shareholders are the main risk-takers in a public limited company.'

Unit trusts and investment trusts

Now that it is becoming more expensive to hire the services of brokers on the Stock Exchange, many small savers are buying units in a *unit trust*. A unit trust is simply a company that collects savings from people and institutions and re-invests their money in buying shares. They tend to specialise in particular areas (e.g. Australia) or particular types of shares (e.g. mining).

For instance, suppose Mr Jones sees an advert in *The Times* asking people to invest in the Hong Kong Securities Unit Trust. He then buys five of the £500 units in this trust. The Hong Kong Securities Trust will use the money it gets from thousands of Mr Joneses to invest in lots of Hong Kong companies as illustrated in Figure 4.13.

By investing in a unit trust you are able to invest in a wide range of companies. The dividend you get will then be determined by the average profitability of these companies.

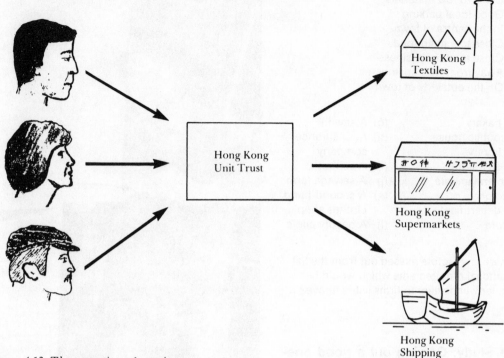

Figure 4.13 The operation of a unit trust.

Summary of the value of the Stock Exchange

1. Companies can attract money from many different sources.
2. The Stock Exchange Council will closely scrutinise companies' records and accounts before allowing them to be quoted. This acts as a safeguard to investors.
3. Lots of small savers can invest on the Stock Exchange becoming part-owners of big companies. (However, broker's fees are very high and this discourages small investors.)
4. Small savers have limited liability, i.e. they do not risk their own personal fortunes.
5. It is easy to buy and sell shares.
6. Large firms wishing to expand can easily borrow money through the organised market of the Stock Exchange.

Location of industry

Firms will usually set up and locate themselves at the site which appears to be best at the time.

Of course, they sometimes choose the wrong spot and this then leads to a lot of problems. There are a thousand and one ingredients that go into a location decision and every firm has its own requirements.

■ Questions

1. Look at the following list of locational requirements and then try to match five which you think are most important with the firms listed below (e.g. you might think that a bakery should be close to where people live, have a good shop window, have good passing trade, low local taxes, and be in a pleasant area).

   (i)   Good passing trade
   (ii)   Quiet location with little passing trade
   (iii)   Low local taxes
   (iv)   A good shop window
   (v)   No shop window
   (vi)   Pleasant area
   (vii)   Away from centres of population
   (viii) Near to where people live

(ix)   Close to raw materials
(x)   Good local parking
(xi)   In the centre of town
(xii)   Close to a main road
(xiii) Close to other businesses
(xiv)   Away from rival businesses
(xv)   On the outskirts of town

(a) A bakery
(b) A public house
(c) A library
(d) A DIY store
(e) An armaments
    factory
(f) A department
    store

(g) A sawmill
(h) An insurance
    company
(i) A school
(j) A sewage farm
(k) A second-hand
    clothes shop
(l) A beauty clinic

2. Are there any factors missed out from the list
   of locational requirements which would be
   particularly important to firms listed above?

■ Case Study: Carving out a good one-man business

East End furniture maker Edward Sanson has one
thing in common with insurance giant Pearl
Assurance. Both have moved to Peterborough to
take advantage of a growing city.

The furniture designer and maker represents the
other side of the coin to the headline-grabbing
Pearl which is bringing 2,000 jobs. But, like Pearl,
he moved because costs were lower and he had
room to expand.

Edward fled the noise and overcrowding of
London's East End for a quieter – and cheaper –
workshop in Peterborough last summer and hasn't
looked back. In London he paid £80 a week for a
cramped back-street workshop which was a third
the size of his current £50 a week workshop.

He said: 'I'm glad I made the move. The price of
property in London is just ridiculous and totally
priced me out of the market. I couldn't afford to
move into a larger workshop.'

He makes high quality office and home furniture
and will show off his best work at a major furniture
exhibition in Covent Garden in May. He hopes
eventually to take on an employee.

(Source: Adapted from *Peterborough Evening
Telegraph*.)

Figure 4.14 Edward Sanson – furniture maker.
Source: adapted from an article in the Peterborough
Evening Telegraph, *12 May 1988.*

Questions

1. List four reasons which you think have tempted
   Edward to move to Peterborough.
2. Explain why two of these might have been
   particularly important.
3. What disadvantages might there be to moving to
   Peterborough (a) in the short term, (b) in the
   long term?
4. In what ways is Edward's case similar to that of
   Pearl Assurance?
5. Why might a firm decide to move from
   Peterborough to London? Give an example of
   the type of business that would be most likely to
   do this.

Factors affecting location

Every firm has some idea of 'the best site'. The best site is the one that *maximises advantages*. This is not always the site where money costs are lowest – for example, a department store *must* be on the high street where property costs are highest.

The following sections examine some of the ingredients of a good location.

Closeness to point of sale

Many firms find it important to be close to their market. They need to be at a point where they can control the sale of their product. Service industries in particular often need to be 'in amongst' their customers. This is as true for commercial services as it is for direct services. Insurance companies, graphic designers (producing business cards, advertising leaflets, etc.) and banks, for example, need to be located in business centres. Hairdressers, retailers and cafés need to be in shopping areas.

Manufacturers also benefit from being close to their markets when transportation costs are high and when products do not travel well. Some products, for example, become much bulkier when the component parts that make them up have been assembled. For this reason, producers such as furniture manufacturers will often be found close to their market.

When products are non-durable such as foodstuffs which go off quickly, they tend to be produced on a local basis, e.g., fresh baked bread and cakes and market garden produce.

Closeness to raw materials

Some firms and industries use a lot of heavy and bulky raw materials. The final product may be a lot smaller and lighter than the ingredients that go into it. Finished steel is a lot lighter than the total quantity of iron ore, limestone and other materials used to manufacture it. Food processing firms are frequently found close to centres of agriculture. In Lincolnshire and Norfolk, for example, there are many large producers of frozen, packeted, canned and bottled foods.

As a general rule products that lose bulk in their production, e.g. steel, food processing, etc., are more likely to be located near their raw materials. Products that gain bulk during their production, e.g. furniture, oil rigs and other heavy mechanical installations, are more likely to be located near to their markets.

Need to be away from centres of population

Some businesses and industries need to be located away from the centres of population because of the social consequences of their activities. Firms which cause a lot of noise because they use heavy power tools, drills and saws might benefit from being where they cause least nuisance. They are likely to have fewer complaints and less inspections.

Other firms such as chemical and nuclear plants can potentially cause serious danger to populations. Because of the Chernobyl nuclear accident in 1986 whole areas of the Russian countryside have been declared unsafe for people to live in. Such industries therefore need to be in isolated areas.

Industries that handle a lot of waste products also benefit from being away from centres of population.

Room for expansion

Some firms need a lot of land to produce on. Obvious examples are farms, mines and quarries. Production lines can be thousands of yards long in industries such as modern breweries, confectionary manufacturing units and car plants. These industries need to be situated where land is plentiful and relatively cheap, and so will locate on the outskirts of towns and cities. If they plan for the future they will buy more land than they need at the time. Avon, a cosmetics firm with their UK plant based in Northampton, for example, originally bought a much larger site than they needed to give them room to spread out at a later date.

Large shopping developments and offices have similar requirements. One reason why a number of large insurance companies and the travel agents Thomas Cook have moved their headquarters to Peterborough from London is because of the availability of cheaper sites.

Government help

Money and other help can be offered by local

and national government bodies to firms to set up in certain areas. For example, money has been made available for new businesses in certain inner city areas and to firms setting up in towns where there has been a lot of redundancies caused by steelworks closing down.

In the 1980s many local councils have tried to boost industry within their boundaries by advertising in national newspapers and magazines. Some councils have gone even further and have carried out research to find out the sorts of facilities that new businesses are looking for. They have investigated which industries are most likely to create jobs and to benefit the local economy. They have then tried to build up these facilities (e.g. building ready-made factory units of the right size and near the right types of roads) in order to attract industry in. York, for instance, has been successful in recent years in building up a microelectronics industry.

National government has also created development zones where industry gets cash support and enterprise zones (usually in run-down areas) where industry does not have to pay certain taxes.

Communications

Distribution expenses may be an important part of a firm's costs and delays and hold-ups can give a business a real handicap. Wholesalers and large-scale retailers will need to be close to major road links. For example, a modern newspaper wholesaler needing to get products to the market at breakneck speed will need branches close to major roads, rail links and airports.

A good selling point for any town will be its closeness to a motorway. Milton Keynes and Telford are particularly good examples of towns that have boomed partly as a result of their motorway links.

Labour force

With the growth of modern technology it is often important for firms to have access to a highly skilled labour force. It costs money to train people and so firms will be keen to set up where a skilled labour force already exists.

Living environment (surroundings)

As we move into the 1990s the environment in which we live is becoming an increasingly important locational factor. People have more money to spend on housing and recreation and more leisure time to enjoy.

There are a wide number of factors involved, including quality of housing, schools, recreation and leisure facilities. If a firm can keep its workforce motivated this will help to keep its training and other costs down and its output up.

Summary of locational factors

You can see that choosing the 'best site' for a business is a complicated decision. Many factors need to be weighed up and it is important to consider long-term as well as short-term factors. In the short term a firm might be forced to choose the cheapest location (in money terms); however, in the long term it is important to take account of a wide range of costs and benefits.

■ Case study: The labour force in York

The following information and data given in Figure 4.15 were produced for a publicity brochure for the York area.

Employment profile

York's working population of 83,000 possesses certain distinct advantages for prospective employers: there is a marked bias towards skilled and professional job functions; the wage rates in the York area are well below the national average; there is a well established tradition of female employment.

The workforce as a whole shows a bias towards skilled non-manual and management functions and shows a profile which in this respect is markedly different from the rest of the North and the Midlands and very similar to the SW and SE Regions.

York is one of the most pleasant working and living environments in the country, yet both living and housing costs are low. House prices are among the lowest in Britain, as are rents. The comparatively low living costs have resulted in low

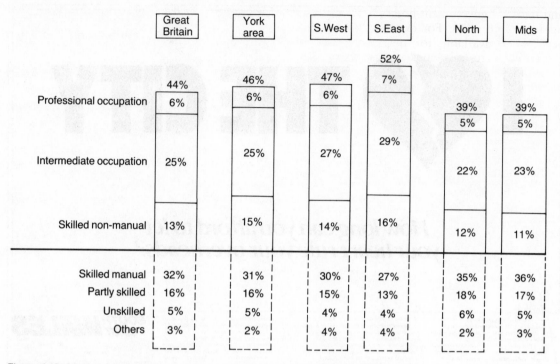

	Great Britain	York area	S.West	S.East	North	Mids
Professional occupation	44% 6%	46% 6%	47% 6%	52% 7%	39% 5%	39% 5%
Intermediate occupation	25%	25%	27%	29%	22%	23%
Skilled non-manual	13%	15%	14%	16%	12%	11%
Skilled manual	32%	31%	30%	27%	35%	36%
Partly skilled	16%	16%	15%	13%	18%	17%
Unskilled	5%	5%	4%	4%	6%	5%
Others	3%	2%	4%	4%	2%	3%

Figure 4.15 Analysis by economically active head of household for the York area.

wage rates combined with a high standard of living.

The high proportion of women who are in employment is indicative of the area's emphasis on modern, clean, light industry. It also reflects a long tradition of women at work that has created an employment orientated female population, which adds strength and diversity to the local economy.

Questions

1. In what ways is the structure of employment in York: (a) similar to the South of England, (b) different from the North and Midlands?
2. Why do you think that the brochure found it important to stress the above points?
3. What main advantages does York appear to have, from the information given, over southern counties?
4. What sorts of firm might be attracted by the employment structure in York?
5. What further information about location would these firms want to have before making a decision about moving?

6. Write a short business report for the directors of Lindsay Microcomputers Ltd, explaining why you think that they should consider locating in the York area rather than the Midlands.

■ Case study: South East Wales, financial services location

Figure 4.16 reproduces an advertisement to attract business to the South East Wales area from London.

Questions

1. What sort of industries do you normally associate with South East Wales?
2. Who do you think has paid for the advert above to be produced?
3. What are financial services?
4. Why do you think that the people who commissioned the advert are trying to attract financial services to South East Wales?
5. Why do you think that financial service

Figure 4.16 *An advertisement to encourage business to move to the South East Wales area.*

companies might be attracted by the advert? List six reasons.
6. What do you think the disadvantages to financial service companies of moving to South East Wales would be?

■ Case study: Locating in Belfast

This study should be tackled in small groups. Figures 4.17 and 4.18 and the data below provide the necessary information. You must select from this what you think will best enable you to present a forceful argument to the activity which follows.

Belfast: facts and figures

Population

Belfast population 500,000 (Northern Ireland total 1,500,000).

Size

The Belfast area covers 60 square miles.

Accessibility

Good motorway connections to rest of Northern Ireland. Good links also to the Republic of Ireland – Dublin is two hours away by road or rail.

Two airports: London to Belfast is 1 hour's flying time. There are 17 flights daily in each direction.

Belfast – Key to a lucrative market

The Northern Ireland Market has an economic significance beyond its relative size. Northern Ireland households spend more than the GB average on food, on footwear and on clothing. Branded products also do better in Northern Ireland than in mainland Britain – which makes the market a profitable place in which to sell. Belfast is the key to capturing this trade.

Purchasing Power

Yes, Belfast's catchment has the purchasing power. More Mercs than the GB average! And a higher penetration of dishwashers, tumble driers, lawnmowers, electric kettles, toasters and coffee makers!

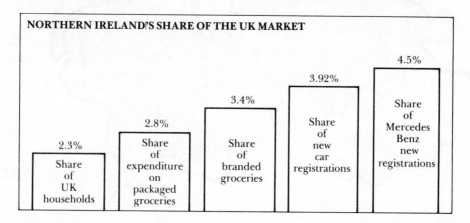

Figure 4.17 Purchasing power in Northern Ireland.

There is a daily passenger/freight boat to Liverpool. Sealink and P&O operate 100 ferry sailings to Scotland a week.

Employment and income

Number of employees in the Belfast travel to work area (1987) is 350,000. Number working in Belfast city centre is 54,000.

Unemployment in the Belfast travel to work area (July 1987) is 63,363 (18.2%).

Estimated average weekly household income (1985) is £208 per week.

Schools/hospitals

The city has 27 nursery schools, 100 primary schools, 18 grammar schools, 29 secondary schools, 11 special schools, 3 further education colleges, 2 teacher training colleges and 2 universities. There are 9 hospitals with 4,278 beds

Leisure facilities

The city has 14 leisure centres, an internationally acclaimed Opera House, 5 other theatres, an international athletics track, an international soccer stadium, an ice rink and 10 golf courses.

Housing

Housing stock in the Belfast urban area is 171,000.

Environment

There is an ongoing programme to pedestrianise and improve city centre streets. Grants are available to improve commercial buildings.

Belfast Enterprise Zone

Set up in 1981 for a ten year period. Up to 1986, 192 new companies have set up in the Zone.

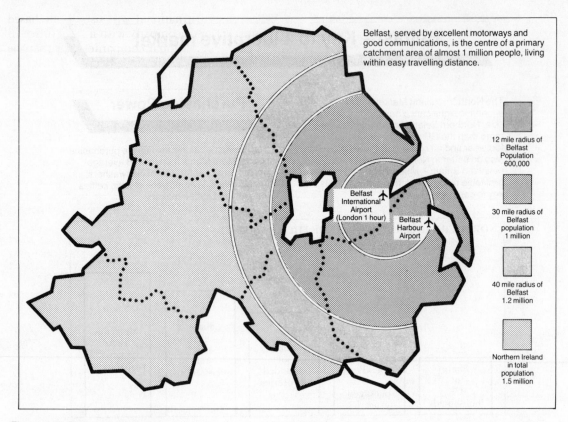

Belfast, served by excellent motorways and good communications, is the centre of a primary catchment area of almost 1 million people, living within easy travelling distance.

Belfast International Airport (London 1 hour)

Belfast Harbour Airport

12 mile radius of Belfast Population 600,000

30 mile radius of Belfast population 1 million

40 mile radius of Belfast 1.2 million

Northern Ireland in total population 1.5 million

Figure 4.18 Belfast catchment area.

Retailing

A recent survey shows that 56% of shoppers in the Belfast urban area shop in the city centre at least once a month; 29% shop in the city centre once a week or more frequently. Major national chain stores in Belfast city centre include Marks & Spencer, Littlewoods, British Home Stores, Boots, Chelsea Girl, Trueform, Argos, Poundstretcher, Milletts, Woolworths, CWS, Burtons, Top Shop, Richard Shops, Wallis, Jaeger, Connect, Dewhurst, Body Shop, Saxone, Dorothy Perkins, Benetton, Thornton's, Fosters, Next, C&A, Thomas Cook, Mothercare and Radio Rentals.

Retail Stores

Belfast's position in company league tables:

Boots	1st
Littlewoods	3rd
BHS	5th
Marks & Spencer	10th overall

There are nine retail stores in Belfast exceeding 50,000 square feet. Belfast's Thursday night late-night shopping is a major feature of retailing.

Retail turnover

Estimated retail turnover generated by Belfast urban area household expenditure plus catchment area is £1,180 million per year.

■ Activity

You work for a major retailing chain selling 'own-brand' groceries. The firm has an important decision to make – to open up a new store in Belfast or not. The store would be located in central Belfast, employing 100 staff (six of whom would be relocated from other parts of the United Kingdom).

Your task is to prepare a presentation for the company board (the class) on why the firm should open up a new store in Belfast. You have been asked simply to outline the main points in favour. In particular you have been asked to select and outline five major locational factors that would make Belfast an attractive choice. You must also produce one overhead projector transparency to go with your talk. Your group will be given ten minutes to make your presentation.

Industrial inertia

Firms locate in a given place because it appears to be the most sensible at the time. As times change, conditions change. A new firm which is just setting up will look for the 'new best site'. However, established firms tend to stay where they are. This process whereby firms become rooted to an existing location is called *industrial inertia..*

It is possible that industrial inertia will lead to a loss of profits relative to what they would be if a firm was prepared to move. However, there are a host of non-financial reasons for firms staying put, including loyalty to an area, loyalty to the workforce, identification with the local community, etc.

In the long term most firms and industries have to change with the times. The way that they do this depends on whether the firm is simply concerned with financial returns or takes into account other non-money factors.

Multinational companies

A *multinational* is a company that operates on a large scale in a number of countries at the same time. The multinational will usually be based around a parent company with a head office in one country. National companies will then be responsible for organising operations in other countries and continents.

An example of this form of organisation is shown in Figure 4.19 for an imaginary petrol company Star International. Star International drills for oil, refines oil and sells oil through its petrol stations.

The multinational may give considerable local power to its subsidiaries. Reports will regularly be submitted and, if necessary, trouble-shooters from the parent company will be sent out to deal with problems.

Multinational companies themselves have considerable power. Some commentators have referred to them as being the third world power after the USA and USSR. Their power rests in the fact that they are:

major employers
major buyers
major producers.

If a multinational sets up in a particular country it can create a considerable amount of employment and income. If it withdraws its operation, it takes away that employment and income. Governments may be reluctant to antagonise multinationals for this reason.

Because of their sheer size and power foreign multinationals may be tempted into certain less than ethical business practices. These practices are particularly questionable when safety is poor, wages are low, taxes are evaded, and local companies are faced by unfair competition. For example, the Union Carbide company (an

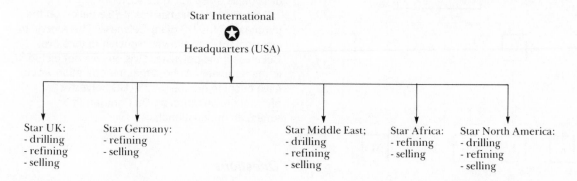

Figure 4.19 The organisation of a multinational.

American multinational) operated a chemical plant close to the centre of Bhopal in India. A serious explosion occurred at the factory causing a cloud of chemicals to engulf the town. Hundreds of people died, and many thousands more suffered from inhaling the fumes. When the plant was investigated it was found that safety was poor and a number of regulations had been broken.

Moreover, in recent years a number of multinationals have been criticised on account of the low wages they pay and the high profits they take out of 'third-world' countries. Pharmaceutical multinationals in particular have been criticised for experimenting with new medicines and drugs in 'third-world' countries.

Multinational companies can also have a destabilising effect on national economies in the way they open up and close down new plants. How this can happen is illustrated in Figure 4.20. AB Holdings is a *holding company*; that is, one that has a majority shareholding in other companies. It owns businesses C and D because it has a 51% shareholding in them. As a result it also owns E, F, G, H and I. Company I is a packaging firm producing tin boxes for the group. If AB Holdings is then taken over by a foreign multinational which already has its own packaging company, the future of company I and its workforce will be in danger.

You will often have heard it said, when one company takes over another, that 'some rationalisation is inevitable'. This usually means that some lines of production are to be cut out (or run down), some production units are to be closed and some jobs are to disappear.

Multinationals sometimes have an enormous amount of power in the market. When they are one of a small number of buyers or sellers they can put a lot of pressure on the people whom they deal with. For example, if there are a lot of small producers of tobacco in a third-world country selling to one large multinational buyer, then that multinational is in a very powerful position. In this situation growers will benefit from joining together to form a marketing co-operative.

■ Case study: Hoechst

Hoechst, the West German chemical giant, is one of the five major chemical companies in the world. Hoechst directly owns 500 chemical-related companies throughout the world, only 60 of which are based in Germany. It also employs 200,000 people throughout the world (including 100,000 in Germany). The Hoechst group operates in 120 countries, selling three times as much outside its home country as within it. Sales by region in 1986 were as follows:

Western Europe	34%
West Germany	28%
North America	13%
Latin America	6%
Australia	2%
Asia	9%
Africa	4%
Eastern Europe	4%
100%	= DM 38,014 million

The range of Hoechst's activities, broken down by division, is given in Figure 4.21.

Recently Hoechst has spent $2.8 billion on the purchase of the US giant Celanese. The American government only allowed Hoechst to take over Celanese if the polyester division was not included in the purchase. Without that the operation would have become number one in US polyester production, outstripping Du Pont (another American multinational).

Figure 4.20 The organisation of a holding company.

Questions

1. Is Hoechst a multinational? Explain.

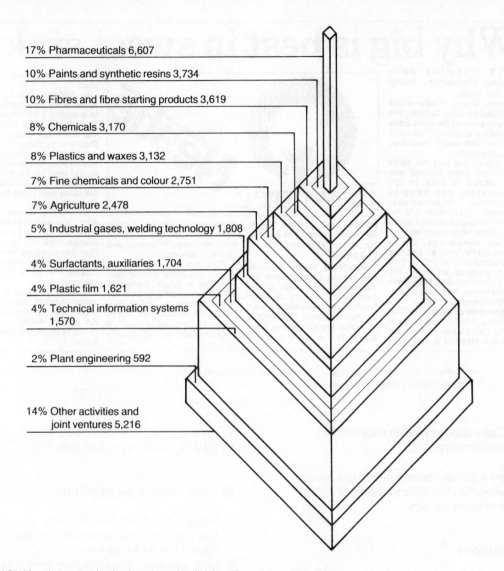

17% Pharmaceuticals 6,607

10% Paints and synthetic resins 3,734

10% Fibres and fibre starting products 3,619

8% Chemicals 3,170

8% Plastics and waxes 3,132

7% Fine chemicals and colour 2,751

7% Agriculture 2,478

5% Industrial gases, welding technology 1,808

4% Surfactants, auxiliaries 1,704

4% Plastic film 1,621

4% Technical information systems 1,570

2% Plant engineering 592

14% Other activities and joint ventures 5,216

Figure 4.21 Hoechst: net sales broken down by division (figures in million DM).

2. What evidence is given above that Hoechst benefits from economies of scale? Describe how some of these economies of scale might operate.
3. Where does Hoechst employ the bulk of its labour?
4. Where does Hoechst sell the bulk of its product?
5. Why do you think that Hoechst produces in a wide range of markets? What benefits does the company get from this diversification?

6. Who benefits from the activities of Hoechst? Make out a list. Explain in detail how two particular groups or individuals benefit.
7. Why do you think the American government would not allow Hoechst to take over the polyester division of Celanese?
8. What evidence would you put forward to back up the argument that 'Hoechst is a powerful business organisation'?
9. What further information would you require to be able to back up this statement?

Why big is best in sweet stakes

CITY investors were arming themselves today for Bar Wars.

From Nestle headquarters overlooking Lake Geneva, the hungry giant of the food trade is seeking an outright takeover of the York-based Rowntree Kit Kat empire.

Forty Kit Kat bars are eaten in Britain every second and the snack is sold in 100 countries, but despite Rowntree's international strength, a full-scale bid for Britain's largest confectionery group had been expected.

Two weeks ago, Swiss chocolate group Jacobs Suchard paid £162 million for a 14.9 percent stake in the business started by Mary Tuke in Walmgate, York, and sold to Henry Rowntree in 1862.

Rowntree's introduced Fruit Pastilles in 1881, Fruit Gums in 1893, Black Magic in 1933, Kit Kat and Smarties in 1937, Polo Mints in 1948, and the Yorkie Bar in 1976. Today, the group's market capitalisation is around £1.5 billion.

Worldwide nearly five million tonnes of chocolate are swallowed each year, manufactured by a host of small family businesses and a clutch of multinationals, the biggest of which are US giants Mars and Hershey and Switzerland's Nestle. Behind them come the two large UK manufacturers, Rowntree and Cadbury Schweppes.

With the European Community adjusting competition laws for a single market in 1992, the chocolate trade is the latest sector to ditch the "small is beautiful" concept in favour of "biggest is best", if only because market muscle increases the chance of survival.

In Britain, the corporate appetite for takeovers surged to a record 1,937 deals worth £27.1 billion last year. Since the Guinness acquisition of Distillers in 1986, the British economy has witnessed a succession of "sector wars" fought from the High Street – Burtons v Debenhams – to the skies now ruled by British Airways.

Suchard's recent "dawn raid" investment in Rowntree marked the opening of manoeuvres to consolidate the continental chocolate market, but also signalled the possibility of a full-scale takeover.

Ironically, it was Rowntree which opened hostilities 20 years ago by manufacturing Kit Kat in Hamburg, Quality Street in Dijon, and Lion Bar in Paris.

Figure 4.22 Battle for supremacy amongst chocolate manufacturers.
Source: Yorkshire Evening Post, 15 March 1988.

■ Case study: Multinationals in confectionery

Figure 4.22 reproduces a newspaper article covering the multinational aspect of the confectionery industry.

Questions

1. Is Rowntree a multinational? Explain.
2. Does the article indicate that confectionery manufacture is totally dominated by multinational companies? Explain.
3. What advantages do large companies have which enable them to produce high outputs at low average costs?
4. What changes are taking place which favour the growth of multinational confectionery manufacture in the European market?
5. What motives might Suchard have for wanting to take over Rowntree?
6. Who stands to lose out from a possible takeover?
7. What is meant in the article by 'sector wars'?
8. Why do 'sector wars' take place?

■ Coursework suggestions

1. Study a local firm which has recently grown in size. Try to find out what major economies of scale it has benefited from.
2. What particular industries have tended to concentrate in your area? How would you explain this localisation?

■ Revision

Complete the following sentences using the words below:

merger	managerial economies
horizontal	commercial
backward vertical	risk spreading
forward vertical	Stock Exchange
lateral	share shops

conglomerate
disintegration
debenture
ordinary share
preference share
financial economies

dividend
internal economies of
scale
external economies of
scale
technical economies

1. A _____ in a company entitles the holder to a dividend before other shareholders.
2. The _____ is a marketplace for second-hand stocks and shares.
3. _____ is the process whereby an existing company sells off some of its interests.
4. A large company is able to hire a specialist accountant, a company secretary, a sales director and a personnel director. The company is reaping the benefits of _____ of scale.
5. _____ integration might involve the joining together of two firms producing different products that are distributed through the same channels.
6. A merger of two businesses at the same stage of production is an example of _____ integration.
7. The reward to a shareholder is known as a _____ .
8. _____ of scale involve improvements to the technique of production such as the employment of specialist machinery.
9. _____ benefit all the firms in an industry.
10. _____ enable a firm to produce a larger output at a lower average cost.
11. A _____ is a large firm producing a range of unrelated products.
12. A soft drinks manufacturer taking over a plant that takes the salt out of sea water would be an example of _____ integration.
13. A _____ holder in a company does not own part of the company. Such a person would simply have lent the company money.
14. _____ economies of scale involve producing a range of products rather than putting all your eggs in the same basket.
15. _____ of scale enable large firms to borrow money at a cheaper rate than that available to smaller enterprises.
16. _____ are opening up on some high streets enabling shoppers to buy and sell company stocks and shares.
17. Being able to buy in bulk is an example of a _____ economy of scale.
18. A brewery buying up a pub is an example of _____ integration.
19. If you own an _____ in a company you will receive your share of the profits after all other groups entitled to a share of the profits have been paid.
20. A _____ is a friendly joining together of two businesses.

CHAPTER 5
The individual and work

Different types of employment

In a modern society based on widescale division of labour there are hundreds of thousands of different occupations and a wide range of different conditions of work. Employees are expected to work under a variety of arrangements including full-time, part-time, flexitime, shiftwork and numerous other practices. Work also takes place in a wide range of organisational structures – large companies, small companies, 'sweat-shops', air-conditioned offices, public companies, co-operatives, etc.

Rewards for work

Job satisfaction is a very personal thing. Some people enjoy doing repetitive work and being told what do to; others look for the freedom to make their own decisions and to work in their own way. Some workers look for enjoyment and satisfaction in their work, whereas others get little satisfaction from their job and look for pleasure outside.

■ Activity

Because job satisfaction is such a personal thing it needs to be investigated by some form of primary research. As a group you should question a wide selection of people to find out what gives them job satisfaction.

Generally speaking you will find that boring, repetitive jobs are least likely to stimulate employees. However, you might find that many people in these jobs work hard and for long hours because they are trying to earn enough money to enjoy the other part of their lives – their leisure hours.

Different types of reward are appropriate in different situations. (You should always bear in mind that for many people work is a reward in itself.)

Basic pay

Basic pay is the amount of money that will be received by the employee before any additional increments or deductions are made. For example, the basic pay may be set at £80 for a 40 hour week.

Overtime

Overtime will need to be paid at a higher rate. The rate will usually depend on how difficult it is to persuade the labour force to work unsocial hours. Whilst overtime worked during weekdays may need to be paid at, for example, one and a half times the basic hourly wage, on a Saturday the rate may need to be increased to twice the basic hourly rate.

Overtime is usually offered by firms where the amount of work varies considerably and it would not be economical to take on more full-time staff.

Bonus pay

Bonus pay is used as an incentive to persuade employees to work harder. Bonuses may be offered to encourage the staff to meet certain targets, e.g. to meet certain production or sales figures. It is common practice to offer a bonus at

Christmas time, or just before the summer holidays when otherwise there would be a temptation to slacken off.

Commission

Salespeople are often rewarded according to the results they achieve. They might, for example, be able to take for themselves 10% of the price of all the sales that they make.

Piece rate

Piece rates may be offered as an alternative to basic time rates. Workers are rewarded according to the output they produce. This is least suitable when work needs a lot of precision and care.

Perks (non-monetary rewards)

Many jobs include a wide range of fringe benefits which do not appear directly in the pay packet. Railway employees and their families, for example, may benefit from free rail travel. Managerial jobs often include perks such as subsidised company cars and phone bills. Other fringe benefits include:

1. Subsidised canteen facilities
2. Free training courses
3. The right to buy the firm's product at discount prices

■ Case study: Job opportunities

Look at the job advertisements given in Figure 5.1, then answer the questions below.

Questions

1. What information contained in the advertisements indicates that these jobs offer a secure future?
2. What fringe benefits are offered by Napcolour Ltd?
3. Write out a letter of application for a job as a Laboratory Assistant with Napcolour Ltd.
4. Why do you think that Hilary Morgan are only offering piece rate earnings once workers have finished their period of training?
5. Apart from wages, what benefits will you get from joining Hilary Morgan?

HIGH STREET
FAST FILM PROCESSING
(Experience desirable but not essential)

Acknowledged as the UK leader in the rapidly growing high street fast film business, with a reputation for the best in quality, we are looking to recruit:

MANAGER
PRINTERS
FULL TIME LABORATORY
ASSISTANTS

For our new Mini Lab opening shortly in Grantham

In addition to a competitive salary we offer:
☆ In depth training
☆ Non contributory pension scheme
☆ 23 days annual holiday
☆ Staff discount
☆ Excellent propsects for promotion.

If you think you can work in a fast moving and stimulating environment with a small, dedicated team of professionals, please apply in writing to:

Mini Labs Recruitment, Napcolour Ltd, Unit 1, Goddard Rd, Astmoor Industrial Estate, Runcorn, Cheshire WA7 1QF.
All interviews will be held locally.

13/5 Ldr

TRAINEE SEWING
MACHINISTS

LEARN WHILE YOU EARN

Age 16 £46.18 per week
Age 17 £57.92 per week
Age 18+ £74.10 per week

With a full order book Hilary Morgan are recruiting for their Training School.

On graduation you will be a skilled worker able to make Bridal and Bridesmaids gowns right through. You will be ready for piecework and have a skilled trade in your hands.

Vacancies for experienced Lockstitch Machinists — former employees very welcome.

Ask for Mrs Wileman at the Station Road entrance or telephone 66125.

HILARY MORGAN
The nation's first name in Bridal Wear

Figure 5.1 Examples of job advertisements.

Income from employment

A host of different factors will determine your pay. These factors will include:

1. *Qualifications and skills.* Employees who have either developed their educational background or who have trained for a number of years to acquire a skill will expect to be rewarded for their expertise. For example, it takes many years of dedication to become a surgeon and so surgeons expect a salary which rewards them for this hard work.
2. *Experience.* Staff who have worked for an organisation for a long time are often paid at higher rates because their experience provides many benefits. For example, in the teaching profession teachers are paid increments annually which compensate for their loyalty and is a recognition of the expertise they have developed in the classroom.
3. *Payment for results.* Some workers have their pay directly linked to their output. In many industries workers are paid on 'piece rates' where their pay is directly linked to the number of items they have contributed to. Salespeople are often paid a commission which relates directly to the sales they have completed.
4. *Overtime.* In some occupations overtime is plentiful and it enables employees to boost their basic pay.
5. *Demand and supply of labour.* If labour is in short supply and the demand for that particular type of labour is strong, employers will be prepared to pay higher wages to engage suitable workers. For example, it has been argued recently that teachers of shortage subjects such as computer studies, maths and science should be paid more.
6. *Location.* It is considerably more expensive for employees to live in the South East than in other parts of the country such as the North East. Many employers recognise this and provide allowances to compensate for costs such as accommodation.
7. *Danger or dirt.* Some jobs are particularly dangerous and others downright unhealthy. In some of these occupations employees might only have a limited period of work. Many employers will take the nature of the work into consideration and try to provide a

suitable pay scale. Examples might include industrial cleaning or diving.
8. *Responsibility.* Those who undertake jobs which involve supervision, decision-taking and influencing the lives of others are often suitably rewarded for this pressure. For example, it would be expected that a production manager would earn more than a production-line worker.

We can apply these pay-determining factors in a number of examples:

1. A *doctor* earns more than a *hospital porter* because of:
   (a) qualifications
   (b) extensive overtime
   (c) greater demand for and limited supply of doctors
   (d) responsibility.
2. A *50-year-old* worker may earn more than a *17-year-old* who does the same job because of:
   (a) skills developed over a long period
   (b) experience
   (c) loyalty.
3. A bank clerk may earn more in the *South East* than a bank clerk in the *North East* because of:
   (a) a greater demand for bank clerks in the South East and, at the same time, a shortage of qualified labour
   (b) the need to compensate for the expense of living in the South East.

■ Question

1. What factors would you expect to influence the wages of the employee in the photograph (Figure 5.2)?

Working conditions

Working conditions vary widely. Different jobs offer different advantages and disadvantages. One organisation listed the following factors as being important in choosing a job:

1. High wages
2. Security of employment
3. A good working environment
4. Good personal relationships with the people you work with

Figure 5.2 Working at the checkout of a supermarket.

5. An interesting job
6. Opportunity to exercise responsibility
7. Good consultative procedures between 'boss' and 'workers'
8. Short working hours
9. Longer holidays
10. Opportunities for promotion
11. Doing an important job
12. Opportunity to use your full ability
13. Having confidence in the people you work with
14. Knowing what is happening, e.g. future company developments

■ Questions

1. Study the list above and try to rank the items in the list in order of importance to you in choosing a job.
2. What other factors would you add to the list?

■ Coursework activity

Design a class questionnaire based upon different factors related to job satisfaction. Interview a selection of people to find out what job satisfaction means to them. Find out how job satisfaction varies between different jobs and different individuals. For example, you may find out that some people get a lot of job satisfaction from employment that you consider boring.

Finding employment

Finding paid employment is not always easy. This is particularly true in some areas of the country where old industries have died without being replaced by new ones. There are a number of sources of information and help for those seeking work, including:

1. parents and friends
2. government employment agencies
3. private employment agencies
4. newspapers and other sources of information.

Family and friends

Family and friends are a good source of information when looking for work. They often know of job vacancies where they work themselves and may be able to put in a good word with the employer. Many firms take pride in their close relationships with groups of families over a number of generations. It also takes a lot of time for a large firm to sift through job applications and interview people for work. If they can cut through this procedure by interviewing the family and friends of existing workers they can save much time and trouble.

Government employment agencies

Government-run employment agencies play a major part in finding jobs for people who are unable to do so by other means.

The job-finding agency established to deal with school leavers is the *Careers Service*. Every school has a careers officer who interviews all potential school leavers during their fifth year. The careers officer works from a local careers office where a list of local job vacancies will be

Figure 5.3 An eye-catching job advertisement

displayed. The careers officer will put school leavers in touch with companies in which they are interested.

The *Employment Service* has brought together the Jobcentre network with the network of unemployment benefit offices. The priority of the Employment Service is to:

1. To give encouragement and help to people who have been unemployed for over six months and to other unemployed people who need such help.
2. To make accurate and prompt payments of benefit to unemployed claimants, at the same time making sure that benefit is paid only to those who are entitled to it.
3. To bring together Jobcentres, unemployment benefit offices and other agencies, particularly by using information technology.

Jobcentres

Jobcentres can be found in prominent places in most towns. Cards advertising jobs are on open display and members of the public can arrange interviews with Jobcentre staff who can then make appointments for job interviews.

Restart scheme

The Restart scheme works as follows. Every benefit claimant who has been unemployed for six months or more receives a letter inviting him or her personally to an interview at a Jobcentre. At these interviews, unemployed people are invited to discuss the problems they face in their search for a job. Each is offered advice and information about the job training and other

Figure 5.4 Classified job advertisements in a local paper.
Source: Grantham Journal.

opportunities which are available. The aim is to try to arrange a course of action that will help the individual to get back to work.

Job Clubs

In a Job Club, a group of unemployed people meet locally to help themselves – and each other – find the best possible jobs in the shortest possible time. The government provides facilities such as free use of telephones, free stationery and postage. Skilled staff are also available to give advice on such matters as how to present yourself at an interview.

The Enterprise Allowance Scheme

Many unemployed people would like the opportunity to set up their own business. Under the Scheme, unemployed people who want to set up in business and are eligible are paid an allowance of £40 per week for a year while the business gets going. They must provide £1,000 of their own capital, which is matched by a government grant. They can also get free business advice.

Private employment agencies

A number of private agencies also recruit workers for companies. These agencies often specialise in particular areas of work, e.g. office, manual, technical or managerial.

These agencies are most widely known in the field of recruiting temporary secretarial help. A secretary signs to work for an agency. The agency then finds a temporary appointment for that person with a company. The company pays the wages direct to the agency which takes a commission from the pay packet before handing it on to the temp.

Newspapers and other sources of information

The classified columns of most local newspapers usually run to several pages. An example of such a jobs section is given in Figure 5.4. National newspapers usually display advertisements for different categories of jobs on specific days of the week. Figure 5.5 lists on what days what types of job will be advertised in *The Independent*.

Some job opportunities nowadays are advertised on the television and radio in programmes related to finding work. Job opportunities are also being displayed by computer links as part of database networks.

MONDAY

■ Computerlink ■ Engineering Appointments
■ Science and Technology Appointments
■ General Appointments ■ Business Contact
■ Independent Classified

TUESDAY

■ Accountancy Appointments ■ Financial
Appointments ■ Banking Appointments
■ Insurance Appointments ■ Secretarial
Appointments ■ Premier ■ General
Appointments ■ Independent Classified

WEDNESDAY

■ Media, Marketing and Sales Appointments
■ Professional and Technical Appointments
■ General Appointments
■ Independent Classified

THURSDAY

■ Public Appointments ■ Education
Appointments ■ Health Appointments
■ Graduate Opportunities ■ Secretarial
Appointments ■ Premier ■ General
Appointments ■ Education and Tuition
■ Independent Classified

FRIDAY

■ Legal Appointments ■ Arts Appointments
■ Retail Appointments ■ General Appointments
■ Entertainments ■ Independent Classified

SATURDAY

■ Travel ■ London Property ■ Country
Property ■ Overseas Property ■ New Homes
■ Gardening ■ Motors/Transport
■ Independent Classified

Figure 5.5 Days on which categories of job will be advertised. Source: The Independent.

■ Activity

For this activity you will interview three candidates in 45 minutes for the post of trainee manager at Marks and Spencer. The activity works best if the teacher arranges for three 'actors' to play the parts of the three candidates. Groups carrying out the interview should be made up of no more than eight. This activity is particularly useful in helping you to understand the way that interviews work.

By the end of the 45 minutes you should have all the evidence required to make a rational decision as to the suitability of each candidate for the post. Your group will be required to give a presentation to the rest of the groups on who you will give the job to and why. In reaching these decisions it will be helpful if you use the job description given below in conjunction with the interview assessment form given in Figure 5.6 and the application forms and résumés referred to later.

The task

1. To draw up a list of qualities that you think candidates should have. Refer to the 'Seven Point Plan' in Figure 5.7.
2. There should be an agreed set of questions which the group thinks will determine whether the candidate has these qualities.

3. The interviewing environment (i.e. the use of desks and chairs) should make both the interviewers and the interviewees feel at ease.
4. Each student should have some form of responsibility.
5. There should be a chairperson with responsibility for the collecting of candidates and introducing the interviewing panel. This person need not be the same for each candidate.
6. Each person on the interviewing panel needs to understand fully the assessment and be prepared to fill one in.
7. The interviewers need to decide how to allocate time. You are allotted fifteen minutes per candidate – do you need all this time or should there be time for general assessment by the panel?
8. If time permits conduct a trial run.

The position

Trainee manager at Marks & Spencer

Background

The Company. One of the top ten companies in the UK by turnover and a leading retailer. The company employs over 50,000 and is fast expanding.

INTERVIEW ASSESSMENT						
Factors	**Rating**					**Remarks**
	A	**B**	**C**	**D**	**E**	
Appearance Personality Disposition Health						
General intelligence Comprehension						
Aptitudes Special Abilities Work Experience						
Interests Hobbies Sports						
Academic						
Motivation						
Circumstances Mobility Hours Limitations						
General assessment						

A – Exceptional;   B – Above average;   C – Satisfactory;
D – Below average;   E – Unsuitable.

CHECKLIST
1. Introduce interviewing panel.
2. Put interviewee at ease.
3. General introduction, what is the job?
4. Training.
5. Expectations of a manager.
6. Has the interviewee any questions?
7. Dismissal of interviewee.

Figure 5.6 Interview assessment form and checklist.

A manager. Managers at all levels would be expected to show responsibility. The company is looking for people who are tough and talented. They should have a flair for business and know how to sell and work in a team.

The training. The first year's training will introduce the new manager to the stores and to working in a management team. In the second year trainees can specialise in personnel, selling or administration.

Salaries: £6,500–£9,000 p.a.

The Seven Point Plan

Many companies advise their interviewers to obtain information by applying the Seven Point Plan devised by the National Institute of Industrial Psychology. The seven points about which the candidates can be questioned are:

1. Physical condition, which may be backed up by a medical examination.

2. Attainments, including academic and past industrial experience.

3. Special aptitudes.

4. Intelligence – the way in which questions of a general nature are answered not requiring any specialist knowledge.

5. Interests, hobbies and other forms of relaxation.

6. Disposition towards authority and towards other workers.

7. Circumstances under which the applicant is living.

Information given to the applicant should include probable earnings or salary and conditions of service.

Figure 5.7 The 'Seven Point Plan' for formulating interview questions.

The candidates

Candidate 1. Sees herself as great management potential and views her present job as adequate training for such a position. This candidate is keen to get on, but not over keen to make the required effort. Thinks she is being overworked in her present employment and working as a trainee manager should be a 'piece of cake'. Her résumé and application form are given in Figure 5.8.

Candidate 2. College graduate keen to enter the world of work. She has spent her summers working at Marks & Spencer whilst at college and has been very impressed by what the firm has to offer. The candidate sees this position as the first step in her career. Her résumé and application form are given in Figure 5.9.

Candidate 3. Tends to think that the world owes him a living and has had a chequered employment history since leaving school. He sees this position as one of the many options available to him in the job market and possibly sees it as a 'cushy number'. His résumé and application form are given in Figure 5.10.

■ Coursework activity: Staff selection

Select two jobs in order to investigate appropriate methods of recruitment of staff to fill these positions. How would you recruit for each job? Compare the approaches – what were the differences? Give your reasons.

Background work

Look at available advertising and select two jobs for study. Use local papers, freesheets and available specialist papers and advertising at Job Centres and employment agencies. Keep a selection of advertisements for the jobs you choose or copy details from cards on display.

Get your teacher to arrange a visit from a personnel officer to talk about his or her firm's methods of recruitment.

If you know an employer or employee with inside knowledge of a job that you are considering, see if they will talk to you. This might be particularly helpful in compiling a job description and deciding on the type of personality and qualifications required.

Details to look for

For each position you are recruiting for:

1. What business or other organisation would require this type of work?
2. What would be a suitable job title?
3. What would be the job description?
4. What sort of personality would be required?
5. What types of qualifications and previous experience would be needed?
6. What would be the closing date for applications?

[*text continues on p. 94*]

```
                              Résumé

PERSONAL DETAILS:
AGE: 22;  Single; British;  Excellent Health

EDUCATION:
      St. Luphen's College          1975 - 1980

Examinations:

          'O' Levels.

          Mathematics              C

          English Language         B

          Religious Education      A

          Design & Technology      A

          German                   C

          French                   B


EMPLOYMENT:

      1980 - present.

      "The Water Garden"        General Assistant


INTERESTS:
      Badminton, Horse Riding, Playing the Piano and Sailing.
```

Figure 5.8 Candidate 1: résumé and application form.

Management requires the ability to lead and organise others. Please list the positions of responsibility you have held, in employment, education or leisure. Indicate, against each, how you have personally contributed and how effective you have been.

```
At St. Luphen's College I was appointed Form Captain each
year from the second year onwards.  I became a prefect in
the Lower Sixth and Deputy Head Girl in the Upper Sixth.
At 14 I represented the school at Badminton and I now play
for a local club.
```

Outline any initiatives you have taken. What have you been able to achieve?

```
I have frequently been left in charge to manage the
"Water Garden", a boutique selling Japanese Water Plants.
I have had responsibility for stock control and the
day-to-day cash sales.
```

Which aspects of your academic work or employment have you most enjoyed and why?

```
Since leaving school I have felt at home in the retailing
environment.  The desire to satisfy customers is very
important, and I believe I can get on well with all levels
of people.
```

Which people, events and experiences in your life have you found difficult to handle?
How have you coped with them and how have you developed as a result?

```
I find it increasingly difficult at work as I feel I am
not adequately rewarded for the level of responsibility
and extra duties that I have undertaken.  It has become
increasingly obvious that I need to work in an environment
with a structured career progression and in one that the
individual is justly rewarded for their efforts.
```

In what ways do you use your spare time? Indicate why and how you became involved.

```
Horse-riding, playing the piano and sailing.
```

What alternative careers have you considered and why?

```
I have not considered any other career outside retailing
as I feel quite satisfied doing the actual work.
```

Please use this space if you have any further information which you wish to add in support of this
application.

Résumé

PERSONAL DETAILS:

AGE: 21; Single;   British; Excellent Health

EDUCATION:	Kingsley Grammar School for Girls.	1976 - 1983
	Hull University	1983 - 1987

Examinations: "O" Levels.

Mathematics	B
English Language	A
English Literature	A
French	A
History	B
Geography	B
Science	B

"A" Levels

French	A
German	B
English	C

B.A. (Hons) Degree in Modern Languages

EMPLOYMENT:

Marks & Spencer   Sales Assistant   Vacation Work

INTERESTS:

Sport - Judo
Travel - Travelled widely throughout Europe.

Figure 5.9 Candidate 2: résumé and application form.

Management requires the ability to lead and organise others. Please list the positions of responsibility you have held, in employment, education or leisure. Indicate, against each, how you have personally contributed and how effective you have been.

```
Being Head Girl at Kingsley Grammar School involved organising
rotas for prefects; contacts with outside agencies; hosting
Governor's meetings; and, making speeches at Prize Giving. My
organisation was thought to be effective and the year generally
successful.
```

Outline any initiatives you have taken. What have you been able to achieve?

```
Travelled widely throughout Europe on completing my "A" Levels.
Completed Stage I exams in Judo.
```

Which aspects of your academic work or employment have you most enjoyed and why?

```
Working at Marks & Spencer during my summer vacations I found the
work most interesting, the firm very caring, and with meeting new
people every day, there was hardly a dull moment!
```

Which people, events and experiences in your life have you found difficult to handle?
How have you coped with them and how have you developed as a result?

```
Moving away from home and friends to go to college was very
difficult. Although at the time it seemed a big move, I certainly
became more independent as a result.
```

In what ways do you use your spare time? Indicate why and how you became involved.

```
I attend local judo and keep-fit classes.
I have recently passed my driving test.
```

What alternative careers have you considered and why?

```
Teaching which involves contact and dealing with people, but the
rewards and career progression do not seem to be as promising as
in industry.
```

Please use this space if you have any further information which you wish to add in support of this
application.

Résumé			
PERSONAL DETAILS:			
AGE: 21; Single; British; Excellent Health			
EDUCATION: Kingsley Comprehensive School 1976-1983			
Examinations:			
'O' Levels		'A' Levels	
Mathematics	B	English	E
English Language	C	History	E
History	C		

EMPLOYMENT:

Red Lion, Kingsley	Bar Person	1983-1985
Viking Insurance	Sales Person	1985-1986
Financial Trust	Trainee Manager	1986-

INTERESTS:

Beer and Wine Making

Figure 5.10 Candidate 3: résumé and application form.

Management requires the ability to lead and organise others. Please list the positions of responsibility you have held, in employment, education or leisure. Indicate, against each, how you have personally contributed and how effective you have been.

I organised a successful summer holiday abroad for half a dozen friends. It required booking, confirming, collecting money and arranging coach travel.
At present, as a trainee manager, I have the responsibility to interview clients for their credit worthiness and to recommend loans. In the same capacity in the loans department I have to chase up bad debtors. I do these jobs to the best of my ability and think that I am reasonably successful.

Outline any initiatives you have taken. What have you been able to achieve?

I started the Duke of Edinburgh Award scheme whilst at school, but was unable to complete due to lack of time.

Which aspects of your academic work or employment have you most enjoyed and why?

Working as a bar person at the Red Lion Inn was most enjoyable. Basically I was left on my own to get the job done, and I was given a large degree of responsibility.

Which people, events and experiences in your life have you found difficult to handle? How have you coped with them and how have you developed as a result?

After leaving school I found living with my parents a very difficult experience. As a consequence I found lodgings near the Red Lion. However after a time this also became too much.

In what ways do you use your spare time? Indicate why and how you became involved.

With a group of friends I usually tour the Real-Ale pubs. I became involved through a natural interest in wine and beer making.

What alternative careers have you considered and why?

Self-employed as one is given a large degree of responsibility and you are your own boss. Unable to pursue this, however, due to lack of capital.

Please use this space if you have any further information which you wish to add in support of this application.

Documents to prepare

1. An advertisement.
2. An application form – if appropriate.
3. Further details for enquirers – include any part of the job description that does not appear in the advertisement.

Final report

You should include as much as possible of the following:

1. Statement of the questions you are considering.
2. The choice of jobs you decided to investigate.
3. Sample advertising of similar positions.
4. Summary of interview with employer or employee if you do one.
5. A description of the recruiting methods used by a firm, if you have visited one.
6. For each job you chose in turn:
   (a) Your advertisement.
   (b) Where you would place it, and why you chose that paper/agency, etc.
   (c) Further details for enquirers.
   (d) Describe how you would proceed when applications were received.
   (e) How many people would you expect to interview?
   (f) How would you choose a shortlist?
   (g) What questions would you ask the applicants?
7. Summarise the differences between your procedures for the different jobs and give your reasons for the differences.

Training

Training for employment is very important. In a modern economy like that of the United Kingdom the nature of work is constantly changing. New technologies mean that new work skills are constantly required. To succeed in business or in a career, people will need to be very flexible about where they work and how they work, and to constantly change the range of skills they use at work. Fewer and fewer people will end their working lives in the same industry or occupation in which they started out. Nobody will be able to rely on an initial burst of training

received as they moved into employment to keep them going throughout their working life.

Many of the jobs created in the last decade of the twentieth century will be open only to workers with skills and qualifications. There will be less need in many industries for unskilled or semi-skilled workers.

There are basically two types of training:

1. *On-the-job training.* Employees develop and improve their work skills whilst actually doing the job in question. For example, word processor operators rapidly improve their skills by constant practice. The apprentice who starts to work on a press soon learns to maintain and repair the equipment.
2. *Off-the-job training.* Employers will often encourage their employees to develop their skills through off-the-job training courses. For example, a trainee may be allowed to attend a day-release course at the local college. This might apply to a wide range of different skills including hairdressing, banking, insurance, electrical work and plumbing.

Government training schemes

In recent years the government has reacted to the high unemployment figures by introducing a number of training schemes. It has, however, been pointed out that training is given far higher priority in countries such as France and Germany.

Training for Employment Programme

From September 1988 the government is bringing together all the existing programmes of training for those over the age of 18 into a single scheme. The aim of the new training scheme is to concentrate particularly on the long-term unemployed to re-equip them with new skills. The scheme will be available for all people who have been unemployed for over six months and to guarantee them a period of training of up to twelve months. The new training scheme will attempt to provide a range of new skills including those required by high technology industries and the skills needed to start up and run a small business.

People wishing to join the scheme will be referred to a training agent. The training agent will then refer the trainee to a training manager who is responsible for planning and directing the training programme. The training manager might be responsible for providing all the training personally or some of the training might be subcontracted, perhaps to an employer. Each programme of training will guarantee that the trainee spends 40% of his or her time on intensive skill training.

Training agents will be paid £15 for each trainee assessed and £20 for each trainee placed with a training manager. Training managers will be paid a weekly basic training grant of £17.50 per trainee. For more expensive training courses the grants will be much higher. Trainees that enter the programme will receive a payment of £10 more than they would from their normal benefits.

The Youth Training Scheme

This scheme is available for 16 to 18 year olds. They are guaranteed a period of on-the-job and off-the-job training. Training is supervised by Training Groups which are supported by government funds but are private organisations.

Classification of employment

In survey work people are often graded according to the occupations they do. The simplest division is that between *manual* and *non-manual* work. Jobs which require physical effort of some kind, such as in a mine or on a building site, are distinguished from those which involve working at a desk. This is mainly because considerable differences often exist in the level of wages, of skills, of working conditions, of attitudes and of prestige attached to manual and non-manual occupations. In a factory, for example, it is not unusual for manual and non-manual workers to use a different entrance, to work different hours, have different lunchbreaks, and to use different facilities.

The most commonly used classification of occupations is that produced by the Registrar-General. This classification divides occupations into five classes:

Class	Occupation
1	Professional and higher administrative, such as lawyers, architects and doctors.
2	Intermediate professional workers and administrative personnel, such as shopkeepers, farmers and teachers.
3	Skilled: (a) Non-manual, such as shop assistants and clerical workers in offices. (b) Manual such as tool-makers and electricians.
4	Semi-skilled, such as bus conductors, farm workers.
5	Unskilled, such as general labourers on building sites.

Since the 1950s there has been a steady decline in the numbers of low-skilled jobs and a great increase in the numbers of professional and lower and middle management positions. There are now more high-status jobs around. Commentators refer to the 'new working class' of workers particularly concentrated in the South of England who have more spending power and access to goods and services.

However, a quite distinct and radically different group has also emerged, labelled the 'underclass'. This group can be found in pockets all over the country and has in the main missed out on the general prosperity. It consists of those people who lack any power and who receive the worst of everything. It includes some pensioners, some single parent families, some poorly educated people and some members of minority ethnic groups.

Professional workers are a loose group of people who generally have to learn a body of knowledge in order to carry out their work, for example doctors and lawyers. They tend to earn high incomes and enjoy a good standard of living but often have to work long hours.

Many traditional working-class jobs have disappeared with the decline of manufacturing and the growth of the service sector of the economy. As a result far more opportunities have opened up for white collar workers. Whereas the old factory system would be characterised by people clocking on in the morning and clocking off at the end of the day, many of the new office and workplaces operate a flexi-time system. All workers are expected to be 'in' at certain key times but they then have the flexibility to work additional hours of their own choice. This has made it increasingly possible for young people who have to take their children to school to find rewarding work.

Another distinction in the workplace is between management and shop-floor workers. Managers have responsibility for a whole department such as production, marketing, accounts, distribution, sales or purchasing, and rarely carry out shop-floor tasks themselves. Many management decisions are relayed to the shop-floor through a supervisor who is responsible for running the operation at ground level.

A business will also employ administrative workers. An accounts clerk, for example, may fill in the ledger on a regular basis, and a secretarial worker will answer the phone and type letters.

Employers, employees and the law

Employers and employees are protected by a number of laws affecting each other's behaviour. Over the years a complex set of rules has developed stretching to thousands of pages in the law books. At this stage, however, you will only need a broad outline of some of these rules. The most important areas concern:

1. Health and safety
2. Equality of employment.

Health and safety

Why is health and safety at work important? In an average year 1,000 people are killed in the workplace and over 500,000 are injured. So for every *working* day, there are four people killed and 2,000 are hurt. There are also many unreported incidents.

'Health is a state of complete physical, mental and social wellbeing, and not just the absence of disease or infirmity.' (World Health Organisation definition.)

'Safety is the state of being safe – freedom from danger, hurt (injury), risk of injury or loss.' (*Concise English Dictionary* definition.)

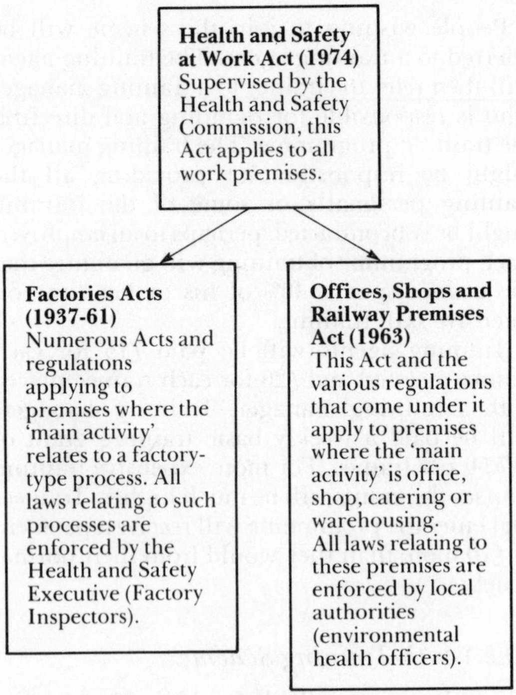

Health and Safety at Work Act (1974)
Supervised by the Health and Safety Commission, this Act applies to all work premises.

Factories Acts (1937-61)
Numerous Acts and regulations applying to premises where the 'main activity' relates to a factory-type process. All laws relating to such processes are enforced by the Health and Safety Executive (Factory Inspectors).

Offices, Shops and Railway Premises Act (1963)
This Act and the various regulations that come under it apply to premises where the 'main activity' is office, shop, catering or warehousing. All laws relating to these premises are enforced by local authorities (environmental health officers).

Figure 5.11 Main legislation relating to health and safety at work.

There are three main pieces of legislation relating to health and safety as illustrated in Figure 5.11.

Health and Safety at Work Act (1974)

1. Sets out duties of *employers* to maintain:
   (a) safe premises
   (b) safe systems of work
   (c) safe plant
   (d) a policy document about safety
   (e) safety training
   (f) to help safety inspectors.
2. Sets out the duties of *employees* to:
   (a) obey safety laws
   (b) to help employers to keep to the law
   (c) to obey the rules set out in the safety policy document.
3. Sets out the duties of *manufacturers* to make sure that all substances or goods produced are safe.
4. *Inspection and enforcement.* Inspectors have wide powers to inspect and examine, to

Figure 5.12 Large companies may employ a medical team who meet regularly with health and safety officers.

request co-operation and information and to sample substances and take photographs. They can also serve notices banning certain activities or requesting improvements.

Factories Act (1961)

The Factories Act has been changed in a number of ways over the years. However, the most detailed interpretation of this Act was given in 1961 and covers:

1. The registration of factories
2. The need to make sure that machinery is safe – the responsibility for this lies solely with employers
3. The employment of young persons
4. Premises, plant and equipment
5. Welfare (see Figure 5.12)
6. Powers to make rules
7. The notification of accidents.

The Offices, Shops and Railway Premises Act (1963)

The main duties of the *employer* are concerned with:

1. Registration of premises
2. The condition of the premises
3. Welfare of staff (see Figure 5.12)

4. Machinery
5. Young people.

Specific requirements of health and safety at work rules

As one would expect, health and safety at work rules govern a wide number of important features of work including:

1. Toilet and washing facilities
2. First aid facilities
3. Employment of young persons
4. Welfare: rest-room, eating and drinking, etc.
5. Environment of work situation: cleaning, temperature, lighting, noise, etc.
6. The safe storage and handling of articles and substances
7. Warning signs
8. Safety committees and safety representatives
9. Accident notifications
10. Rules about hoists, lifts and escalators
11. Rules about machinery (different types of machinery have different rules)
12. Fire hazards (covering fire escapes, fire practices, alarms, etc.)
13. Electricity regulations
14. Use of liquid petroleum gas
15. Asbestos
16. Industrial diseases
17. Fork lift trucks.

■ Coursework activity

The Health and Safety at Work Act states that:

'It shall be the duty of every employee while at work:

a to take reasonable care for the health and safety of themselves and of other persons who may be affected by their acts or omissions at work; and
b as regards any duty or requirement imposed on his employer or any other person by or under any of the relevant statutory provisions, to co-operate with them so far as is necessary to enable that duty or requirement to be performed or complied with.'

Working as a group you should make a list of all the ways that these duties apply in work situations with which you are familiar. For example, some of you may work in a bakery where it is necessary to wear some form of hair cover.

Equality of employment

Women form about 40% of the workforce today, and yet they are seriously under-represented in the professions and in managerial positions. On average they earn less than 70% of men's wages and are far more likely than men to be engaged in part-time work.

The Sex Discrimination Act (1975)

The Sex Discrimination Act gives rights to *both* men *and* women. Unlawful discrimination means giving less favourable treatment because of someone's sex or because they are married, and can be either direct or indirect. The Act also covers victimisation:

1. *Direct sex discrimination* means being treated less favourably than a person of the opposite sex is (or would be) treated in similar circumstances, for example under a policy to appoint only men to management positions.
2. *Direct marriage discrimination* means being treated less favourably than an unmarried person of the same sex, for example under a policy not to recruit married people for a job that involved being away from home.
3. *Indirect sex discrimination* is less easy to identify. It means being able to comply with a requirement which on the face of it applies equally to both men and women, but which in practice can be met by a much smaller proportion of one sex. For example, organisations may be indirectly discriminating against women if access to certain jobs is restricted to particular grades which in practice are held only by men.
4. *Victimisation* means being treated less favourably than other people because you have in good faith made allegations about discrimination in relation to the Sex Discrimination Act or the Equal Pay Act.

The Act also relates to training. There must be no unlawful discrimination against people applying for training.

In advertising a job there should be nothing in the wording or presentation of advertisements to give the impression that only men or women or single people are required. However, there are a number of instances in which it *is* possible legally to discriminate on grounds of sex or race (for example, advertising a male or female acting role). Complaints about advertisements should be taken to the Equal Opportunities Commission.

In work you are entitled to equal access on equal terms to promotion, transfer of jobs and training, and you are entitled to an equal chance to join a trade union or professional organisation.

Complaints

A person who thinks he or she has been treated unfairly with regard to sex discrimination must lodge a complaint with the Central Office of Industrial Tribunals before the end of the period of three months beginning when the act complained of was committed.

An industrial tribunal is a relatively informal 'court' which will usually take place somewhere near to where you live. There is a legally qualified chairperson and two ordinary members of the public with experience of industry and commerce. You can either present your own case to the tribunal or seek help from the Equal Opportunities Commission.

If the tribunal finds in your favour it can do any or all of the following things:

1. Make an order declaring your *rights*.

2. Order that you be paid *compensation*. This could include lost earnings, expenses, damages for injury to your feelings or damages for future loss of earnings.
3. Recommend the person or organisation you complain against to take a particular course of *action* within a specified period, for example to consider you for promotion within the next year.

■ Activity

For this activity three members of the class will represent officials on an industrial tribunal. Other individual members of the class will represent employers and employees in the following cases. The tribunal, after questioning the two parties, must decide on the rights and wrongs of the case and what action should follow:

Case 1: Jane Dempsey v. Midshire County Council

The following advert recently appeared in national publications advertising a job in the primary school where Jane works.

Deputy Headship

Committed primary teacher wanted to take on this post of responsibility. We are looking for someone with a broad range of interests and experience. The successful applicant should be able to take charge of music, drama and boys' PE.

Jane had been working at the school for ten years, already ran the school music department and had a keen interest in drama. She felt that she would not be given a fair opportunity at interviews for the job.

Case 2: Donald Smith v. Household Insurance

Donald had been working for the firm for three years. Mrs Smith had brought up their child for two years before deciding to return to work. Donald's firm has a crèche for firm's employees of two years and over. When he applied to put the child in the crèche he was told that he could not do so because the crèche was only for the children of female employees.

Case 3: Bosco Rajic v. International Sales

Bosco has been working in the marketing department of the company for several years. Recently the company advertised for an international sales officer who would be in charge of departments in Brussels, Rome and Paris. The job entails a lot of travel. Bosco applies for the job but is not selected for interview, though a number of those who are have far less experience. However, Bosco notices that they are all single people.

The Equal Pay Act (1970)

The 1970 Equal Pay Act promised equal pay for equal work by 1975. However, employers devised a number of strategies to get round the Act, such as the separation of male and female workers and the attachment of extra 'responsibilities' to male employees (such as heavy lifting).

In 1984 the Equal Pay (Amendment) Regulations were introduced. These Regulations allow an employee to claim equal pay with a colleague of the opposite sex on the basis of work of equal value. A number of cases relating to 'equal value' are coming before the courts.

■ Case study: *Hayward v. Cammell Laird*

In this case Julie Hayward, a canteen cook, was the first employee successfully to claim equal pay for work of equal value when she compared her job with that of some of her male colleagues – painters, joiners and thermal insulation engineers – also employed at the shipbuilders Cammell Laird.

■ Coursework suggestion

How effective has legislation been in creating more equality at work? This activity would involve collecting newspaper articles and facts and figures related to changes that have taken place over the last twenty years. For example, how have women's earnings as a percentage of men's changed over the period?

The Race Relations Act (1976)

Another area where equality is important is that of race. The Race Relations Act 1976 sets out to eliminate discrimination of any type on the grounds of race. Discrimination is against the law in a wide range of areas including employment, training, recruitment and promotion. This Act is reviewed by the Commission for Racial Equality, which makes recommendations and suggestions to the government about ways of updating the Act. Individuals who feel that they have been discriminated against in matters relating to employment can take their grievances to a court or industrial tribunal. The Commission for Racial Equality will, if asked, provide help and advice on such issues.

■ Revision

Complete the following sentences using the words below:

basic pay
overtime
bonus pay
commission
piece rate
perks
Job Centres
Restart
Job Clubs
industrial

private employment agencies
on-the-job training
off-the-job training
Youth Training Scheme
professions
Health and Safety at Work Act
Factories Act
Sex Discrimination Act
Equal Pay Act
Enterprise Allowance Scheme

1. An _____ tribunal is a small court responsible for dealing with grievances between employers and employees.
2. _____ is the standard rate of pay before extras

such as bonuses are added on.
3. The _____ are occupations which usually involve the learning of a body of knowledge in order to pass an entry qualification.
4. _____ is acquired at work.
5. Under the _____ scheme every benefit claimant who has been unemployed for six months or more receives a letter inviting them personally to attend an interview at the Job Centre.
6. People who have been out of work for a few weeks and can put up £1,000 of their own capital can apply to join the _____
7. Additional fringe benefits that go with a job are known as _____
8. _____ is usually paid at a rate well over the basic rate.
9. Amongst other things the _____ sets out the duties of employers to maintain safe premises.
10. The _____ deals with the registration of premises, the condition of premises, the employment of young persons and other features related to the safe operation of factories.
11. Under a _____ system employees will be rewarded according to the number of units they produce.
12. The _____ guarantees all school leavers a period of work experience.
13. _____ may be acquired at a local technical college.
14. At _____ job vacancies are displayed on cards.
15. _____ frequently operate in providing part-time secretarial work.
16. The _____ sets down that employees must be given equal opportunities in the provision of training at work.
17. The _____ did not originally lay down the principle of equal value calculations.
18. _____ have been set up to encourage unemployed people to help each other to find jobs.
19. _____ is frequently given as an incentive to sales people.
20. _____ is often used to encourage employees to meet production targets.

CHAPTER 6
Employee and employer relationships

An *employer* is someone who hires someone else to work for him or her. An *employee* is someone who works for an employer. Employers and employees frequently form organisations to represent them and to protect their interests.

Industrial relations

Employers and employees need to have some system for communicating their views and requirements to each other. The aims of a business, for example, may be to win more orders and to make more sales. Employees working for that business, on the other hand, may be more concerned with having a longer holiday break and improving their wages. A forum of some description needs to be set up to make these dif-ferent viewpoints known. Employers and employees need to come together to discuss and negotiate their needs and problems (see Figure 6.1). Arrangements for such industrial bargaining vary a lot.

■ Case study: The need for industrial relations in a changing industry

British Rail is a good example of a company in which industrial relations are important. As conditions on the railways have changed there has been an urgent need for discussion between employers and employees.

The railways were once one of the country's biggest employers. In the 1950s half a million people worked on the railways; in 1989 there are just over 150,000 (see Table 6.1).

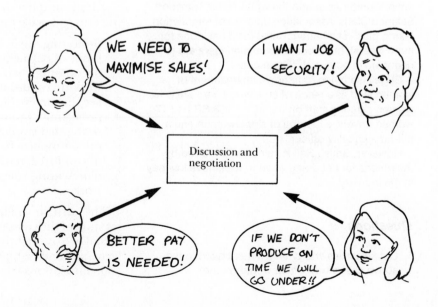

Figure 6.1 Industrial relations: a meeting point for expressing views.

Table 6.1   Changing face of the railways

	December 1962	December 1968	March 1987
Number of employees	502, 703	317,478	166,989
Passenger route miles	12,915	9,471	8,912
Passenger miles travelled (millions)	19,728	17,835	19,150

As steam trains disappeared and hundreds of miles of branch lines closed, so work on the railways changed. Firemen were no longer needed, although the second man in the cab remained until after the 1981 and 1982 rail strikes. Nor were guards needed any longer on freight trains as more traffic was carried in containers, but the biggest job losses came because fewer trains were travelling over fewer miles of track. In the early sixties Dr Beeching recommended that a wide number of loss-making railway lines should be closed.

In 1968 the number of job descriptions for railway workers was reduced from 170 to five. The eight-hour day was abolished to be replaced by more flexible hours and one-man trains were brought in. As British Rail tried to bring in such changes it met considerable opposition and industrial unrest. Only recently have unions and management come close to agreeing that railway guards can retrain as engine drivers.

Changes are also taking place in the way that management actually negotiates with the unions – the National Union of Railwaymen, the train drivers' union Aslef and the white-collar Transport Salaried Staffs' Association. Instead of negotiation taking place at a national level (as it has done for many years), hundreds of local managers are to negotiate directly with the unions.

BR is also trying to improve its treatment of women staff as a result of criticism. There are now women catering staff on trains; in 1988 BR had 17 women drivers, a handful of signalwomen and a full-time equality officer.

However, British Rail is still often criticised by the unions for not doing enough to remove low pay in the industry.

Questions

1. List six issues and changes mentioned in the above case study which would require negotiation between British Rail and its employees.
2. How many unions are there in the railway industry? Why are there several unions?
3. What evidence is given in the text that the railways are in decline? What evidence is there that railways are not in decline?
4. How are arrangements for negotiation between employers and employees changing? What do you consider to be the advantages and disadvantages of this change?
5. Give an example of a grievance that an individual railway employee might want to take up with British Rail. Outline what you consider to be an 'ideal' arrangement for discussing this grievance with British Rail officials.

Trade unions

Trade unions are groups of working people who have something in common – they are all employees rather than employers. They may also have in common a skill, a trade, an industry, an employer or an occupation. Trade unions are organisations formed, financed and run by their members in their own interests, and several have existed for over 100 years. Trade unions today consist of many groups from bank managers to bank clerks, from school-caretakers to schoolteachers and lorry drivers to civil servants.

A trade union will try to protect its members' interests in a wide number of ways including:

1. protecting their levels of wages and other forms of payment;
2. negotiating their hours of work and other working conditions;
3. keeping an eye on health and safety at work;
4. protecting promotion opportunities and seeing that employees get fair treatment;
5. providing benefits for members who are ill, unemployed, retired or injured;
6. representing members in any dispute at work.

The British trade union movement is a mixture of different types of union. They can be broadly divided into 'craft', 'industrial', 'general', and 'white-collar' unions. However, you must appreciate that this classification is only of limited use because many unions can quite easily fit into more than one category.

Craft unions

The earliest trade unions in the last century were usually made up of skilled workers. They formed themselves into groups such as the Union of Jewish Bakers to try to protect their members' working conditions. They often insisted on long periods of training and members paid quite high contributions to the union. In return members received sickness, injury, and other benefits as well as a pension. An example of a craft union today would be the Musicians' Union.

Industrial unions

Industrial unions recruit their members from a single industry whatever their trade or occupation. This type of organisation is more commonly found in countries like Sweden and Germany. A major advantage of an industrial union is that it simplifies the process of negotiation.

General unions

General unions will organise employees from a variety of industries and occupations. These unions are usually associated with semi-skilled and unskilled workers, e.g., the General, Municipal, Boilermakers and Allied Trades Union (GMB).

White-collar unions

White-collar workers are those employees who carry out non-manual work, such as secretarial staff and bank clerks. The term 'white-collar' is used to distinguish them from 'blue-collar' employees who carry out manual operations, traditionally wearing blue overalls. White-collar unions have seen the biggest increases in membership in the late twentieth century, as more people have become involved in office and administrative work, and as these groups have become more prepared to join unions. Examples of white-collar unions include the teachers' unions such as the National Union of Teachers and the civil servants' union, the Civil and Public Servants Association.

Trade union representatives

It is not possible for each employee individually to negotiate with management on every issue or grievance that occurs. Neither management or workers would want this. Instead trade unionists elect or appoint representatives who negotiate on behalf of all the members. Those representatives can be divided into two groups:

1. *Union representatives,* often called shop stewards. They are elected by union members at their workplace and their task is to represent the views of trade unionists to the employer. They are not paid by the union since they work at their own job when not on union business. They are trained by the union to carry out their union duties.
2. *Full-time officials,* who are either elected by trade unionists or appointed by the union. They work full-time for, and are paid by, their union.

To do the job well, trade union representatives need skill in talking to members and in gaining a clear view of their problems. They must be able to speak at and organise meetings, be able to present arguments to management and have an understanding of accounts, production levels, the market and basic economics. They must also have a good knowledge of present laws concerning health and safety, dismissal, redundancy and employment in general. The job of a trade union representative is therefore an extremely demanding one.

■ Case study: The work of a shop steward

Many people, even trade unionists, talk of the 'union' as some distant body, too remote to be interested in the problems of individual workers. It isn't. The union is for everyone. The union steward is a workmate and your branch secretary could be as well. They are there to speak for their members on every issue which affects them on the job (with the exception of basic pay, which is negotiated at national level). So if there is a problem, or doubts about some aspect of the job, go to the union steward for advice. Figure 6.2 shows this clearly.

Figure 6.2 *The work of a shop steward.*
Source: *NUPE Publications.*

The official trade union organisation

In general, full-time union officers are organised in most unions in three or four grades (see Figure 6.3). At the top is the General Secretary who is an elected official. Next come the national officers, who are usually promoted from within the union and operate from their union's headquarters. The third layer of officers run the union at regional or district level. They are responsible for the first-line officers who not only organise the union at local level, but also are closely involved with the union membership at the place of work and the local branch. The first-line officers represent the vast majority of all full-time officers.

The annual conference

National officials are responsible for arranging the Annual General Meeting (often called the Annual Congress) of the union. At this meeting delegates from the shop-floor meet to discuss and pass resolutions setting out the policy of the union. This annual meeting is very important because if the union truly represents its members it will listen to and then carry out their wishes. They will discuss a wide range of matters ranging from wages and safety to education and giving help to workers in other countries.

The unofficial union organisation

Disputes and disagreements often boil up very quickly on the office, shop or factory floor, and then quickly die down. The official union structure is often felt to be too slow in moving to deal with such problems. Employees are usually represented at the workplace by a shop steward who usually deals with such matters. Sometimes the shop stewards will ask the employees if they want to take industrial action without first getting union permission. This is known as unofficial action and the national union will not offer financial or other support.

In large factories and other workplaces there will be a shop stewards' committee supervised by a leading shop steward called a *convener*.

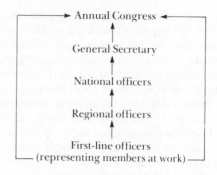

Figure 6.3 *The organisation of a trade union.*

Trade unions and disputes

The mass media often give the impression that trade unions set out to create industrial disputes. In Britain the number of disputes is remarkably low when compared with other countries. The vast number of trade unionists have never been on strike.

Trade union representatives help to ensure the smooth running of industry. Wherever people work or meet together, disputes and grievances will occur, and in industry the problems of new technology, complicated payment systems and work that lacks stimulation are bound to create dissatisfaction. Many of these everyday problems are easily dealt with by meetings, discussion and bargaining.

It is the trade union representative who expresses the view of the employees. Shop stewards often say that most of their activity is concerned with preventing disputes or strikes, but such information is not reported in the newspapers.

Disputes usually occur when all the available channels of discussion and negotiation have been tried after many hours of talks. Reasons for disputes are usually very complicated and you need to be cautious about saying that one party is 'wrong' or 'right'. If the causes of disputes were simple, then disputes would rarely occur.

Negotiation

The way that collective bargaining takes place varies from plant to plant. *Collective bargaining* means that representatives of employers and employees get together to discuss and bargain.

At one extreme negotiation may just involve two people. This is a very common arrangement – the personnel manager and a representative of each trade union will have short meetings every week. Most collective bargaining over major issues, however, involves inter-party negotiations. These can range from fairly small groups on each side of the bargaining table to over 20 representatives from management and a similar number from different trade unions.

It is important to remember that talk and discussion is the major tool of industrial relations, not industrial action.

Types of union action

Non-cooperation

This can take the form of working without enthusiasm, a go-slow or a work-to-rule. Working to rule means sticking firmly to the rule book. Workers might, for example, stick rigidly to the safety or working rules which they normally ignore.

Overtime bans

This is a weapon that needs to be used carefully because employees lose earnings and employers pay out less in costs. It is most effective when management has important orders to meet.

Strikes

Strikes are the ultimate weapon of a trade union and occur when employees withdraw their labour. A strike will normally involve some form of picketing activity. A picket is a union representative who stands outside the place of work to explain to people why the strike is taking place and why they should not go into work.

Sit-in/work-in

In response to being made redundant workers continue working and lock out the management.

Types of employer action

Employers and management can themselves take industrial action to put pressure on employees. This includes the withdrawal of overtime, mass suspensions, changes in working standards and piecework rates, locking workers out, the closing down of enterprises and the removal of plant and machinery at the workplace. The withdrawing of overtime or mass suspensions, for example, is sometimes used by management to put over the point to union negotiators that it proposes to stand firm on a particular point.

■ Case study: Industrial action in the textile industry

Figures 6.4 and 6.5 reproduce a newspaper report covering a strike at Courtaulds during June 1988.

Questions

1. What evidence is presented in the article that the textile industry has had very little previous industrial action?
2. What is the dispute about?
3. What form of industrial action have the employees taken?
4. What evidence is there that the employees' action has the support of the union?
5. Why do you think that management is not prepared to accept the union's demands?
6. What is the function of the two pickets shown in Figure 6.5?
7. What incentives are employers offering to get people back to work?
8. How do you think that management and trade unions should go about settling this dispute?

■ Case study: Responding to management

You are the representative of the employees in a small factory. You have just received the memo in Figure 6.6 from the production manager. You must discuss this memo and then set out a reply.

'It's 40 years behind the times – but better late than never,' Courtaulds worker Len Clark said. He is due to retire next year and out on strike for the first time.

Yesterday was the third day of the first major textile dispute for more than half a century. And Mr Clark – who has heaved cotton bales into machines all his working life – is a strike enthusiast. He will retire happy if the dispute boosts wages which even the company acknowledges should 'rise appreciably'.

Across Lancashire, 21 mills are idle as 3,500 workers on the Courtaulds spinning payroll adapt to life on strike. Yesterday the company was pinning its hopes on a drift back to work. Letters have been sent to all workers, telling them their job – and the 6.5 per cent pay offer rejected in a secret ballot – is available to all who cross picket lines. The lure of further productivity cash through mill-by-mill deals is also dangled.

But outside the gates of Maple No. 1 mill in Oldham, a young striker screws up his letter and kicks it defiantly into the gutter. 'Voting with my feet,' he quipped.

Alfred Wiseman – a mill labourer who earns £83.50 a week – is forthright in his denunciation of the workers' previous moderation. 'For years we've been the laughing stock of other trade unions. It's the textile workers that have accepted low rises without a whimper. It's taken us 50 years to wake up – but we're ready for a fight now.' Many small textile unions have disppeared leaving one main union. Mr Wiseman says that there is a new breed of union official: 'Union blokes who are cleverer than the gaffers and know how to add up.'

Mick Smith, who feeds cotton into large machines, held up his payslip and said: 'Look – £80.90 for 39 hours plus two hours overtime. It's peanuts.'

Bill Iveson, personnel director at the strikebound mills, says the company would be irresponsible 'to place future business in jeopardy by paying more than we can afford.'

Figure 6.4 Industrial action in the textile industry. Source: The Independent, *June 1988.*

Figure 6.5 Picketing at Courtaulds.
Source: Ged Murray, The Independent, *June 1988.*

MEMORANDUM

From: Production Manager

Ref: PB/NLC

To: TU Reps

Date: 9.4.89

Subject: New layout changes

Following the work study done by our consultants it has been decided that there should be a new production layout. The layout will be designed to eliminate certain unnecessary movements of manual workers and to introduce new equipment.

The introduction of this new layout will have certain consequences:

1. There will be no movement from individual work stations except during authorised breaks or in cases of emergency.

2. With the introduction of new equipment it will be necessary to reduce the work force by 20%.

3. The improved layout and consequent cost reductions will result in bigger profits which will in the long term create more job security and other benefits for employees.

Figure 6.6 Memo from the production manager.

■ Activity

For this activity four members of the class will represent the management team and four will represent a local shop stewards' committee. The purpose of the meeting is to discuss four cases which potentially may lead to industrial disputes. Each case will last for a maximum period of 15 minutes after which time the teacher will debrief the class and explain what might have happened next. The company the issues are focused around produces bridal wear.

Case 1

The company wants to suspend eight workers from a particular section. The supervisor had reported that this particular group had been taking more than the allowed time for their tea breaks. When the section had been given an official warning by the personnel officer they claimed that they had been picked on because the supervisor had a grudge against one of their members over a family dispute. The next time the section had taken a break the toilets had been vandalised and obscene drawings had been placed on the washroom mirror depicting the supervisor.

Case 2

The firm has just received a new order which will mean that it is able to use all of its existing machinery and workforce at full stretch. Work is guaranteed for the next three years. The firm had previously said that it was only prepared to offer a 4% wage increase rather than the 6% that was asked for because of the cost of employing machinery and workers that were not fully engaged in work 100% of the time.

Case 3

The factory usually closes down on Friday afternoons to tidy up and prepare for the next week. A Royal visitor will be opening a new workshop close to the factory on the Thursday afternoon. Employees have requested that they are given the Thursday off and work on Friday afternoon instead.

Case 4

The firm wants to bring in a new computerised system in the buying and ordering department.

There are two women working in this department who have both been with the company for over 30 years. The new system will mean that only one of them is required to work the computer. How will you resolve this issue?

The Trades Union Congress

The trade unions as a group have their own organisation known as the Trades Union Congress (TUC). Every year delegates from the various unions meet together at the Annual Congress to debate and discuss general union policy.

The TUC also has a permanent body of national officials under the leadership of a president. The TUC puts forward the unions' point of view to the government, the CBI and other major groups, and has a major interest in employment laws, training and conditions at work.

However, trade unions do not simply concern themselves with matters related to employment. They also debate issues such as education, political freedom and the international economy, as well as running their own educational courses and giving cash donations to various causes.

Employers' associations

Just as employees have formed and joined trade unions in order to protect their joint interests against employers, so employers have formed and joined their own organisations. Examples are the Confederation of British Industry (CBI) and the National Farmers' Union.

Employers' associations have two main functions:

1. To represent employers in dealings with trade unions;
2. To give help and advice to employers on a wide range of issues such as training, paying tax, etc.

In some industries an employers' association will bargain with trade unions to establish a minimum wage for a given period of time. Individual employers will then negotiate additional payments at company, plant or workplace level with shop stewards.

Most employers' associations today operate mostly at a regional rather than a national level.

The Confederation of British Industry

This body was set up to provide a national organisation giving the view of employers. The CBI acts as a mouthpiece for the employers to present their opinions and feelings to trade unions, government, the media and other interested parties.

The CBI collects and makes known information about a wide range of matters. Its *Industrial Trends* survey is published quarterly giving up-to-date information about the state of business. The CBI also produces a magazine *CBI News* giving employers up-to-the-minute information on a wide range of business issues.

The CBI has a permanent staff involved in collecting statistics, processing information, publishing articles, and dealing with queries from industrialists. The CBI is led by a Director General.

Professional associations

A professional association provides membership based upon exclusiveness for professional workers in order to enhance the status of their work. There are many types of professional association reflecting the wide range of professions, and many were incorporated under the Companies Acts or by Royal Charter. Their functions may include:

1. Acting as an examiner of standards and providing study facilities and guides. For example, prospective bankers undertake exams organised by the Chartered Institute of Bankers.
2. Control of entry into the profession.
3. Preserving a high standard of professional conduct in order to protect the public.
4. Providing members with technical information and keeping them in step with existing knowledge.

With more specialisation in professions and larger numbers working in the services sector, professional associations have increased in numbers in recent years.

ACAS

The Advisory, Conciliation and Arbitration Service (ACAS) was set up in the 1970s to act as a third party in industrial disputes. It can do this in a number of ways:

1. *Conciliation* is a process through which an independent outsider, such as an ACAS official, tries to act as a new channel of communication between employers and employees. The conciliator will usually meet the parties separately before trying to bring them together.
2. *Mediation* is a stronger process whereby a mediator proposes the basis for a settlement. However, the parties involved do not have to accept it.
3. *Arbitration* involves both parties agreeing to accept the recommendations of an independent body like ACAS.

The government and industrial relations

Smooth industrial relations are an important ingredient in a prosperous economy. The government will frequently meet with representatives of employers and employees to discuss issues of national importance. The government will actively seek the co-operation of trade unions and employer organisations in launching new initiatives such as training schemes, health and safety laws and many other matters.

■ Coursework suggestion

Study the process of negotiation at a local firm When do employers and employees meet? What do they discuss?

■ Revision

Complete the following sentences using the words below:

employer	general
craft	CBI
TUC	Director General
first-line officer	employee
ACAS	industrial
negotiation	annual conference
mass suspension	work-in
professional associations	mediation
Jewish Bakers	white collar
Sweden and Germany	unofficial action

1. Employees may resort to a _____ in situations when they are threatened with redundancy.
2. An _____ is someone who works for somebody else.
3. The _____ is the national employers' organisation.
4. Employers may as a last measure resort to a _____ if they want to put pressure on trade unions.
5. A _____ union will be made up of highly skilled workers.
6. _____ does not have the support of the union.
7. A _____ union will take members from several trades and industries.
8. The _____ is the national organisation representing trade unions.
9. In countries like _____ industrial unions are the typical form of union organisation.
10. The top official in the CBI is the _____
11. An _____ is someone who hires labour.
12. The government set up the body _____ to try to bring employers and employees involved in disputes together.
13. _____ are the typical form of employee organisations for doctors and lawyers.

14. The Union of _____ was an early example of a craft union.
15. The fastest growing unions in recent years have been the _____ unions.
16. Rank-and-file members of a trade union have the opportunity to express their feelings to a wide audience at the _____ .
17. _____ involves an independent party trying to impose its own guidelines for the settlement of a dispute.
18. _____ represent everyday trade unionists at their place of work.
19. _____ involves getting employers and employees together to discuss and bargain.
20. An _____ union would involve all the workers in the same industry regardless of their particular job.

CHAPTER 7
Distribution

Distribution is the process of moving goods and services to the places where they are wanted. It may involve just one step, or any number of steps. The local baker might supply bread directly to customers. In contrast, the furniture store may supply chairs and tables produced in Scandinavia which have passed through a number of hands and have been stored two or three times before arriving at their final destination. The transport network helps to bring the system of distribution together.

Industrial products (machines, bulldozers, expensive computer systems, etc.) are commonly sold by the maker direct to the user. Consumer goods (clothes, food, games, sports equipment, etc.) are more usually distributed through retail shops. The maker could supply the shops direct, but to do this the company would need a large salesforce. An alternative is to use *wholesalers* who buy in bulk and can be served by a small salesforce. The wholesaler is part of the chain of distribution and is a link between the manufacturer and the retailer, as shown in Figure 7.1.

Manufacturer → Wholesaler → Retailer → Consumer
(maker)   (storer)   (final seller) (user)

Figure 7.1 The chain of distribution.

■ Case study: A race against time

At seven o'clock in the morning the first British newspapers are being sold by Sophie Enjolras from her kiosk in Paris. The timetable for getting them there is shown in Figure 7.2. Eight hours earlier, these papers would have been rushed in

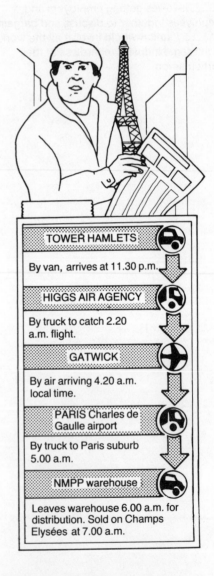

TOWER HAMLETS
By van, arrives at 11.30 p.m.

HIGGS AIR AGENCY
By truck to catch 2.20 a.m. flight.

GATWICK
By air arriving 4.20 a.m. local time.

PARIS Charles de Gaulle airport
By truck to Paris suburb 5.00 a.m.

NMPP warehouse
Leaves warehouse 6.00 a.m. for distribution. Sold on Champs Elysées at 7.00 a.m.

Figure 7.2 Distributing British papers abroad.

publishers' vans to Higgs Air Agency's depot in London. From there, along with 30,000 other British papers, they are transported to Gatwick in time for the 2.20 a.m. chartered flight to Paris.

Arriving at a Paris airport the papers are hurtled down the motorway to reach their destination by 5.00 a.m. At the Paris warehouse (organised by an IPD subsidiary Nouvelles Messageries de la Presse Parisienne – NMPP), the vans are unloaded by 120 packers to be broken down into bundles to be sent to the 5,000 retailers throughout France.

International Press Distributors (IPD) has virtually cornered the market for British newspaper sales abroad. In all, over 300,000 British newspapers are sold abroad each day. They all pass through the warehouse of Press Packers International, an IPD subsidiary, off Fleet Street.

Questions

1. In what way can the distribution of British newspapers overseas be seen as a race against time?
2. What forms of transport are used to deliver British newspapers to Paris?
3. List four sets of employees that would be involved in the distribution of these newspapers.
4. Who is mainly responsible for organising the distribution process?
5. Would you describe the distribution of newspapers overseas as taking place in a competitive climate? (Explain your answer.)
6. Identify:
   (a) a manufacturer of British newspapers;
   (b) a wholesaler of British newspapers (for the overseas market);
   (c) an overseas retailer of British newspapers.
7. How is your local newspaper distributed? (Carry out a piece of investigative research to uncover the stages in its distribution, the timetable involved in getting it from production to the consumer, etc.).

Wholesaling

There are many ways of distributing products, some of which involve the services of the wholesaler. Local wholesalers will normally be positioned on the outskirts of a town.

1. because rates and rents are cheaper;
2. because there will be less traffic congestion;
3. there will be room for expansion.

The main similarity between a wholesaler and a retailer is that they are both concerned with selling goods. However, whereas retailers sell to consumers, wholesalers sell to retailers.

Types of wholesalers

General wholesalers

Most wholesalers will be like the wholesale warehouses described above.

Cash-and-carry wholesalers

Most small retailers buy a large proportion of their stock from a *cash and carry*. The retailer is responsible for transporting his or her own goods from the wholesale warehouse to their premises. They are able to buy the goods at a discount.

The inside of the wholesalers is very similar to a large supermarket, except that goods are packed in bulk and the premises are sparsely decorated. Normally the retailer will have to show some form of identification.

Voluntary groups

Some wholesalers have organised *voluntary groups* (see Figure 7.3). A voluntary group is an organisation set up by wholesalers and is made up largely of small retailers who have agreed to

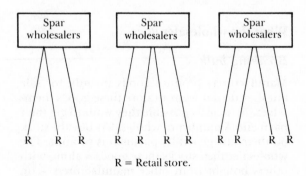

Figure 7.3 *The organisation of a voluntary group.*

buy most of their stock from the group whole-saler. For instance, the retailers might have to purchase 70% of all their supplies from group wholesalers. More information is given later in this chapter about voluntary groups from a retail angle.

Co-operative Wholesale Society (CWS)

The Co-op does most of its own wholesaling. Co-operative retail stores buy their goods from the Co-op wholesalers, and the profits made by the wholesalers are then shared out amongst the retailers in proportion to the amounts they have bought from the CWS.

Wholesale produce markets

Some markets perform a wholesaling function:

New Covent Garden – fruit, vegetables and
                     flowers
Smithfield   – meat
Billingsgate   – fish

The people who produce such items, e.g. market gardeners, farmers and growers in the case of fruit and vegetables, deliver them to wholesale sellers at these London markets. Buyers repre-senting firms like Smedleys, Waitrose and Birds Eye come to the market to buy in bulk for their firms.

Direct selling

We must remember that in modern Britain many large firms will cut out the middle stage. Tesco's, for example, do their own wholesaling.

What the wholesaler does

Breaking bulk

Manufacturers produce goods in bulk for sale but they do not want to store these goods them-selves. As soon as possible they want to get their payment. A number of wholesalers buy the stock off them and generally payment is prompt. The wholesaler then stocks these goods – along with others bought from other manufacturers – on their premises ready for purchase by retailers, as illustrated in Figure 7.4.

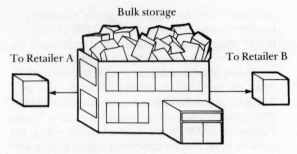

Figure 7.4 Breaking bulk.

Simplifying the process of distribution

The chain of distribution without the wholesaler would look something like Figure 7.5. Manufac-turer 1 has to carry out four journeys to supply R1, R2, R3 and R4. He has to send out four invoices, advice notes, statements, etc., and has to deal with four different accounts. The same situation applies to each of the manufacturers, so that in total sixteen journeys are made and sixteen sets of paperwork are involved.

The wholesaler can simplify the costs and processes of distribution in the following ways:

1. Cutting down on transport journeys and costs;
2. Cutting down on paperwork, e.g., invoices, administration and costs.

The chain of distribution with the wholesaler would look something like Figure 7.6. With the wholesaler everything is simplified. Each manu-facturer has only one journey and one set of paperwork. The wholesaler has four journeys and four sets of paperwork to organise, but the whole process is greatly simplified.

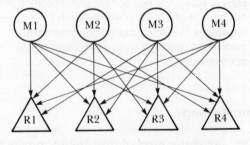

M = Manufacturer   R = Retailers

Figure 7.5 The chain of distribution without the wholesalers.

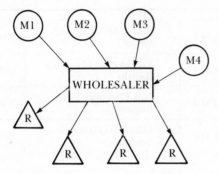

Figure 7.6 The chain of distribution with the wholesaler.

Offering credit

Without credit, buying and selling goods would be very difficult. Traders do not always have money available – often they will need to sell goods before they can pay for them. The wholesaler will help out the retailer by selling goods on credit for later repayment.

Storage

Most retailers only have a limited amount of storage space (see Figure 7.7). The wholesaler can be looked upon as a huge store cupboard for the retailer. Provided the retailer agrees to take supplies at regular intervals, the wholesaler will perform this important storage function. With the growth of cash-and-carry facilities it has become easier for the retailer to stock up on supplies that are running down.

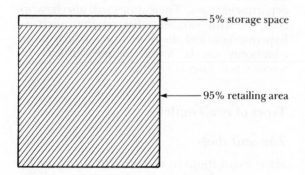

Figure 7.7 Storage space in a small retail outlet in comparison to retail area.

Packing and labelling

The wholesaler will sometimes finish off the packaging and labelling of goods, perhaps putting price tags on goods or brand names for supermarkets.

Offering advice

Being in the middle of the process of distribution, wholesalers have a lot more information at their fingertips than either the retailer or the manufacturer. In particular, wholesalers know what goods are selling well. With this in mind they can advise:

1. Retailers on what and what not to buy;
2. Manufacturers on what and what not to make.

The organisation of a wholesale warehouse

Wholesale warehouses are usually situated in large open buildings. They are divided up into office space and storage space (see Figure 7.8). The offices will include:

1. *Orders department* – for dealing with retailers' orders;
2. *Sales department* – for promoting the business to attract customers;
3. *Purchasing department* – for buying in stocks from manufacturers;
4. *Accounts department* – for keeping records of all purchases and sales, all the payments made to and by the company, and all money owed by and owed to the company;
5. *Despatch department* – for packing up the orders;
6. *Transport department*.

The wholesale warehouse is usually a sparsely decorated building full of shelves packed with boxes and cartons. The shelves are laid out so that the packers can quickly make up a correct order. The packers go round the shelves filling trolleys with ordered items.

A packer will be presented with an order form like the one in Figure 7.9. The shelves are numbered in a corresponding way to the numbers on the order form so that the packers have no problems in finding the goods.

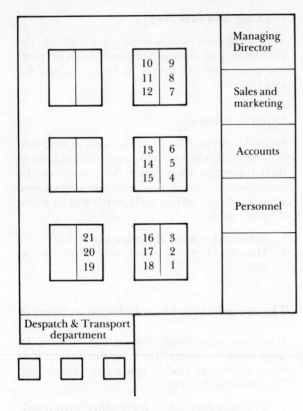

Figure 7.8 The layout of a wholesale warehouse.

ITEM 1	Round Milk Chocolate Biscuits	200
ITEM 2	Round Plain Chocolate Biscuits	150
ITEM 3	Milk Chocolate Finger Biscuits	300
ITEM 4	Plain Chocolate Finger Biscuits	100

Figure 7.9 The layout of an order form.

Resale Price Maintenance

Before 1965 manufacturers were able to tell retailers the exact price they should sell items for. In the 1965 Resale Prices Act this price fixing was made illegal, and since that time retailers have been free to set their own prices, leading to a growth in competition.

Growth of competition

The last twenty years since the abolition of Resale Price Maintenance have seen the growth of a high degree of competition between retailers. A modern high street will be made up of many different types of store, ranging from the small corner-shop to large supermarkets and department stores. These shops will also have to compete with various other retailers such as hypermarkets and discount stores which more commonly can be found on the outskirts of towns where rates are cheaper.

Types of retail outlet

The unit shop

Many small shops in this country are owned by one person whose business interests are confined to that single shop. These small retailers often set up in business by putting their savings into

■ Coursework suggestions

1. How is a local wholesale warehouse organised? How are orders gathered and made up? Who does what in the warehouse? What items are stored? Who are the suppliers and customers?
2. What channels of distribution are used by local retailers?

Retailing

The French word 'retailler' means 'to cut again'. We have already seen that the wholesaler breaks bulk supplies from the manufacturer. The retailer then cuts the bulk once again to sell individual items to consumers.

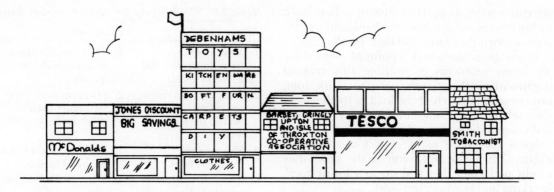

Figure 7.10
The many faces of
a small retailer.

starting up the shop. They then buy their stock by borrowing money from the bank and paying it back when they have sold their goods.

From the businessman's point of view, there are many problems to running this type of organisation. Proprietors have to work long hours carrying much of the load of the business themselves. They have to do many different tasks demanding a great deal of specialist knowledge – they have to be a 'jack-of-all-trades'. Figure 7.10 illustrates some of the tasks they might perform – they add up to a lot of back-breaking and exasperating work.

From the customer's point of view there are many advantages of shopping at the corner-shop as opposed to a larger supermarket; there are also disadvantages. We can weigh up the advantages and disadvantages in Table 7.1.

Supermarkets and hypermarkets

Many people like to shop in the small corner-shop rather than in a faceless hypermarket in a dreary industrial estate on the outskirts of town. They prefer the personal service provided in their own local shopping area. Prices may be a little dearer and queues longer but shopping is more enjoyable.

A supermarket is defined as a store with at least 2,000 square feet of selling area using mostly self-service methods and having at least three check-out points. The first Tesco supermarket appeared in 1947, and since then supermarkets have rarely looked back while corner stores have tended to die out. Most corner-shops that were in good locations have now turned into mini-supermarkets but many have been taken over by the supermarket chains.

The first *hypermarket* was opened in Britain in the mid 1960s. Hypermarkets have an extremely large selling area and offer a very wide range of household goods at discount prices. As well as food and clothing they stock lines as diverse as DIY equipment, motoring accessories, cosmetics, children's toys, hardware and many other items. They aim to provide cheaply all the basic shopping needs of an average household. They may also contain restaurant facilities and stock consumer durables like television sets at a discount. They are usually located on the outskirts of towns where building land and rates are cheaper. To encourage custom they advertise

Table 7.1 Weighing up the value of the unit shop.

Advantages	Disadvantages
1. You can get nice friendly service, and a chat or gossip.	1. They can at times be crowded with long queues.
2. They are convenient, providing a local 'round the corner' service.	2. Prices on most items are higher than in supermarkets.
3. You save on transport fares.	3. They provide a limited choice of brands.
4. They often allow people to buy goods on credit ('on the slate').	4. They have a limited range of goods.
5. They can buy in special items for regular customers.	
6. They might offer a delivery service.	

widely, often offer cheap petrol, have large car parks and many special offers.

The sheer size and number of hyper- and supermarkets is badly affecting the small independent traders' livelihood. They find difficulty competing price-wise but are finding various ways around it. For example, many are diversifying into more specialised areas, e.g. health foods or delicatessens, or are making the design of their stores more 'olde-worlde'.

Meanwhile, hypermarkets and supermarkets are using all the latest technology to full advantage. Computerised till service directly feeds into a central computer which prints out for the customer an itemised bill. At the same time the information about what goods have been sold

Figure 7.11 Voluntary group organisation.

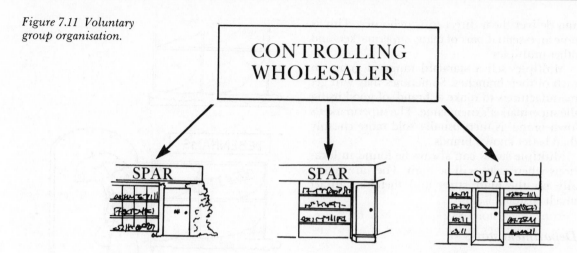

fed into the computer means that the ordering department is continually aware of which goods are in stock and what needs reordering so that there should never be any shortages.

Often supermarkets will encourage custom by advertising *loss-leaders* in their shop windows. A loss-leader is a good which is either marked down by the supermarket from its buying price or it is sold at no profit at all. Only a small number of the items sold by supermarkets are loss-leaders but the aim of selling them is to give the impression that all your items are cheap. A shopper seeing that coffee is 5p cheaper in one supermarket than in another might falsely expect all prices to be cheaper in the first store.

Voluntary groups

Wholesalers have found that with the growth of supermarket chains that do their own storage they have been cut out of a lot of business. In order to fight back they have formed themselves into *voluntary groups*. A voluntary group is a system of distribution organised by a wholesaler or a number of wholesalers and a number of retailers. Corner-shops often join these voluntary groups and trade under names like Mace, VG, Spar, Wavyline, etc. (see Figure 7.11).

The group wholesaler buys goods in bulk from manufacturers at discount prices and is able to pass these low prices onto the retailers. These then sell at prices which compete with those charged by other stores. Each of the retailers in the group is expected to buy a certain percentage of their supplies from the group wholesaler. Individual stores can get loans from the group wholesaler to redecorate their premises and they all benefit from the advantage of trading under the group name.

Voluntary group prices are quite competitive and as a result many small retailers now trade in this way. However, shoppers often criticise voluntary groups for selling only a very limited range of goods.

Chain stores

Chain stores (or multiples) can be found in most towns up and down the country. We can always recognise a Marks & Spencers, Boots or Woolworths by the design of the front of the building.

Most chain stores work on the basis of charging a low mark-up and selling a high turnover. The founders of Tesco's, Sir Jack Cohen, who started off as a market trader in the East End of London, worked to the idea of 'pile them high and sell them cheap'. Tesco's have always worked to this principle. Marks & Spencers started off as a penny bazaar in a Leeds market in 1884.

Multiple stores have a central head office responsible for ordering goods and supervising the administration of the whole chain. By ordering in bulk from a central head office the multiple is able to buy goods cheaply from manufacturers.

The firm usually has its own transport fleet which can pick up goods from the manufacturers and deliver them direct to warehouses. This is now an essential part of many supermarkets and other multiples.

Multiples sell a standard range of goods in each of their branches. Sometimes they will get manufacturers to make a 'brand' of good using the supermarket's own name. The supermarket's 'own brand' is then usually sold more cheaply than better known brands.

Multiple stores can always be found in locations where sales will be high. They are generally on the high street and therefore attract much custom.

Department stores

Department stores, like the chain stores, are to be found on 'prime sites' on high streets in most towns and cities. A department store:

1. is divided into separate departments each with a departmental manager and staff;
2. provides a very wide range of services so that customers can do all their shopping under one roof (one famous London department store claimed that a customer could buy anything from a pin to an elephant);
3. provides a high standard of service and comfort with carpeted floors, pictures on the walls, restaurant and cafe services, art galleries, exhibitions and displays, as well as polite service to customers;
4. often charges slightly higher prices for quality goods (it also charges higher prices to cover its high overheads such as high rates in the city centre).

By shopping in a department store customers are able to get all their needs met in the same building. In Selfridges in London, for example, shoppers can have their hair cut, order theatre tickets, buy a painting, have a meal and buy a whole range of household goods. This will save travelling from store to store and is a handy way of shopping in bad weather.

Department stores also run credit accounts for well-known customers, and some stores also run a delivery service.

Franchising

In America one-third of all retail sales are made through firms operating under the franchise

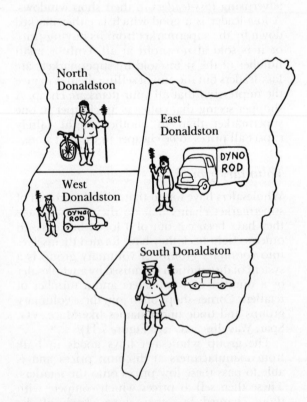

Figure 7.12 Franchising gives a local monopoly.

system. It is a method of selling that is becoming increasingly popular in Britain.

A *franchise* is permission to market a product in a specified area. The person taking out the franchise puts down a sum of money as capital and is issued with equipment by the franchise company to market the product or make the product which the franchise company deals in. The firm that sells a franchise is called a *franchisor* and a person taking out a franchise is called a *franchisee*. The person taking out a franchise has the sole right of operating in a particular area (see Figure 7.12). Table 7.2 lists the various advantages of the system for both franchisor and franchisee.

Franchising is common in 'fast-foods', examples being McDonalds and Spud-u-Like. A further example, in the plumbing business, is Dyno-Rod.

Discount stores

Today specialist firms like Argos and Comet concentrate on selling large quantities of consumer durables at discount prices. The aim of these stores is to produce a high level of total profit by means of a very high rate of turnover of stock. As the name implies, they attract custom by the discounts they offer.

Co-operative retail societies

There are over ninety co-operative retail societies operating in various parts of the United Kingdom. There used to be several hundred, but over

Table 7.2 Advantages of the franchise system.

Advantages to the franchisee	Advantages to the franchisor
1. Trades under a well-known name.	1. Franchisors do not risk their own capital.
	2. Supply equipment and training courses.
2. Has a local monopoly.	3. Take a percentage of the profits.
3. Works for him or herself, is own boss and the profits are mostly his or hers.	4. Have people working indirectly for them who will work long hours because they are also working for themselves.
4. Is supplied with equipment.	

5. Receives training.

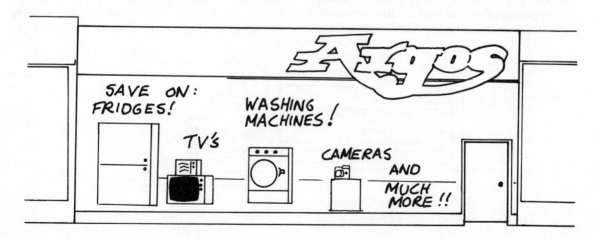

the years many of the smaller societies have joined together. The largest one is called the CRS and has its headquarters in Manchester. There are also a number of smaller societies, such as the Greater Nottingham Co-operative Society, which runs a number of shops in the East Midlands.

The Co-ops have always tried to do more than just run a shopping business. They set out to serve the local community in a variety of ways. For example, a Co-op will often support a local education service for members, subsidise health care and other social services, as well as financing co-operative theatre ventures and recreational facilities.

The first retail co-operative was set up in 1844 by a group of twenty-eight weavers in Rochdale, Lancashire, who were fed up with being paid low wages in tokens which they could only exchange in company-owned shops where prices were high. They clubbed together to buy foodstuffs from a wholesaler which were then sold to members. Profits were shared out among the members in the form of a dividend according to how much each had spent in the shop.

To become a shareholder in a modern co-operative retail society you need only buy a £1 share. Shareholders are entitled to attend meetings, to have a say on policy and to elect the officers of the local society.

For many years the Co-ops tended to share out their profits by giving a dividend to members, often by issuing stamps to shoppers with every purchase. These stamps were stuck in books and books of stamps could be traded in for cash or used to make further purchases. Today, only a few societies issue stamps. Instead, the Co-ops tend to plough their profits back into improving their stores in order to provide a better service.

The CRS, for example, has opened up a number of 'Leo' hypermarkets in various parts of the country.

The Co-ops are preparing for the 1990s by making their stores bright and attractive and by selling a wide selection of goods. Although they have closed down a number of smaller shops, a main aim of the retail co-operative still is to serve the local community. This may involve providing milk delivery, a funeral service or an education service.

Direct selling

Strictly speaking when we refer to direct selling we mean that a manufacturer is missing out the wholesaler and retailer and selling directly to the consumer. A straightforward example of this occurs when the farmer sells part of his crop at the farm gate (see Figure 7.13). Direct selling is a very fast growing way of retailing because it increases the cut of the profit made by the manufacturer.

However, we must be very careful how we use the term direct selling. The most commonly quoted examples of direct selling are mail-order and direct response advertising, but these more often than not do not provide perfect examples of direct selling. Mail-order firms usually buy the commodities that they sell through their catalogues in bulk from manufacturers (We discuss mail-order further below.) Direct response advertisers – such as firms that advertise in newspapers, in leaflets delivered through people's letter boxes and in television advertisements giving the address of the firm – are also often wholesalers who buy in bulk from manufact-

Figure 7.13 An example of direct selling.

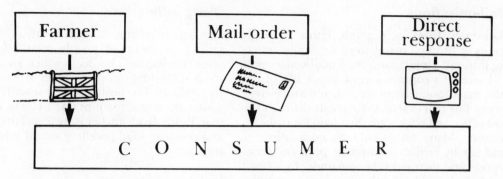

Figure 7.14 Direct selling – simplifying the chain of distribution.

urers. It is therefore probably more accurate to say that direct selling means simplifying the chain of distribution to miss out the retailer (see Figure 7.14).

Manufacturers can themselves cut out middle men by owning their own retail units. Examples of this are breweries with their own public houses, oil companies with their own petrol stations and shoe factories with their own shops (see Figure 7.15).

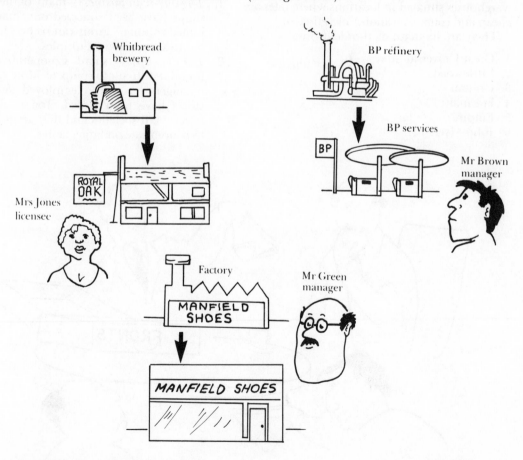

Figure 7.15 Manufacturers with their own outlets.

Mail-order firms

Mail-order firms sell goods either through agents or through members of the public ordering through a free catalogue. A mail-order agent will receive a commission of about 10% of the sales made. Some firms have their own delivery service but others send their goods through the post office and which are then paid for cash-on-delivery. Many goods sold by mail-order are paid for by credit. A customer pays an initial deposit and then pays the remainder by a fixed number of weekly instalments. Customers who are not satisfied with goods they receive can return them.

Mail-order goods give good value for money because by cutting the middle man out firms can sell goods at competitive prices. Mail-order firms are able to use computerised methods for handling orders and stocks and sell from large warehouses situated in locations where rates are cheap and communication links efficient.

There are six main mail-order firms:

1. Great Universal Stores } two biggest
2. Littlewoods
3. Grattan
4. Freeman
5. Empire
6. John Myers

'Party' selling

One way of selling through agents is by 'party' selling. A group of people meet informally, often in someone's house, to which an agent for the party-selling company comes to demonstrate its products. The host or hostess usually receives commission or a discount on products. Lingerie (e.g. Pippa Dee), kitchenware (e.g. Tupperware) and cosmetics and jewellery are all sold by this method.

The future of retailing

We have seen that over the last twenty years retailing has become increasingly competitive. Large firms that can cut costs have increasingly pushed out the older types of retailers or made them change their ways.

1. *The one-man business* – many of the corner-shops have been squeezed out, many have joined voluntary groups and others have sold out to supermarket multiples.
2. *The Co-ops* – small Co-operatives have found it difficult to compete. More specialist managers have been employed and many stores have been closed. Today, there are fewer retail societies and they are beginning to concentrate on larger stores.

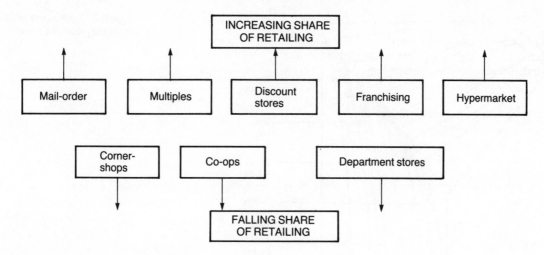

Figure 7.16 Prospects for various retail operations.

3. *Department stores* still concentrate on service but many of the regional stores are now selling cheaper lines.
4. *Multiples* increasingly dominate the retail scene for goods which can be sold in bulk.
5. *Discount stores* are increasing their share of the sales of consumer durables.
6. *Franchising* is branching out from 'fast-food' into many other areas.
7. *Hypermarkets* are regularly packed with shoppers who like to buy a week's goods 'all in one go'.
8. *Mail-order* and *direct selling* have increased enormously.

The changing fortunes of these types of retailing are outlined in Figure 7.16.

■ **Coursework suggestion**

Study your local shopping area and draw up a map of the retail outlets. Try to explain the pattern and locations of the shops that you find there.

■ **Case study: The Net Book Agreement**

Although resale price maintenance has been abolished for most goods in this country this ruling does not apply to book sales (in 1988). This means that publishers are currently able to set the price at which retailers sell books.

At present, when someone spends £12.95 on the average hardback book, the money is typically split as follows (although the exact percentages taken by authors and retailers can differ): 5% on distribution, 10% to the author, 15% to the printer, 25% to the publisher and 45% to the retailer (see Figure 7.17). The retailer would in fact be in a good position to offer a discount of up to £3 on an average hardback book.

Questions

1. What arguments could be put forward for keeping the Net Book Agreement?
2. What arguments could be put forward for abolishing the Net Book Agreement?
3. How would you go about making a decision as to whether the Net Book Agreement should be kept or abolished?

■ **Case study: The growth of large-scale retailers**

In the early 1950s magazines had to explain to their public what a supermarket was: 'All goods are put on open counters and customers circulate with specially constructed pram-like baskets. They cannot leave the store ... except by passing the cash desks where they pay for the goods in their baskets.' All because in 1950 Jack Cohen, ex-market stallholder made good, had opened his first

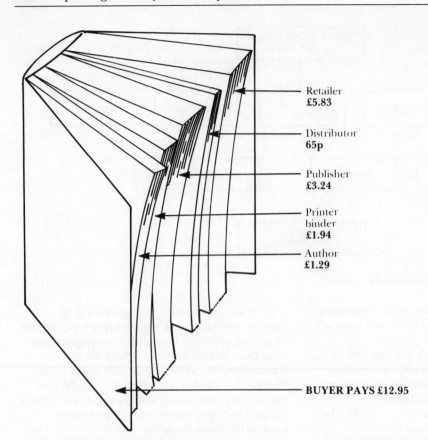

Figure 7.17 Who gets what from the price of a book.

Retailer
£5.83

Distributor
65p

Publisher
£3.24

Printer
binder
£1.94

Author
£1.29

BUYER PAYS £12.95

Tesco supermarket. By the late 1950s there were more than 4,000 supermarkets overall, accounting for almost one-tenth of all grocery outlets.

In those days supermarkets were on a much smaller scale than those we know today. Tesco's current chairman remembering the 1950s says: 'Manufacturers delivered to each store, none of which had much storage capacity. During the summer you had to keep the butter in the lavatory – it was the coolest place.'

In 1965 Resale Price Maintenance was made illegal. This meant that manufacturers could no longer fix the prices at which goods were sold. This opened the door for competition and economies of scale, and efficient distribution and stock management became the battle weapons.

Since then the trend towards large-scale retailing has increased. The seventies saw the introduction of superstores. First it was Asda, MFI and Queensway; then followed the hugely successful DIY chains like B & Q and Sainsbury's Homebase. Today even more new out-of-town retailers are joining the battle.

The high street, in many instances, is fighting for its life. Forty years ago there were less than three million private cars on Britain's roads. In 1962 research revealed that 43% of shoppers went to the shops on foot and another 38% by bus. Only 10% went by car. Today a very high percentage of shoppers go by car.

Questions

1. What would you consider to be the three most important developments that have made possible the growth of large-scale retailing?
2. How would you expect the balance of power (e.g. the ability to arrange discount purchases) between manufacturers and retailers to have changed over the last forty years?
3. How would you expect each of the following to have benefited/lost out as a result of the growth of out-of-town retailing?
   (a) A pensioner living in a flat at the centre of a

large housing estate on the outskirts of town.

(b) A shop sign writer.

(c) A cash-and-carry wholesaler.

(d) A door-to-door seller.

(e) The owner of a small corner-shop situated close to a new superstore.

(f) School students living close to the hypermarket.

(g) A bus company.

(h) Shareholders of Tesco's.

What further information would you require to give more elaborate answers to the above?

4. Explain how superstores might have benefited from:

(a) economies of scale

(b) better distribution

(c) better stock management.

5. Carry out a piece of research to find out the following:

(a) Why do people shop at superstores?

(b) What are the implications for the local community of the growth of superstores?

Part (a) requires the development of a questionnaire to find out where people shop and why they choose to shop at superstores. You would need to build up some background information, e.g. a map showing the location of superstores, data to show what percentage of iyour local population use different methods of travelling to shops, etc.

Part (b) requires an investigation of various groups and individuals affected by the growth of superstores. How many new jobs have been created/how many jobs have been lost in the area? Which other groups have had spin-off benefits/losses, e.g. builders, advertising agencies, other local shops, etc.?

■ Case study: Armchair shopping

The days of remote-control shopping from the home or office have arrived. Technology allows us to sit in front of a personal computer and television screen, call up details of a range of goods, key in an order and pay for it by an electronic command to our bank. The goods also can be delivered from factory to home, missing out the retailing chain. (See Figure 7.18.)

A range of sellers offer thousands of items, mostly branded goods such as domestic appli-

ances, cameras, furniture, china, silverware and cars. Discount prices, with cuts of 20% or more, are part of the sales system.

One of the experiments in teleshopping was run by Tesco's at Gateshead in the North-East. It was initially restricted to a group of consumers who found it difficult to get to the shops, including the disabled and elderly. Display units were set up at three convenient locations linked to a Tesco store computer. Orders could then be put through and free home deliveries made from Tesco's Gateshead store.

A number of mail-order organisations have now been successfully running armchair shopping schemes for a number of years.

Questions

1. Which stage of the chain of distribution is missed out by armchair shopping?

2. List six groups which would benefit from armchair shopping, giving a different reason in each case.

3. List six groups which would lose out from the development of armchair shopping, giving a different reason in each case.

Site location of retail outlets

Choosing a site is one of the most important decisions made by a retailer. What makes a good location varies from business to business.

■ Case study: Where should I locate?

Granby is a rapidly expanding town in the East Mdlands. The current population is 30,000 but this is expected to rise to 40,000 over the next ten years. This is partly due to the development of a fast rail link to London which has opened up the possibility of commuting. Employment is high in the town and incomes are increasing. There are also an increasing number of children and old people in the town. The nearest rival shopping centre is 30 miles away and as a result Granby gets many shoppers from the surrounding villages.

The map in Figure 7.19 outlines part of the central section of Granby including Market Place, Castlegate, a section of the High Street and Vine

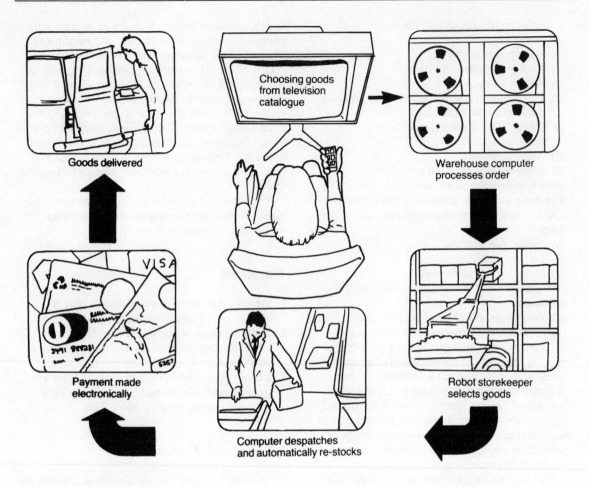

Choosing goods from television catalogue

Goods delivered

Warehouse computer processes order

Payment made electronically

Computer despatches and automatically re-stocks

Robot storekeeper selects goods

Figure 7.18 Armchair shopping.

Street. The local council has carried out a frequency survey to count the number of people passing along these roads in an hour on an average shopping day. The results are shown below:

Castlegate (church shop side)	80
Castlegate (bakery side)	100
Vine Street	100
High Street (Marks & Spencer side)	1,100
Market Place (Marks & Spencer side)	420
Market Place (antiques side)	310

Figures also show that for Castlegate and Marketplace 2 out of 10 passers-by will be shopping on that street. For the High Street, 4 out of 10 passers-by will be shopping on that street. For Vine Street only 1 out of 10 passers-by will be shopping there.

The costs of being on the High Street will be more because of higher rents and local taxes paid to the council. Market Place is the next most expensive location. There is not a lot of difference in costs between Vine Street and Castlegate.

Questions

1. The following businesses are thinking of setting up in Granby:
   (a) an off-licence
   (b) a second-hand dress agency
   (c) a well-known women's clothes shop
   (d) a children's toy shop
   (e) Thornton's (sweet shop)
   (f) Trustee Savings Bank
   (g) a butcher

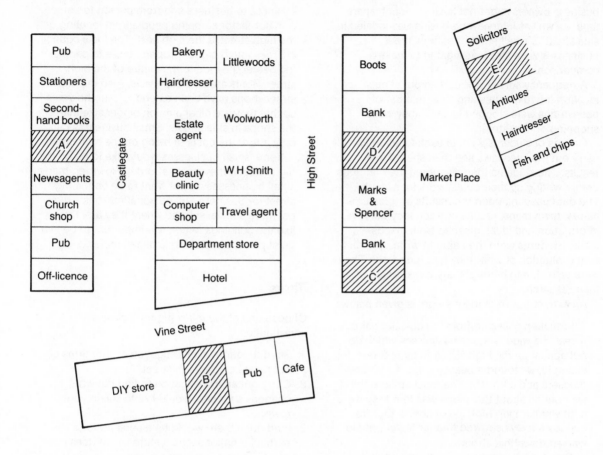

Figure 7.19 Granby shopping area.

Working in small groups try to decide which of the locations A, B, C, D or E would be the best for each of the above. Why do you think that the locations you have chosen are the best?

2. Which location on the map would you regard to be the best one for a new café? Explain your reasoning.
3. Which location on the map would you regard to be the worst one for a bank? Explain your reasoning.
4. What sorts of businesses would be most likely to make profits by setting up at location D?
5. What sorts of businesses are most likely to set up at location A? Explain your reasoning.
6. Select a line of business which you would like to set up in. Which location would you set up at? Explain your reasoning.

■ Coursework suggestion

A group of students set out to answer the question: Why is it that many small businesses do not locate on the High Street?

If you look at the high street of any major town or city, you will find that it is dominated by major chain stores owned by big companies – Boots, W H Smith, Woolworth, etc. There are very few one-off shops on the high street.

In order to investigate why small businesses do not locate on the high street the students set up a questionnaire to be answered by a wide range of businesses at different locations. Because the students felt that there would be a lot of individual reasons why firms chose their locations they left most of the questions open ended. It was decided not to ask too many questions because the business owners might not have too much spare time. As well as interviewing businesses located in side streets a small number of high street businesses were also investigated to make a comparison.

A frequency survey was carried out at each location for 10 minutes and a set number of pedestrians were stopped to see if they were shopping on that street.

Groups of students went to each location to carry out the interviews and then shared their results. The students then discussed their findings before writing up their coursework individually. The data used included the results of questionnaires, town maps, results of frequency surveys, information and ideas gleaned from discussions. Students were then able to write up their own evaluation of what they had found out. They were also able to highlight any weaknesses of their research.

An extract from a student's work is given below:

'Information collected from the questionnaire revealed a wide range of businesses which do not appear on the high street. In Lime Street, for example, we found a beauty clinic, two hairdressers and a florists. The most striking thing we noticed about the shops was that they were a lot smaller than high street shops. Our frequency surveys showed that far fewer people walked down this street.

'People in these shops mentioned all sorts of reasons why they preferred not to be on the high street. For example, the beauty clinic said that they liked the peace, a car park was very close, they were in an old building with character, and it was a nice street and in a conservation area.

'The florists thought that their part of the street was quite busy anyway (they can be seen from the high street), and that there was a car park nearby. They said that the main reason why they were not on the high street was because of the high costs such as business rates which are high in the middle of town.

'The hairdressers said that it would be too costly on the high street. They felt that costs were much lower on Lime Street. There was a major disadvantage in that it was out of the way so that it is difficult to attract new customers....

'... This sort of information tells us a lot about why small businesses do not locate on the high street. Of course the reasons will vary from business to business and from person to person. A major factor stopping people from locating on the high street is the high cost. The local council charges much higher property taxes to people the nearer they are to the centre of the high street. Rents are also expensive. Also the high street shops have been extended over the years so that they are all of a much bigger size than the shops in side streets. Small businesses can only afford the costs of being off the high street.

Some small businesses would like to be on the high street if they could afford it. However, many small businesses do not want to be on the high street for business and personal reasons – they get more specialist trade where they are, they like the buildings better, it is important to be in a quiet place, car parking is better, etc.....'

Tasks

Choose one of the following for a class investigation:

1. Set out your own investigation of why firms do not locate on the high street.
2. Carry out an investigation to find out what changes shoppers would like to see in your town.
3. Find out if there would be a demand for a particular national chain store which does not as yet operate from your town.
4. Choose a class selection of 20 products. Each member of the class should then try to uncover the route by which each product has been distributed for a class presentation.

■ Revision

Complete the following sentences using the words below:

supermarket	retailer
franchising	unit shop
credit	turnover
discount stores	loss leaders
mark-up	distribution
department store	storage and breaking
voluntary group	bulk
to cut again	Co-operative Wholesale
cash-and-carry	Society

Resale Price
  Maintenance
wholesaler

discount
party selling

1. The _____ shares out its profits amongst its retail stores according to how much they spend with it.
2. _____ is often given for prompt payment or bulk purchases.
3. The abolition of _____ opened the doors for competition in retailing.
4. A _____ facility enables retailers to pick up their own supplies.
5. The difference between a seller's buying price and selling price is known as the _____.
6. Items sold at less than their cost price in order to attract custom are known as _____ .
7. A self-service shop with at least three check-out points is known as a _____ .
8. _____ is often used for underwear sales.
9. The total value of a firm's sales is known as its _____.
10. To 'retail' means _____.
11. The process whereby goods are transferred from manufacturer to wholesaler, to retailer, to consumer is known as _____.
12. The local corner-shop owned by a sole trader is called a _____.
13. _____ sales is the normal method of dealing in business.
14. Shops specialising in consumer durables which are sold at low prices are called _____ .
15. _____ are two of the functions of a wholesaler.
16. Fast-food firms will often sell their goods through the _____ system.
17. The _____ is placed in the middle of the process of distribution.
18. A _____ offers many shopping services under one roof.
19. Mace is an example of a _____.
20. The _____ sells goods to the final consumer.

CHAPTER 8
Marketing

Everybody is familiar with a street market, where buyers and sellers meet up to bargain and trade. The term 'marketing', however, has a far wider use. A market can be described as any situation in which buyers and sellers come into contact, as in Figure 8.1. Goods or services will normally be exchanged for money, or promises to pay money at a later date.

When developing products it is important to pay close attention to customers' wishes. In simple terms *marketing* is responsible for making sure that people want to buy what you want to sell.

However, the times, the market place and the demands of your customers change, and in order to stay in business and be successful it is vital to keep up with and be aware of these changes. If you do not, you will produce goods that no one wants to buy, and as sales fall so will profits.

Research and development of products and services goes hand in hand with marketing them. In other words marketing must be tied in with the need to develop new products and to change old ones. For example, suppose a firm producing coffee develops a new blend which it thinks will be popular. It also hopes to sell the coffee in a new rectangular shape jar which will cut down on packaging and storage costs. However, when the firm tests the product on the public it finds that they love the coffee but hate the jar – and therefore the firm has to sell the product in the old round topped jars. Later the firm may be able to develop a new square shaped container which the public does like.

Although marketing products may be expensive and will increase the selling price, at least by doing the research you will be safer when it comes to selling your product. There is no point in developing a product, however attractive it is, that nobody is prepared to buy. A classic example of this was a small battery-run vehicle that was developed in Britain in the mid 1980s called the C5. The product was a brilliant idea but it had technical faults and customers were not prepared to buy it in large numbers at the asking price. More elaborate marketing would have told the business not to go ahead with the project and this would have saved them substantial sums of money.

The life cycle of a product

Spending money on marketing needs to be linked to the *life cycle* of a product. In its infancy a product needs to have a lot of money spent on promotion so that people are aware of its existence. Once the item becomes better known it will tend to promote itself. Marketing managers must then decide whether to continue with

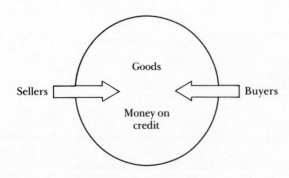

Figure 8.1 The market place.

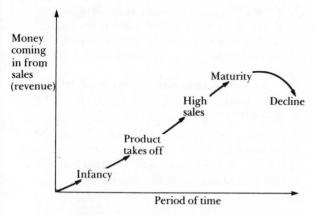

Figure 8.2 The life cycle of a product.

heavy advertising expenditure or to switch to promoting other less well known lines.

Eventually products will reach a period of maturity when sales revenue is at a maximum. The length of time for which this period lasts will vary between items. Some products have a short lifespan because they are temporary crazes, e.g. recordings of television theme tunes and videos of the latest 'hit' film. Others have much longer lifespans – Smarties and Coca Cola will probably be around for a long time.

An understanding of the lifespan of a product (see Figure 8.2) makes it possible for the marketing manager to plan promotion and advertising in order to get the maximum sales revenue per £ spent on marketing.

The marketing mix

The main ingredients in marketing a product are:

1. advertising
2. selling
3. distribution methods
4. after-sales service (particularly for durable goods)
5. pricing.

These combine to make the *marketing mix* (see Figure 8.3).

The idea behind the marketing mix is that it is necessary to combine your marketing ingredients in such a way that will give you the biggest market share. Of course, the correct mix will vary from product to product. The mix which a firm chooses will depend on how much money it has available for marketing, the stage the product is at in its life cycle, what competing firms are doing and many other things.

When launching a new product it might be important to keep prices low and advertising expenditure high. Later on it may be possible to increase price and lower advertising expenditure. Consumer durables might need extensive expenditure on after-sales service. Keeping distribution costs down will always help a business to develop a competitive edge.

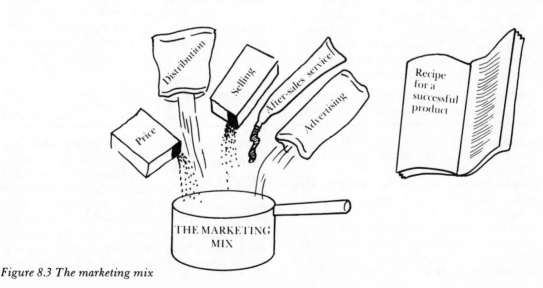

Figure 8.3 The marketing mix

■ Questions

Which elements of the marketing mix would you concentrate most on in marketing the following products:

1. A video recorder in a highly competitive market?
2. A new national chain of quick fitting car exhaust replacers?
3. A local clothes shop?
4. A new chocolate bar?
5. A new exclusive fridge freezer?

Market research

Market research involves collecting, recording and making sense of all the available information which will help a business unit to understand its market. It sets out to answer the following questions:

1. Who makes up the target audience?
2. What do they want?
3. When do they need it?
4. Where does it sell best?
5. How can it be taken to them?
6. Why do they want/need it?

Market research helps firms to plan ahead rather than to guess ahead. In business demand is always changing and therefore it is essential to know how things are changing.

Market research requires a special form of skill. Specialist market research companies are often employed becaue they have the necessary experience, and also because such research takes up a lot of time. They can be used to find out information in the following areas:

1. *General.* This would include up-to-date statistics about the size and nature of the market – the age, sex, income level, geographical distribution, social status, etc., of customers; the percentage of the market controlled by different companies in the industry, how goods are distributed in the industry, what trends, laws, etc., are likely to change the industry in the future.
2. *Sales.* This would include information about sales and sales methods. Are the sales people as effective as they should be? Are the best possible sales methods being used?

3. *Product.* What do customers think of the product? Who buys it and why? The product itself and its packaging will be tested. The market researchers will also look at competition.
4. *Advertising.* How effective is the advertising and public relations? Is there scope for improvement?

The investigative approach used by market researchers lays down some useful guidelines for any piece of fieldwork. This approach is discussed in detail in the following sections.

Data gathering

Basically this involves collecting as much information as possible about the market, usually before any further steps are taken. It involves both *desk research* and *field research*.

Data is divided into *primary* and *secondary* categories. Primary data is collected in the field. Secondary data is gathered from all the material that is at present available on the subject, and is always studied first when doing desk research.

Desk research

This involves the search for secondary data, whether published or unpublished. A good place to begin is with a company's records: production, sales, marketing, finance, etc. Other sources of secondary data are government publications, trade journals, materials produced by business groups, and information available from major commercial research organisations such as Gallup.

Field research

This involves the search for primary information.

The most common way to gather field data is by means of *sample surveys*. It involves taking a census of a small sector of the population which represents all of a particular group: e.g. married working women in Bristol aged 30–45 are taken to represent all urban, married working women in the UK. *Convenience sampling* is taking information from any group who happen to be handy, those walking down a high street for example. *Judgement sampling* is slightly more refined; the interviewer would select high street respondents on the basis of whether or not they appear to belong to a particular segment of the population, say middle-class business people. *Quota sampling* deals with specific types of respondents, working class male Asian youths aged 14–19, for example.

The most popular method of extracting information from people is by means of *questionnaires*. They are usually conducted by post, telephone or in person. Questionnaires are easy to administer and easy for respondents to deal with. They simplify the analysis of results, and can provide surprisingly detailed information. However, they are easy to 'cheat' on and a market research agency will ensure that 'control questions' have been built in to check that the questionnaire has been filled in in a suitable fashion.

1. *Postal questionnaires.* These are easy to administer but unfortunately they yield a poor response. They are rarely used on their own; more often, they are used to support a programme of telephone or personal interviews. Benefits include relatively low cost, no interviewer bias and reaching people who are otherwise inaccessible. Disadvantages are the 'hidden' costs – paper, envelopes, printing, postage, clerical and researcher time, design and editing the results – are all expensive.
2. *Telephone interviews.* These are ideal when specific information is required quickly. However, for consumer research it is a biased method because it is limited to households which have telephones. The benefits are that it is easy to set up and the response is quick. The disadvantages are that you need a trained tele-interviewer, you do not get a spread of the total population, and the interview can come to a quick end by someone putting down the receiver.
3. *Personal interviews.* In a structured interview, the interviewer has to follow a set pattern of questions and responses (e.g. ticking boxes). In semi-structured interviews the order and wording of the questions are laid out in an interview guide but the response is open ended, and interviewees are allowed to reply in their own words. Unstructured interviews are what they sound like – certain topics are covered in a relaxed fashion.

The benefits of personal interviews are that by using trained interviewers you are able to get a high percentage of usable interviews. It is the most popular and widely-used form of gathering information. The disadvantages are the high cost and difficulty of getting trained interviewers. This method also takes a long time and semi-structured and unstructured interviews are difficult to analyse for hard facts.

■ Coursework activity

Designing and carrying out a market research questionnaire is a demanding task.

As a group try to find out if there would be a demand for a new clothes shop in your town. What sorts of clothes is there a gap in the market for? How much do people spend on clothes? [This question could be answered by interviewing people (primary research) and by examining figures for household expenditure at the local library (secondary research).] Where would people like the shop to be? How do existing shops operate? Where do they get their supplies?

You should spend some time writing out a list of questions that you think are suitable. Then discuss them in class to produce a combined questionnaire. The class can then collect data by going out together as a group to research the questionnaire.

Advertising

Any type of publicity is advertising. In Britain, the body that spends most money on advertising is the government which has all sorts of messages to put over to the public. As well as trying to sell things to people the government will use advertising as a means of informing people about their rights and obligations.

Most adverts do more than just give out information – you wouldn't see an advert for a breakfast cereal that just told you about the ingredients of the packet. Most adverts go further and contain a persuasive message. Some people argue that persuasive advertising is a

Figure 8.4 Two views of advertising.

waste of resources because it adds to the cost of a product.

Other criticisms of advertising are that:

1. Small firms with only a small amount of money available are not able to compete effectively with large firms with a large advertising budget.
2. Advertising costs money and this cost will be passed on by the firm to the consumer.
3. Adverts are not always truthful and may mislead the public.
4. Adverts might encourage people to spend money and get into debt.
5. Some advertising is offensive to some people (see Figure 8.4).

The good things about advertising are:

1. From a company's point of view it enables them to make more profits and hence more sales.
2. By enabling producers to sell more products to a wider market advertising makes it possible for Mass production to take place. Mass produced goods can be made cheaply and their prices will, therefore, be lower to customers.
3. From the customers' point of view, adverts help to inform them about the range of goods and services available to them.
4. Some people argue that advertising helps to make life more colourful.
5. Advertising helps us to show that competition and choice exist.
6. Advertising helps to pay for newspapers, magazines, radio and television. Without advertising in these media, some might go out of business and others would increase in price.

Advertising agencies

Just as a firm might employ a specialist market research firm to find out about the market it may employ an advertising agency to publicise its product (although many large firms will contain both these functions in their own in-house marketing department).

For advertising to be successful it must:

1. reach the right audience;
2. be attractive and appealing;
3. cost little in relation to the extra sales made.

The advertising industry divides the population into groups. The most important type of grouping it uses is that which depends on income. If a firm is advertising a product which it thinks will appeal to high-income earners, it will use media which this group is most likely to come into contact with, e.g. the firm might choose to place an advertisement in an expensive glossy magazine which research has revealed is typically read by this income group. Alternatively, if the firm is trying to market a product which it believes will appeal to those on low incomes, it will use media which this group is most likely to come into contact with, e.g. bus shelter advertising or advertising during certain television programmes.

The advertising agency will have wide experience in planning the layout of the advertising campaign. Producing an attractive campaign depends on the flair of the advertiser.

The extra sales made as a result of an advertising campaign should bring in far more money than the cost of the advertising, as shown in Figure 8.5.

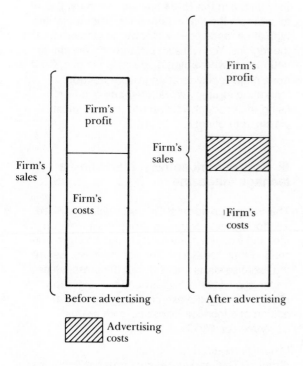

Figure 8.5 Increased profits through advertising.

Advertising media

There are many media through which advertising can take place. The type of media used will depend on how effective they are felt to be and how much they cost to use.

Television advertising

This is the most expensive method of advertising. The cost depends on the length of the advert and the time of the day that it is shown. This type of advertising will reach a very large audience but it is only generally used by firms that make very large sales or ones that are launching something new.

National newspapers

Once again this sort of advertising will reach a very wide audience but is an expensive way of advertising. The type of paper a firm chooses to advertise in will depend on the product for sale. For example, if a firm was trying to attract the attention of young upwardly mobile middle-class buyers it would need to research which type of paper this group generally read.

National radio

Once again this medium reaches a very wide audience. Firms using this medium must consider the type of audience that will be listening to the radio at different times of day.

Local newspapers and radio

These media take in a local network of people. It is cheaper to advertise using local media than to advertise nationally and therefore it is a particularly useful form of advertising for firms that operate on a regional basis. Also many large companies will test new products in pilot regions before contemplating a national sales campaign, so the local network is a good way of promoting a new product.

Direct mail

Direct mailing is a very important part of retail selling in modern Britain. The compiling, maintaining and renting of lists of names and addresses is big business. There are over 100 companies which make their living from renting out lists of names and addresses to companies that want to operate a direct mail shot.

Direct mailing involves sending material direct to the name and address of a potential customer. Research has shown that householders read quite a high proportion of letters that are sent to them directly with the first post.

Magazines

Magazines are not as widely bought as newspapers but they have a longer lifespan. Magazines are usually kept for several weeks and may be read for years in various waiting rooms and surgeries.

Trade journals

Trade journals are specialist magazines which are produced for people in a particular trade such as *Construction Weekly* and *Poultry Farmers Monthly*. They are a good cheap way of advertising direct to a trade.

Posters and bill-boards

In the late 1980s this form of advertising has come back into fashion. The British Telecom share issue which was advertised in thousands of bus shelters up and down the country was particularly successful, and modern poster hoardings use a system of slats whereby adverts are continually being changed.

Cinema

With the decline of cinema audiences this type of advertising has become less popular although it is still used by local businesses as a cheap method of advertising. Large firms will also pay to have material used in a film in order to increase their sales and some films are made to create a retail demand for toys and other items.

Point-of-sale

For many businesses a shop window or display will act as a lure to attract customers. This is particularly true of smaller businesses. Supermarkets and other concerns will also set up displays such as sweets on the check-out to encourage impulse buying.

Exhibitions

A trade exhibition is a good way for a firm to attract business. It is also a good way for a local business to advertise itself to other local businesses.

Word-of-mouth

For many businesses word-of-mouth is the best recommendation. If you can attract a few initial customers who will spread the word your business can rapidly pick up. This is sometimes known as a 'whispering campaign'.

■ Case study: Marketing a film

Your advertising agency has been given the account to market a new film, *Young Love in New York*. The film combines a young-love story and a modern music soundtrack. Market research has revealed that the main age range who will watch the film are in the 15–34 bracket. You must first of all promote the film in London in order to get the high attendance figures that will sell the product to the regions. You will also be targeting the film at youngsters with a high disposable income. Cost is not a major consideration in your London marketing strategy. What methods of advertising the product will you use that will most please your client?

■ Coursework activity: Marketing a teenage magazine

This is a group activity. The class will be divided into four groups and each group must work on their individual activity for 35 minutes before presenting their ideas to the rest of the class. Before the exercise starts you will read the press release and this will set the background to the group work. (Before starting the exercise look at a recent edition of a teenage magazine such as *Just Seventeen* or *My Guy*.)

Materials required:

Group 1: The market research group will require pens and lined paper.

Group 2: The poster designing groups will need either one or two sheets of A1 card. They will also need some felt-tip pens. The group also requires some existing magazines which portray images of young people, two pairs of scissors and one Pritt Stick.

Group 3: The radio jingle group will require some lined paper and pens and a portable tape recorder.

Group 4: The writers group will need some lined paper.

Press release

'News has just come in that the teenage magazine *Just Sixteen* has run into financial difficulty. The sales of the magazine have been falling for the last two years and the publishers are now making a loss. Staff of the magazine have decided to form a workers' co-operative so that they own the business and share in the profits. The new magazine will cater for the needs of today's teenagers and will come onto the market in the spring under the title *Modern Times*.'

Group 1: Market research

Your research group has been allocated the task of finding out the sort of magazine that teenagers would be prepared to buy. You should develop a questionnaire of about 12 questions to discover the sorts of stories and features that teenagers would be interested in reading about in a new magazine. You must bear in mind that your magazine will be for both girls and boys.

Your presentation should explain the following points to the class:

1. How you chose your questions and what they were.
2. Who you will use the questionnaire on (how many people, what age, etc.).
3. How you will deliver your questionnaire (e.g. stopping people in the street, through the post, etc.).
4. When you will do your questionnaire – what day, what month, etc.
5. Where you will do your questionnaire.

Group 2: Poster design

Your group can either use the picture in the magazine provided or draw its own pictures to produce a poster for the new magazine to be called *Modern Times*. The poster should present positive images of young people, and that the magazine is concerned with issues which are of interest to modern teenagers. It should also show that the magazine will cost 50p and come out on Wednesdays.

Group 3: Radio jingle production

Your group must produce a radio jingle for the magazine *Modern Times*. The jingle should show that the magazine is for both boys and girls and presents positive images of young people. It should include the facts that the magazine will cost 50p and will come out on Wednesdays. It should also be presented using interesting voice effects and, if possible, some form of musical effect.

Group 4: Writing a story

Your group has thirty minutes to write an outline for a story that will be presented in a picture strip. The story should be of interest to both boys and girls and should present positive images of young people. The story should also cover issues which are of concern to modern teenagers.

Sales promotion

You should promote a product in such a way that the people who buy it remember your product's name and qualities even when competitors start trying to promote their product. You should time your promotion campaign to 'break' when customers are most likely to buy and you are ready to supply. Posters, press advertisements, radio commercials and even TV commercials are all important media.

The best publicity is 'word of mouth' – personal recommendation. 'Word of mouth' publicity is free in one sense, but it has to be earned. You must look upon every customer as a potential sales representative. This keeps you on your toes. A satisfied customer can bring you in more customers; a dissatisfied customer can do you a great deal of damage.

After-sales service

After-sales service is important for durable goods such as motor vehicles, central heating systems, photocopiers and other items of equipment. Offers of after-sales service may be an important part of the promotion of a product. An example of this would be a car sales firm offering a free service after a given number of miles.

Another aspect of after-sales service is the handling of enquiries and complaints from customers. Some firms will send out circulars encouraging customers to comment on a particular product or service.

The advantage of running an after-sales service is that once you have managed to gain your customers' confidence you are better able to keep their loyalty.

Distribution

This subject is dealt with at length in Chapter 7. It is important to develop the most effective system of distribution relative to the amount of money spent on it.

Pricing

Pricing is an important part of the marketing mix. Different pricing policies will be used at different times and in different markets:

1. *Promotional pricing* – a new product might be sold at a low price to encourage the consumer to try a good or service.
2. *Profit maximising* – some firms will set a price that maximises short-term profits. This might be a good idea if the firm wants to make quick profits in the short term. In the long term high profits might attract competition and public concern.
3. *Cost-plus pricing* – some businesses find it convenient to add a percentage for profit to their cost figures, e.g. if a firm worked on the basis of adding 20% to its costs for profits and produced a tractor at a cost of £20,000 it would then retail the tractor for £24,000.

4. *Sales maximisation* – some businesses are more interested in having a big market share than in having high profits. They might then charge a price which enables them to maximise sales whilst breaking even on the product line.

Price and non-price competition

Firms compete with each other in many different ways. Trying to undercut a rival's prices is an obvious way of trying to get a competitive edge. However, there are a range of far more subtle methods including:

1. providing a better service;
2. providing a wider range of items;
3. offering after-sales service;
4. providing better quality;
5. siting at a more desirable location;
6. offering discounts, free gifts, etc.

■ Coursework activity

Study one of the following markets to find out the relative importance of price and non-price competition:

1. national newspapers
2. local taxi firms
3. local bakers

■ Activity

Why does the electricity supply industry have to market electricity? In order to consider this question you are provided with some background information and a task to carry out related to a marketing activity.

Background information

1. The rate of growth of electricity sales had been declining over many years and in 1980 the 'trend' actually reached zero growth (see Figure 8.6).
2. During this decline the average price of electricity increased in real terms (i.e. compared with inflation).

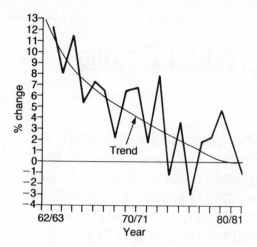

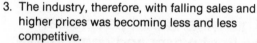

Figure 8.6 Percentage change in total electricity sales (to 1980).

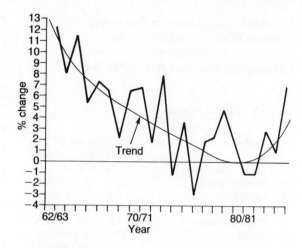

Figure 8.7 Percentage change in total electricity sales (beyond 1980).

3. The industry, therefore, with falling sales and higher prices was becoming less and less competitive.
4. Like any other business organisation having to achieve acceptable financial results when faced with rising costs and falling sales the electricity supply industry had three main opportunities:
   (a) to increase prices;
   (b) to cut costs;
   (c) to improve its sales position.
5. Whilst (a) and (b) were both necessary, tremendous success has been achieved by the industry in improving the sales position. Aggressive marketing to sell products that would use electricity has reversed the trend since 1980 (see Figure 8.7).

The task

Your task is to promote actively one of the new products being marketed by East Midlands Electricity. You are to develop part of a marketing plan to sell Quartz Linear Lamp Heaters in the West Lincolnshire district of East Midlands Electricity. The tasks which you are expected to complete are:

1. To target customers (who are you selling to?)
2. To design a promotional plan (how will you promote your product?)

Your main aim will be to stimulate the customers and produce 'lead enquiries' which will be serviced

by sales people visiting the customer's premises to discuss the benefits of the product.

To help you to set out your plan you will need certain additional background information:

Table 8.1   Numbers of non-domestic customers

Warehouses	90
Public buildings (including leisure centres, libraries)	280
Churches	420
Pubs and clubs	460
Industrial	1,400
Farms	2,300
Shops and offices	5,200
Total	10,150

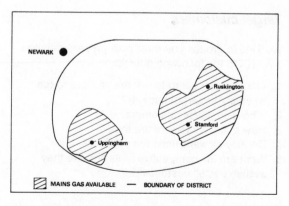

Figure 8.8 Sketch map of the area.

1. a sketch map of the area (Figure 8.8);
2. details of the product (Figure 8.9);
3. numbers of non-domestic customers (Table 8.1);
4. approximate costs of advertising (Table 8.2).

Table 8.2   Costs of advertising (approximate).

		£	
1.	Television (Central)	600	30 sec off peak
		3,000	30 sec on peak
2.	Local radio (Trent)	55	30 sec spot
3.	National press	5,000	per insertion
4.	Local press	500	per insertion
5.	Free trade press	200	per insertion
6.	Electricity account stuffers	750	(one for each non-domestic customer)
7.	Direct mailing:		
	(a) Package (envelope, leaflets, etc.)	300	per thousand
	(b) Post Office delivery (selected addresses)	130	per thousand
	(c) Hand delivery (selected areas)	20	per thousand
8.	Telephone sales	10	per hundred calls
9.	Exhibitions/displays:		
	(a) Small	250	
	(b) Medium	1,500	
	(c) Large	4,000	
10.	Posters (bus sides, advertising boards, etc.)	500	per poster
11.	Leaflets	250	per thousand
12.	East Midlands electricity shops (Grantham, Melton Mowbray, Oakham, Stamford, Bourne, Sleaford)	Free	

Target customers

Working in groups you must now prepare detailed answers to the following questions:

1. Who are you going to sell the product to (i.e. what is your target market)?
2. Where are these customers?
3. How many customers are there?
4. Do they all want/need the product?
5. What are the competitive fuels and are they available to all customers?

Product Details

The Quartz Linear Lamp Heater is a new concept in space heating. It directs heat precisely where it is needed, unlike any other heater on the market by using a high temperature source at a short wave length.

This means that people can be kept warm and comfortable without wasting energy on heating unoccupied space.

For low occupancy buildings and those used intermittently the Quartz Linear Lamp will be ideal.

In addition the efficiency of this low cost heater with its "spotlight" capability means low running costs, and the installation is quick and easy.

Figure 8.9 Details of the product.

INSTALLATIONS

CHURCH

SQUASH COURT

HALL

SMALL HALL

WORKSHOP

SPORTS HALL

APPLICATIONS

INTERMITTENT HEATING
- **Community Buildings**

Churches, Halls etc.

- **Commercial Buildings**

Canteens, Farms, Garages, Libraries,
Museums, Squash Courts, Storerooms
All types of hall—Exhibition, Lecture,
Recreation, Sports etc.

- **Industrial Buildings**

Factories, Mills, Warehouses, Workshops etc.

ZONE HEATING
- Areas within buildings
- Individual work positions

SPECIAL CONDITIONS
- Anti-condensation
- De-icing
- Frost Protection
- Hazardous areas
- Temporary heating

**TECHNICAL INFORMATION AND
ASSISTANCE AVAILABLE**

MONERGY '86

QUARTZRAY Limited

32 AMBLESIDE ROAD, FLIXTON, MANCHESTER M31 3PH
TELEPHONE: 061-748 6765 & 6764
REGISTERED DESIGN Nos. 999500 & 1017760

GET MORE FOR YOUR MONERGY

QUARTZRAY Limited

QUARTZ LAMP ELECTRIC RADIANT COMFORT HEATERS
MODELS 0183 AND 0184S

Model 0183 in Dark Brown
Also available in Silver Birch Grey

Model 0184S in Silver Birch Grey
Also available in Dark Brown and Stainless Steel

Features
- Outstanding long throw performance gives comparable warmth for lowest load.
- Optical accuracy of flood lighting directs heat where needed over long distances.
- Heat penetrates damp atmospheres with little loss compared to that from conventional radiant heaters.
- Heat feels comfortable without giving typical hot head effect.
- Full swivel and tilt plus plug-in fixing for maximum flexibility.

Model 0183 has a choice of lamp sizes and this combined with a four pin plug as standard allows a variety of ratings with simultaneous or individual switching under either manual, time, or temperature control.

Model 0184S is a single 1½ kw heater designed specifically for use in the more confined areas but is also a useful supplement to the Model 0183 in large installations. Temperature Control available.

Design Service available on request.

Standard Heater Specification

Model 0184S is fitted with a 1½ kw Rubisol® lamp, plus 10A plug and socket, plus guard.

Model 0183 can be fitted with a combination of 1 kw and 1½ kw Rubisol® lamps to make ratings of 3 kw, 3½ kw, 4 kw or 4½ kw.

Unfiltered lamps available if combined heating and lighting required.

4 pin plug and socket with maximum rating of 25A.

Both Models

Heater box and bracket in high quality heat resistant paint.

Super purity anodised aluminium reflectors.

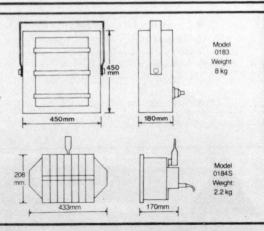

Model 0183
Weight:
8 kg

450 mm
450mm
180mm

Model 0184S
Weight:
2.2 kg

208 mm.
433mm
170mm

Promotional plan

Working in groups you must now plan your strategy of promotion. In order to do this you must answer the following questions:

1. If the customers are not all the same do you need a different message for each type? Give examples.
2. Which media/activities are suitable? Give reasons.
3. If you have a budget of £8,000 over a 3 month period how much would you spend on the various media or activities? Draw a pie chart to present your conclusions.
4. Expand where possible on your promotional activities. For example:
   (a) If you are proposing exhibitions/displays where would you hold them and when?
   (b) If you are using the Post Office delivery service where would you get your addresses from?

■ Revision

Complete the following sentences using the words below:

market	informative
life cycle	direct mail
market research	after-sales service
marketing mix	distribution
convenience sampling	promotional
judgement sampling	cost plus pricing
quota sampling	profit maximising
primary research	sales maximisation
secondary research	postal questionnaires
telephone interviews	persuasive

1. A _____ is a situation where buyers and sellers come into contact.
2. A _____ advert attempts to convince people that a product is worth buying.
3. New products are often launched using _____ pricing.
4. A good system of _____ is required to bring goods and services to consumers.
5. _____ can be used to target advertising at specific individuals.
6. Maturity is at the peak of the _____ of a product.
7. _____ pricing can be used to gain a dominant market share.
8. _____ is essential to find out who your potential customers are and what they want.
9. Looking up information in a book is an example of _____
10. _____ involves taking information from any group that happens to be handy.
11. Pricing, after-sales service and selling are three ingredients in the _____
12. The success of _____ depends on people having the time to talk to you.
13. If you added 10% on to your cost of production this would be an example of _____ .
14. _____ is important when selling durable items.
15. The government often uses _____ advertising to put over important messages.
16. _____ would involve selecting people to question who appear to fit into a certain group.
17. Interviewing people yourself would be an example of _____ .
18. _____ have a number of hidden costs such as paper and administration expenses.
19. _____ may be a successful short-term pricing policy.
20. _____ deals with specific types of respondents, e.g. 50 middle-aged insurance salespeople.

CHAPTER 9
Consumer protection

In everyday life we enter into a contract on each occasion that we buy a commodity or are provided with a service. The relationship of the buyer to the seller is set out by rules which are backed up by law. A society which had no rules for the protection of buyers and sellers would be open to dishonest dealings. The law of the land is intended to provide a stable framework through which providers of goods and services and consumers can exist together secure in the knowledge of a 'safety net' protecting their relationship.

The need for consumer protection

Before the 1960s, consumers had very little protection under the law. They had to rely on their own common sense. The Latin expression *Caveat emptor* – 'Let the buyer beware' – applied.

Individual traders and business organisations provide goods or services for consumers who

then provide payment. The legal system exists to provide a framework within which transactions can take place and also to provide a means of settling disputes. As large and well developed organisations often deal with relatively small consumers there is a need for the law to make sure that this inequality in bargaining power is not abused.

Disputes can arise for a wide range of reasons, as outlined in Figure 9.1. These are discussed further below:

1. *Damaged or poor quality goods.* Many people buy goods which do not function properly. They may have been damaged in transit or they may be of poor quality and not suitable for the purpose for which they were intended.
2. *Goods not matching descriptions.* Goods may not match the description on the packaging or the information provided in an advertisement.
3. *Manufacturer's negligence.* Faulty manufacturing processes or bad design might lead to the personal injury of the consumer or damage to other goods. For example, a faulty electrical component might cause fire and/or injury.
4. *Breach of contract.* This could include the failure of the supplier to supply, a failure to meet the required quality, or a failure to supply by a given date. For example, a shop selling bridal gowns might fail to supply the bridal dress by the agreed date.
5. *Consumer safety.* Goods might not be safe and could cause injury to consumers.
6. *Unfit food.* Eating unfit food can have particularly unpleasant consequences and con-

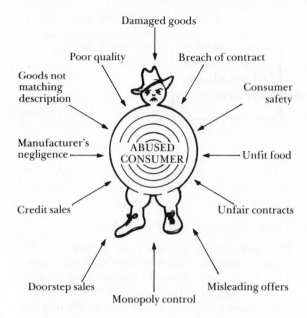

Figure 9.1 Reasons for consumer complaint.

sumers need to be protected from this.

7. *Misleading offers.* Consumers could easily be misled by offers, bargains and their rights concerning sale items.

8. *Unfair contracts.* Contracts could contain exclusion or disclaimers which might make the relationship between the seller and the buyer unreasonable. It would be unacceptable for a firm to disclaim responsibility for an injury caused by their own negligence.

9. *Doorstep sales.* Guidelines need to exist to protect clients who might have been intimidated into buying goods from doorstep salespeople, particularly if these goods have been bought on credit.

10. *Credit sales.* Customers 'buying now and paying later' over an extended period leave themselves open to abuse. They could well be charged excessive interest rates, pay large administration costs or be tied to an expensive maintenance agreement.

11. *Monopoly control.* Monopolies and mergers produce a situation where one or a few companies control a market. Lack of competition could be to the disadvantage of consumers because monopoly firms might limit the quantity and quality of their product and raise prices.

The legal process of consumer protection

The consumer may need help to ensure that he or she gets a fair deal. The legal opportunities to obtain justice against certain practices may be provided by the following.

Criminal law

The criminal law deals with cases where the law of the country has been broken. These laws attempt to protect members of society and to punish offenders whose actions have been harmful to the community. Cases might, for example, be brought to court for dishonesty and for selling unhygienic foodstuffs. Punishments could be fines, imprisonment or both.

Civil law

The civil law is concerned with disputes between individuals and groups. Laws have been built up over the years dealing with buying and selling activities.

Laws related to contracts set out the obligations that individuals have to each other every time they enter into an agreement, while the law of torts protects individuals and groups from each others' actions, particularly if an individual or group suffers injury as a result of these actions.

Individuals and groups enforce their rights by suing in the courts.

Consumer laws

Numerous Acts of Parliament are concerned with various aspects of consumer protection. Though it is not necessary to know each Act in detail, it is necessary to understand the general effects and reasons for the more important Acts. Figure 9.2 shows the three main areas covered by Acts of Parliament.

Unfair business activities

Fair Trading Act 1973

This Act set up an Office of Fair Trading with a Director-General in charge. They keep a constant watch over monopolies and restrictive

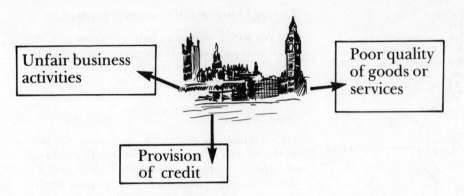

Figure 9.2 Main areas of consumer protection covered by Acts of Parliament.

Unfair business activities

Poor quality of goods or services

Provision of credit

practices. If they discover traders who persist in breaking the law they can require them to make assurances to cease their illegal activities.

The Restrictive Practices Act 1976

Traders who restrict competition by making agreements with other traders in the same line of business must register their agreement with the Office of Fair Trading.

Competition Act 1980

The Director-General of Fair Trading can investigate the activities of any business organisation in the UK if it is operating anti-competition policies which are preventing or distorting competition.

Poor quality of goods or services

Sale of Goods Act 1979

Sellers must provide goods which are of 'merchantable quality', i.e., they must not be damaged or broken. Goods sold must also be fit for the purpose intended. If you bought a pair of shoes and they fell apart at the seams within a week, they would not be fit for the purposes for which they are sold.

By this law you can expect replacements if goods do not meet the requirements you specify to the seller. For example, if you buy parts for your Mini from a garage on the understanding that they are to fit a Mini and find that they, in fact, would only fit a larger car, you would be within your rights to ask for money back or a replacement.

Trades Descriptions Act 1968

The description of the good is part of the contract that the buyer makes with the seller. This Act makes it a criminal offence for a trader to falsely describe their goods. The type of case that is most frequently prosecuted under this Act is when second-hand car salespeople turn back the mileometer on used vehicles.

The Trades Descriptions Act is thus fairly self-explanatory. Descriptions of goods and services must be accurate. Terms like 'waterproof' and 'shrinkproof' must be genuine.

Food and Drugs Act 1955

This law is concerned with the contents of food-stuffs and medicines. The government needs to control this area so that the public is not buying harmful substances. Some items have to carry warnings – kidney beans, for example, *must* have clear instructions that they need to be boiled for a fair length of time before they can be eaten. There are various substances which are not allowed to be included in medicines.

The Act also lays down minimum contents for various foodstuffs. For example, a sausage can only be called a sausage if it contains a certain amount of meat The same applies to items like Cornish pasties and beefburgers.

Weights and Measures Act 1963

The aim of this Act was to establish a uniform system of weights and measures and to make sure that pre-packed items contained an indication of the quantity within the pack. It made it an offence to give short weight or measurement.

Provision of credit

Consumer Credit Act 1974

Under this Act all businesses involved in some way with credit have to be licensed by the Office of Fair Trading. Adverts have to state the annual percentage rate (APR) so that consumers can compare the true cost of one credit offer with another. It became illegal for traders to send you a credit card you have not asked for and, if you are refused credit, you can ask for the name and address of the credit reference agency that has reported you as a bad risk. You can then put the matter to rights if it has been based on false information.

■ Case study: Applying the Sale of Goods Act 1979

Figure 9.3 illustrates what might happen if goods you buy are not fit for the purposes for which they were sold. As a consumer you are protected by the Sale of Goods Act 1979.

■ Case study: The law and consumers

Read the following passage carefully and answer the questions which follow it.

What the law says about buying things
When you buy something you and the seller make a contract. Even if all you do is talk! The seller – not the manufacturer – must sort out your complaint.
    The law has three rules:

1. Goods must be of *merchantable quality.* This means they must be reasonably fit for their normal purpose. Bear in mind the price and how the item was described. A new item must not be broken or damaged. It must work properly. But if it is very cheap, second-hand or a 'second' you cannot expect top quality.
2. Goods must be *as described* on the package, a display sign or by the seller. Shirtsleeves should not be long if marked 'short' on the box. Plastic shoes should not be called leather.
3. Goods must be *fit for any particular purpose* made known to the seller. If the shop says a glue will mend china, then it should.

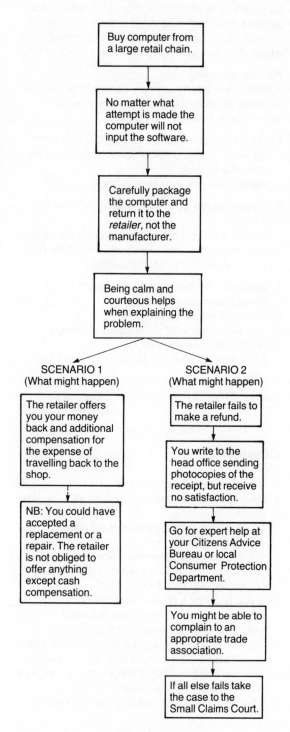

Figure 9.3 Following up the Sale of Goods Act.

All goods – including those bought in sales – are covered (food too) if bought from a trader, for example from shops, in street markets, through mail-order catalogues or from door-to-door sellers.

If things go wrong

If there is something wrong with what you buy, tell the seller at once. If any of the three rules have been broken, you may be able to:

1. get a cash payment to make up the difference between what you paid and the reduced value of the faulty item, or
2. reject it and get your money back.

If you both agree, you may get a replacement or free repair.

Exactly what you are entitled to depends on how serious the fault is and how soon you tell the seller. You are not entitled to anything if you:

1. examined the item when you bought it and should have seen the faults;
2. were told about the faults;
3. simply change your mind about wanting it;
4. did the damage yourself;
5. got it as a present (the *buyer* must make the claim).

Source: Office of Fair Trading and Central Office of Information, HMSO.

Questions

1. What is meant by a contract?
2. Having bought something, explain why the law doesn't help if:
   (a) You simply change your mind about wanting the product.
   (b) You damage the product yourself.
   (c) You were told about faults in the product before you bought it.
3. If you find that a present that has been given to you is faulty, what should you do about it if you want the seller to correct the fault?
4. If you buy what you are led to believe is a new coat labelled 'shrink proof wool size 8', explain how the purchase might break each of the *three* rules discussed in the passage.
5. Why do we need consumer protection laws?

Label	Name of label	What does it show?	Examples of where it can be seen
BS 1970			

Figure 9.4 *Consumer protection symbols.*
Source: *British Standards Institution.*

■ Activity

Where would you see each of the symbols shown in Figure 9.4? Copy out and fill in the figure to show:

1. The name of each label (for example, BS 1970 is the number of the British Standard for hot water bottles).
2. What it shows (for example, BS 1970 shows that a manufacturer has used the correct materials, and made a hot water bottle in the right way).
3. Where it can be seen (for example, BS followed by a number can be seen on many products, e.g. lamp posts, manhole covers, plugs and sockets, and car number plates).

Sources of consumer help and advice

There are numerous sources of help and advice for consumers and these provide opportunities for people to follow up complaints and grievances. It is therefore important to consider carefully the circumstances of each grievance before deciding the most appropriate way forward.

Government or local authority departments

The Office of Fair Trading

The Office of Fair Trading was set up to look after the interests of consumers and traders. It publishes a wide variety of information, talks to businesses and encourages them to issue Codes of Practice to raise the standards of their service. Traders who keep breaking the law must give the OFT an assurance that they will mend their ways. The OFT keeps an eye on anti-competitive practices, monopolies and mergers and might suggest changes in the law.

National Consumer Council

This organization looks carefully at consumers' interests and represents the consumer to the government, nationalised industries, public services and businesses. It also carries out research and publishes its recommendations.

Citizens' Advice Bureaux

Though these are funded by public money, they are independent and there are about 900 of them up and down the country. Consumer protection is only one part of their work which covers many aspects of day-to-day life. CABs will often agree to act as a 'go-between' in disputes between traders and consumers.

Trading standards departments

Local authority departments will investigate complaints about misleading prices, inaccurate weights and measures, and about consumer credit.

Environmental health departments

These departments enforce legislation covering the health aspect of food, e.g. unfit food, unhygienic storage, preparation or serving of food.

Consumer and consultative councils of nationalised industries

Nationalised industries are vast monopolies with the potential to put consumers in a weak position. These councils represent consumers and aim to prevent the misuse of monopoly power and bridge the gap between the industry and its customers.

Organisations which try to maintain and improve standards

British Standards Institution

This organisation is financed by voluntary subscriptions and government grants. Its primary concern is with setting up standards which are acceptable to both manufacturers and consumers. Goods of a certain standard are allowed to show the BSI kitemark which will indicate to consumers that the product has passed the required tests.

Professional and trade associations

These organisations promote the interests of their members as well as the development and professionalism of a particular product or service area. In order to protect consumers their members often agree to abide by voluntary codes of practice. These codes aim to keep up standards and will often set up funds to safeguard consumers' money. For example, the Association of British Travel Agents (ABTA) will refund money to holidaymakers should a member company fail to deliver.

Independent consumer groups and the media

Consumers' Association

This Association examines goods and services offered to the public and publishes the results of its tests in *Which?*. This magazine was founded in 1957 and has developed a circulation of over half a million. It has become an invaluable source of information for consumers.

National Federation of Consumer Groups

The Federation is a co-ordinating body for voluntary local consumer groups. Local groups might survey local goods and services, publish reports and campaign for changes.

Media

There is no doubt that, when consumers' rights and obligations are abused or when dangerous goods are brought into the market place, feelings run high. The media through TV programmes such as 'That's Life' and 'Watchdog' as well as the radio and newspapers have become an increasing focus for campaigns and justice. High TV viewing figures in particular clearly demonstrate the public interest.

■ Case study: A *Which?* investigation of the mortgage market

The chart given in Figure 9.5 is a response to a comprehensive survey by *Which?* on the performances of building societies and banks when lending for house purchase. *Which?* used a variety of ways to assess the services provided in the hope that consumer response might persuade institutions to improve their services where necessary and also help consumers to make better decisions.

Study the survey carefully and then answer the questions below.

	Overall	Providing size of mortgage required	Providing type of mortgage required	Interest rate charged	Keeping me informed	Speed of offering mortgage	Efficiency and service	Helpfulness and courtesy	Arranging home valuation	Providing other services e.g. insurance	Cost of arranging mortgage	Mortgage terms and conditions	Interest rate % APR
Abbey National	O	O	X	O	O	O	O	O	O	X	O	O	10.8
Alliance & Leicester	O	X	O	X	O	O	O	O	X	O	O	O	11.0
Anglia	O	O	O	X	O	√	O	O	O	O	O	O	11.1
Britannia	O	O	O	O	O	O	O	O	O	O	O	O	11.0
Cheltenham & Gloucester	O	√	O	O	O	O	O	O	O	O	O	O	10.8
Halifax	X	O	O	X	O	X	O	O	X	X	X	X	11.0
Leeds Permanent	O	O	O	X	O	O	O	O	O	O	O	O	10.9
National & Provincial	O	O	O	O	O	O	O	O	O	O	O	O	10.9
Nationwide	O	O	O	X	O	O	O	O	O	O	O	O	11.1
Woolwich	O	O	O	O	O	O	O	O	O	O	O	O	11.0
Barclays	√	√	O	O	√	√	√	√	√	√	√	√	10.7
Lloyds	√	O	O	√	O	√	√	√	√	√	O	√	11.1
Midland	O	O	O	√	O	O	O	O	O	O	O	O	10.8
National Westminster	√	O	√	√	O	O	O	O	O	√	√	√	10.9
Insurance companies	O	O	O	√	O	O	O	O	O	O	√	√	—

Key:
X = below average
O = average
√ = above average

Figure 9.5 A Which? *report on the mortgage market.*
Source: Which?, *April 1988.*

Questions

1. Which institutions performed well in the survey? Explain why.
2. Which institutions performed badly in the survey? Explain why.
3. Why do you think that banks generally performed well in the survey?
4. Is the survey easy to understand?
5. Would the survey influence your decision if you were looking for an institution to provide you with a mortgage?
6. What dangers are caused by 'surveys'?

■ Case study: A *Which?* investigation of the small automatic car market

Study the survey of small automatic cars given in Figure 9.6 and then answer the following questions.

Questions

1. Which is the safest car in the test?
2. Which car performs (a) best, (b) worst? Explain your answers.
3. Could you add any points to those listed in the chart?
4. Would this guide influence your choice of car? Indicate why.

■ Case study: Stop and think before you pay in advance

Study the following passage from a leaflet issued by the Office of Fair Trading and answer the questions below.

'Pay now – receive the goods later. This is an everyday way of shopping. Some things – a new kitchen or furniture, perhaps – have to be specially ordered. You might be buying a "service" such as a package holiday or a season ticket for a keep-fit club. Or you can shop from home through a mail-order catalogue or newspaper advert. But are you waving goodbye to your money? Paying in advance has its risks. And if the firm goes out of business you'll probably get little or nothing back. Even reputable firms can run into trouble and there will rarely be any warning. There are rogues about too.'

Questions

1. Identify occasions when you, your family or friends have had to pay either a deposit or for the full cost of an item in advance of receiving it.
2. List some of the risks associated with paying in advance.
3. Set out some simple rules or guidelines that one should use if asked to pay in advance.

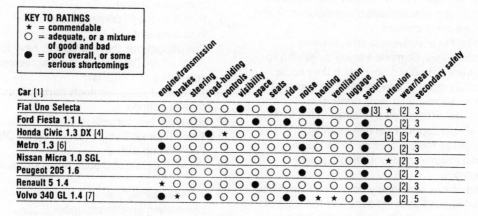

Figure 9.6 A Which? *report on small automatic cars.*
Source: Which?, *April 1988.*

■ Case study: Buying by post

Study the following extract from a leaflet issued by the Office of Fair Trading and then answer the questions below.

'Many people find it difficult to get to the shops regularly – perhaps because the nearest town is too far or because they are housebound. For these people, and many others, buying by post is a godsend. On the other hand, there can be drawbacks: you may have to wait for longish periods for goods and, in some cases, you are asked to send off money before you have seen them.'

Questions

1. Identify the categories of people who might find it difficult to regularly visit shops.
2. What are the main drawbacks of mail-order?
3. List the types of mail-order you have come across. Describe the types of advert or publication they use.

■ Coursework suggestions

1. For this activity you need to work in groups. Each group should discuss an area of consumer durables which comes within their experience and list the points they look for in a good quality commodity of that type. The group should then compile a survey, test it upon a target group of people who use this commodity and present a '*Which?*' type of table capable of influencing the decisions of consumers.
2. Consider the effectiveness of consumer protection laws. Compile a study by talking to consumers to find out how much they know about their rights. Survey traders to find out if they know about their legal rights and obligations. Present your findings in the form of a newspaper report. Interviews can be presented as feature articles. Draw up an editorial to summarise your findings and conclusions.
3. You may know someone who has been involved in a consumer/trader incident. List the facts of this incident and clearly indicate the rights and wrongs of the parties involved.

4. Arrange to see a solicitor to discuss consumer rights. Ask him or her about the position of the consumer, whether there is a need for law reform and whether consumers are well protected. Make sure that you prepare a good list of questions.

■ Revision

Complete the following sentences using the words below:

personal injury	kitemark
bargaining power	be fit for the purpose
Food and Drugs Act	intended
calm	Trade Descriptions Act
Parliament	resolving disputes
contract	fines
exclusion clause	credit transaction
prices	Director-General
CABs	National Consumer
trade association	Council
torts	Consumers' Association

1. The legal system is a mechanism for _____.
2. Consumer protection overcomes the inequality in _____ between small consumers and large organisations.
3. Bad design might lead to the _____ of the consumer.
4. An unfair contract might contain an _____ .
5. 'Buying now and paying later' could be used to describe a _____.
6. Monopolies have the power to limit supply and charge excessive _____.
7. Punishments in criminal law include imprisonment and _____.
8. The obligations that individuals have to each other when they enter into an agreement are contained in _____ law.
9. The law of _____ protects parties from each other's actions.
10. Statutory law consists of Acts of _____.
11. The 1973 Fair Trading Act set up an Office of Fair Trading with a _____.
12. Under the Sale of Goods Act goods sold must _____.
13. A trader falsely describing goods is committing an offence under _____.
14. Under the _____ it is a criminal offence to sell food unfit for consumption.

15. When taking goods back you should always be _____.

16. The _____ represents the consumer to the government.

17. There are over 900 _____ up and down the country.

18. The symbol of the British Standards Institution is the _____.

19. ABTA is an example of a _____.

20. *Which?* is published by the _____.

CHAPTER 10
Markets for goods and services

The three stories reproduced in Figure 10.1 appeared on the front page of the *Grantham Journal* on Friday 6 May 1988. They show the continual change in the market place - old products and services go out of fashion and new ones come in. Things are constantly changing and buyers and sellers respond to these changes.

Aveling Barford is an engineering firm producing dumptrucks and other heavy use vehicles. It faces stiff international competition and felt that it had to cut down its costs to make it more competitive. On the other hand, Grantham is a boom town for housing. Electrification of the east coast railway line has developed its commuter potential. Meanwhile Tip Top is closing down because Woolworth have looked at the profit figures and decided to concentrate their investment on their best lines.

300 to be jobless

JUST after the Journal went to Press last week, Grantham was stunned by news of 300 redundancies at Aveling Barford.

On page 3, we look back at the ups and downs of a major employer in the town.

And we bring up to date the story that only weeks earlier brought repeated denials from the firm's bosses.

A TWO-THOUSAND home estate, incorporating a shopping centre, industrial estate and community centre, could be built in Grantham if South Kesteven District Council give the go-ahead.

D. W. L. Bocock Lincoln Ltd were due to submit plans yesterday (Thursday) for the £50 million development between Barrowby Road and Great Gonerby.

by Richard Bijster

"We believe Grantham will become one of the most sought after areas in the country over the next decade," said Bocock's chairman Mr Dennis Bocock.

This latest project includes a proposed 900-home estate on 108 acres of Buckminster Trust land on part of the same site.

The owners of the latest 130 acres wish to remain anonymous.

Tip Top closing

HIGH Street drug store Tip Top — opened about a year ago — is closing down with the loss of three jobs.

Woolworth Holdings, parent company of the Superdrug Stores, bought the Tip Top chain in January for £13 million. A spokesman confirmed closure on May 21.

Five members of staff have been offered work at the Isaac Newton Centre store.

Figure 10.1 Differing fortunes.
Source: Grantham Journal, *6 May 1988.*

Demand

In a modern economy money is central to many of our activities, the things we buy, the places we visit and many of the pleasures that we enjoy. Goods and services that we have to pay for all have a price and therefore an element of scarcity. These economic goods have been produced by factors of production (land, labour, capital) which are themselves scarce because payments have to be made to use them.

Free goods such as air are in plentiful supply and, because they are not scarce, we do not have to pay a price for them. The goods and services we receive at the end of the day are determined by the prices we have to pay for them as well as the incomes we receive. We are therefore only going to buy goods and services that:

1. we want;
2. we can afford.

If you are on a particularly low income you may not be able to afford all of the goods you want. You might then have to make decisions to forfeit some goods in favour of others. We all have our personal preferences and we prioritise these in our mind according to what we can afford. For example, if I had an income of £5:

1. I could go to the pictures, or
2. I could go to a football match, or
3. I could buy an LP, or
4. I could buy a shirt.

I feel that I would gain the most satisfaction from going to a football match, so I make that decision and forfeit the alternatives. Next week I might choose differently and do something else.

It is therefore clear that any individual's behaviour is based upon both preferences and ability to pay. This is known as *demand*. Demand for a particular product is therefore determined by the collective desire of all individuals and/or organisations wanting the product who are in a position to afford it.

Demand is the desire for a commodity supported by one's ability to pay a stated price for it.

We are all influenced by prices. If the price of a particular good is too high, we might not buy it. We are not going to be happy paying that price for it as our satisfaction would then be disproportionate to the payment we have made. If prices for that good fell, we are more likely to buy it. If they fall dramatically, we might even buy more than one. For example, look at the following demand schedule for records:

If the price of singles was £3.50 Fred would not buy any.

If the price of singles was £3.00 Fred would buy 1 every week.

If the price of singles was £2.50 Fred would buy 2 every week.

If the price of singles was £2.00 Fred would buy 3 every week.

If the price of singles was £1.50 Fred would buy 4 every week.

If the price of singles was £1.00 Fred would buy 5 every week.

This shows clearly that Fred buys more as the price falls. His demand increases when the price is lower. From this schedule we can construct a chart as in Figure 10.2 showing Fred's buying preferences for singles at the various prices. Note that the demand curve slopes downwards from the top left-hand corner of the diagram towards the bottom right.

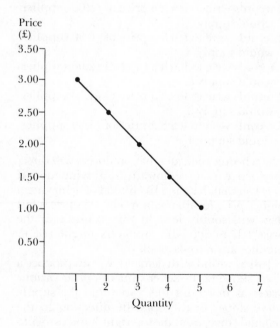

Figure 10.2 Fred's demand for singles (per week).

Supply

One of the most crucial decisions that any firm has to make is 'how many to produce'. Firms usually have an element of flexibility about the number of items they can make and their production decisions would be largely dependent upon the price that they can obtain. If producers are receiving a good price for their goods, it is likely that they will expand output even at the expense of increasing costs (overtime/factory expansion, etc.) and direct more *resources* into production. Conversely, if producers are only receiving a poor price, it might not be as profitable for them to supply to that market and they could well consider alternatives.

Let us consider the example of Fred again and try, in a hypothetical way, to relate a sole supplier's feelings to a sole customer. If the price of singles was £3.50 this supplier would be willing to develop the business and supply 6 singles onto the market. At lower prices he or she will be reluctant to supply so many. Just as we developed a demand schedule for Fred we can show a supply schedule for the producer:

If records were to fetch a price of £3.50 supplier would supply 6.

If records were to fetch a price of £3.00 supplier would supply 5.

If records were to fetch a price of £2.50 supplier would supply 4.

If records were to fetch a price of £2.00 supplier would supply 3.

If records were to fetch a price of £1.50 supplier would supply 2.

If records were to fetch a price of £1.00 supplier would supply 1.

The schedule indicates that producers will direct productive resources towards supplying more if they feel that there is a likelihood of achieving a higher price for their commodity. As prices fall they will supply less. In this example, if the price fell to 50p, the producers might fail to produce any records at all.

Just as we did with demand, we can produce a chart showing the seller's intentions at various prices as in Figure 10.3. Note that the supply curve slopes in the opposite direction to the demand curve, from the top right-hand corner to the bottom left-hand corner.

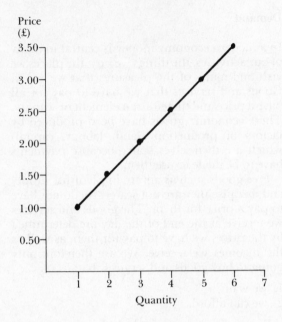

Figure 10.3 Producer's supply curve for singles per week.

The meeting place

A market is not just the stall-based trading area that we associate with the term, but has a much wider meaning. It is any situation whereby sellers come into contact with buyers.

We have seen that the forces of supply influence sellers and the forces of demand influence buyers. If our sole producer meets up with Fred, we can consider what will happen. If the supplier set the price at £3.00, he or she will produce 5 records but Fred would only buy 1. There are therefore 4 left over and this is what we call excess supply. At £2.50 there is an excess supply of 2 because the supplier wishes to produce 4, but Fred will only buy 2.

At £2.00 the supplier produces 3 and Fred wants 3. Clearly there is then harmony or *equilibrium* in the market as Fred's wishes have matched the supplier's intentions. At a price lower than £2.00 Fred would want more than the producer would be willing to supply and there would be excess demand. At a price of £1.00 Fred would like 5 records but the producer would only be willing to supply 1. There would be an excess demand of 4.

We can now match up both the demand and

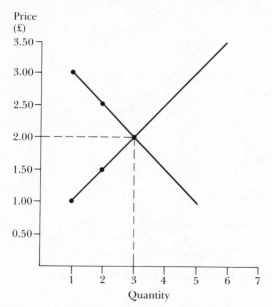

Figure 10.4 Matching up demand and supply curves.

supply curves to show how these relationships have created the equilibrium price. This is illustrated in Figure 10.4. Consider now the following situations:

1. If you draw a line horizontally across at £2.50 to cut both the demand and supply curves, are you in an equilibrium position? How would you explain the position at £2.50? What do you think will happen next?
2. If you draw another horizontal line at £1.50 to cut both the demand and supply curves, are you in an equilibrium position? How

would you explain the position at £1.50? What do you think will happen next?
3. If you draw a line horizontally across at £2.00 to cut both the demand and supply curves, are you in an equilibrium position? How would you explain the position at £2.00? What do you think will happen next?

Equilibrium is a situation from which there will be no tendency to change in the short period because forces are in balance.

The price system

Clearly the equilibrium price reflects a situation when a price at which consumers are willing to pay matches the price at which producers are willing to sell. It reflects demand and scarcity of resources. Many who are in favour of the price system argue that this relationship between consumers and producers is an important one because it guides resources into their most efficient uses (see Figure 10.5).

Others might argue that the market mechanism is not a 'fair' allocation of resources and that it requires state intervention to provide a socially acceptable outcome. Opponents of the price system would argue for instance that incomes are distributed unfairly so that richer people can grab the lion's share of scarce resources. They would also argue that prices do not accurately reflect 'real' costs of production.

■ Case Study: Labour plans 'public enterprise culture'

Read the extract from a newspaper article given in

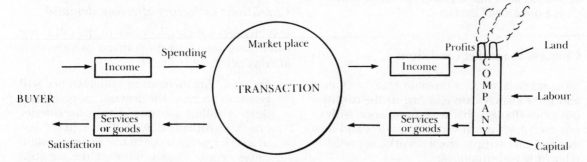

Figure 10.5 How resources are allocated and directed to profit-making activities through the forces of demand and supply.

State-backed garages, est-ate agencies and building companies should be set up by a future Labour government to challenge private enter-prise, a Labour policy group has told the party leadership.

The public sector should demonstrate its ability to offer high quality services in areas where the market often fails the consumer, promoting a 'public enterprise culture' the group says.

'Examples include estate agency, car maintenance and garages, and house mainten-ance,' according to the group.

Figure 10.6 Extracts from a newspaper article.
Source: adapted from an article in The Independent, *15 May 1988.*

Figure 10.6 about a view held by some members of the Labour party, and then answer the questions below.

Questions

1. In what ways could the market be failing the consumer?
2. Why do you think that estate agents and garages have been quoted as examples of the market failing consumers?
3. What other examples could be added to the list?
4. What evidence would you expect the Labour group to be basing its case on?
5. What evidence could be used to refute their argument?
6. Do you think that a 'public enterprise culture' is a good idea? Explain.

Changes in market conditions

Most markets are in a constant state of change and these changes are reflected in the continu-ous price changes that we have to cope with in our everyday lives. If we are to understand how demand and supply theory works we need to relate it to real situations.

A *movement along* a demand or supply curve takes place when a price changes. For example,

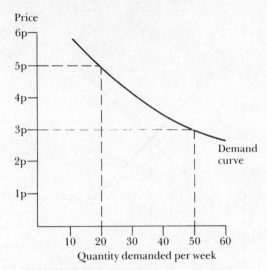

Figure 10.7 Movement along the demand curve.

if a price fell from 5p to 3p more would be demanded at 3p, and though demand has ex-tended other things remain the same. This is illustrated in Figure 10.7.

However, sometimes events can take place which can bodily *shift* either the demand or the supply curve so that more or less will either be demanded or supplied *at every price*. This situ-ation is illustrated in Figures 10.8 and 10.9.

Note that any increase in demand or supply at each price causes either the demand curve or the suply curve to shift to the right (Figures 10.8(a) and 10.9(a)). Any decrease in demand or supply at each price causes either the demand curve or the supply curve to shift to the left (Figures 10.8(b) and 10.9(b)).

Conditions or factors affecting demand

It is changes which take place in the following conditions that cause the demand curve to shift at every price:

1. *Incomes.* An increase in real incomes will generally increase the demand for goods and services unless a commodity is an inferior one (e.g. synthetic fibre clothing). In the case of inferior goods a rise in real incomes might cause people to buy more of the superior alternatives.
2. *Tastes, fashions and habits.* Consumers are

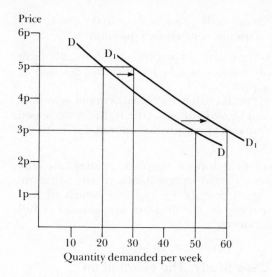

Figure 10.8 (a) Increase in demand.

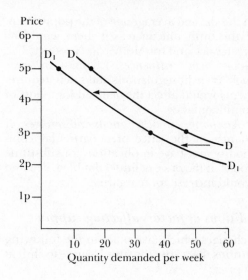

(b) Decrease in demand.

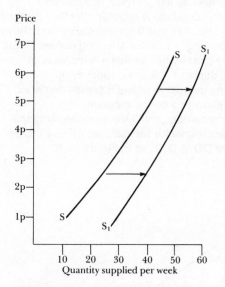

Supply has moved from SS to $S_1 S_1$ meaning
that more is now supplied at each price and the
supply curve has shifted to the right.

Figure 10.9 (a) Increase in supply.

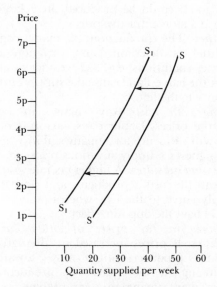

Supply has moved from SS to $S_1 S_1$ meaning
that less is now supplied at each price and the
supply curve has shifted to the left.

(b) Decrease in supply.

influenced by personal feelings towards
goods. In the mid-seventies skateboards were
popular with the young. Today there are
new crazes.
3. *Advertising.* Advertising campaigns attempt
   to influence consumers' preferences and thus
   increase their demand for particular com-

modities.
4. *Seasonal influences.* A long hot summer
   might well increase consumer demand for
   particular types of drinks. In a severe winter
   demand could increase for heating appli-
   ances and energy.
5. *Population.* Demand might vary in relation

to the size and average age of the population. If the birth rate increased there would be greater demand for Mothercare products.

6. *Government influences.* Changes in areas such as credit regulations and safety requirements would affect the demand for a host of commodities.

7. *Price changes in other goods and services.* A change in the price of a particular commodity may have implications for substitute goods. If the price of butter doubled, demand would increase for margarine.

Conditions or factors affecting supply

It is changes which take place in the following conditions that cause the supply curve to shift at every price:

1. *Technology.* This might well improve both production techniques and cost efficiency so that goods could be produced on a larger scale at a more attractive price.

2. *Weather.* The production of many commodities is determined by variation in weather conditions, e.g. bad weather might affect the harvest and cause the supply curve to move to the left.

3. *Changes in costs.* Any change in raw material prices, labour costs, factory rents, etc., will influence a company's ability and willingness to supply at various prices.

4. *Taxes and subsidies.* A higher tax rate would increase the costs of producing and move the supply curve to the left, whereas subsidies would have the opposite effect.

5. *Changes in the prices of other commodities.* If prices increased in alternative markets, producers might move towards producing in those areas of production rather than staying in their present area. They would then be moving resources towards producing for the higher priced markets.

Effects of changes in the conditions of demand and supply

When we look at realistic or actual situations, by considering our price theory we can anticipate the impact these events will have upon the markets for various goods and services. Whenever you are presented with a situation which

points towards changes in market conditions you must ask yourself two questions:

1. Is the change in market conditions as a result of changes in a factor affecting demand or supply?

2. Has this change increased demand or supply and moved curves to the right, or decreased demand or supply and moved curves to the left?

Never just draw a diagram. A diagram only shows a partial representation of any situation. You must describe in your own words what is happening in the diagram and provide a full explanation.

■ Case Study: The effect of an advertising campaign

First, you have to ask yourself whether an advertising campaign is a factor affecting demand or supply. You can see from our discussion above that advertising is a factor affecting demand. You then have to ask whether this will increase or decrease demand. Clearly a successful advertising campaign would increase demand. You can show this on the diagram. The advertising campaign will increase demand and the demand curve for the product will shift to the right from DD to D_1D_1 as in Figure 10.10.

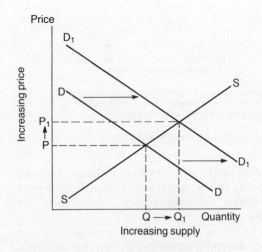

Figure 10.10 The effect of an advertising campaign.

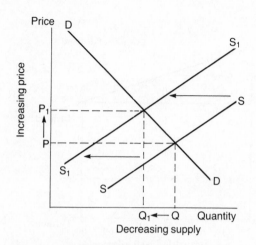

Figure 10.11 The effect of bad weather on the market for coffee.

■ Case Study: The effect of bad weather on a cash crop

What would happen to the market for coffee if extreme variations in weather conditions severely reduced the Brazilian crop? Clearly, bad weather in this instance would be a factor affecting the supply of coffee and would reduce the potential supply to markets.

Supply is now reduced at every price and moves to the left in Figure 10.11 from SS to S_1S_1. Bad weather has reduced the quantity on the market from Q to Q_1 and the shortage is reflected in a higher commodity price which has risen from P to P_1.

These changes in market conditions and the circumstances they portray show that the market mechanism is at the heart of our economy. It is clear that through this system production decisions are taken and resources are allocated.

■ Case Study: The leisure industry

The phenomenon known as the 'leisure boom' has been with us since the mid-1970s. The Sports Council has recently put together a *Digest of Statistics* looking at this growth. The report showed that between 1977 and 1983 there had been a 25% increase in sports participation, that

the number of local authority sports centres had grown from 20 in 1972 to 1,500 in 1987, and that sport not only employed more people than either the coal or gas industries, but also generated £6.75 billion of expenditure in 1987.

Consider Table 10.1 which lists consumer expenditure on a variety of items and then answer the following questions.

Table 10.1 Selected categories of UK consumer expenditure in 1985

	£m
Motor vehicles	9,916
Beer	8,347
Cigarettes	6,115
Electricity	4,860
Furniture and floor coverings	4,639
Sport, including gambling	4,366
Bread	4,051
Gas	4,046
Menswear	3,981
Spirits	3,861
Wines and ciders	3,847
Sport, excluding gambling	3,207
DIY goods	2,616
Newspapers and magazines	2,273
Pets	1,278
Records	783
Bingo admissions	288
Cinema	125

Source: Sports Council 1987.

Questions

1. Which of the above expenditures would you regard to be on leisure activities? How much in total would you say is spent on leisure activities?
2. Draw a chart showing a breakdown of leisure activities into different categories (by per cent). Compare this with the breakdown of leisure expenditure for (a) yourself, (b) other members of your class.
3. Why do you think that there has been a general increase in demand for leisure activities? Give as many reasons as possible.
4. Would the increase in demand for leisure apply to all leisure activities?
5. (a) Name one product associated with leisure for which demand has increased during the last ten years. (b) Illustrate by means of a

demand-and-supply diagram how the market has responded to this change. Explain your diagram.

6. (a) Name one product associated with leisure for which demand has fallen during the last ten years. (b) Illustrate by means of a demand-and-supply diagram how the market has responded to this change. Explain your diagram.

Measurement

In order to measure the impact of a price change upon a market, economists use the term *elasticity*. The term refers to the extent that either the quantity demanded or the quantity supplied changes as a result of a price variation and this degree of change is dependent upon the shape of either the demand curve or the supply curve.

Elasticity of demand

This is the measurement of the extent that the quantity demanded changes if the price is altered. Its formula is:

$$\text{Elasticity of demand} = \frac{\text{\% change in the quantity demanded}}{\text{\% change in price}}$$

For any commodity which has many substitutes and whose demand responds easily to price changes, the elasticity of demand will be larger than 1 and demand is said to be *elastic*. This is illustrated in Figure 10.12 which shows the effect of a 25% increase in price on such a commodity.

Demand has fallen considerably as a result of this 25% price increase. Consumers have responded to the price increase by moving away from this commodity towards substitute goods. The knowledge that demand in one's market is elastic enables producers to understand how consumers may respond if they put up prices.

In contrast, a good which has very few substitutes and for which demand responds very little to a price change would have an elasticity of demand of less than 1. In this instance demand would be *inelastic*. This situation is illustrated

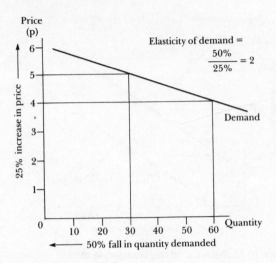

Figure 10.12 Elastic demand.

in Figure 10.13 which shows the effect of a 20% fall in price on such a good.

Though the price has fallen by the significant margin of 20%, demand for this commodity has not increased by as much. Again this is a useful guide for the decision-maker as it indicates how the market reacts to price changes. In this particular situation it might not be worthwhile for the business to make the price cuts.

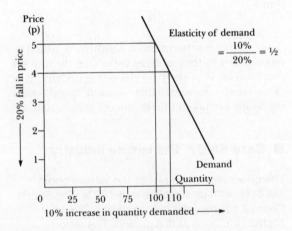

Figure 10.13 Inelastic demand.

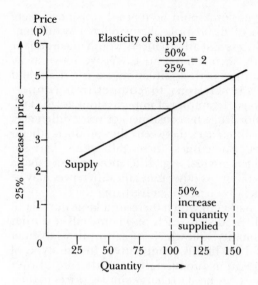

Figure 10.14 Elastic supply.

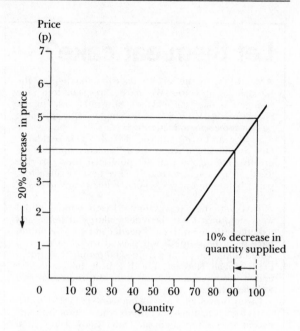

Figure 10.15 Inelastic supply.

Elasticity of supply

This is the measurement of the extent to which the quantity supplied changes if the price is altered. Its formula is:

$$\text{Elasticity of supply} = \frac{\% \text{ change in the quantity supplied}}{\% \text{ change in price}}$$

If suppliers respond readily to small price changes by producing a lot more when the price goes up or by producing a lot less when the price falls, supply will be elastic. Supply will be elastic if the elasticity of supply is larger than 1. Figure 10.14 indicates that firms in an elastic market would find it easy to respond to price changes and vary their levels of production. They probably either work well below their capacity or keep large stock levels.

If firms have severe difficulties varying their output levels, their supply will be inelastic. Supply will be inelastic if the elasticity of supply is less than 1. Even though price has fallen by 20% in Figure 10.15, the supplier has only decreased the quantity supplied by 10%. They may be reluctant to lay off resources and could be surveying the situation in the long run.

■ Case Study: Does the price system help?

Study the letter reproduced in Figure 10.16 which appeared in *Pravda*, and answer the questions below.

Questions

1. Using diagrams explain how the price system might have helped to solve some of the problems outlined by the letter writer.
2. What problems might have been caused by using the price system in this situation?
3. Describe at least three situations in which shortages occur in this country, and three situations in which consumers only have a limited choice.
4. Explain how government intervention might help in these situations.

Competition

The success of price equilibrium where prices are determined by the forces of demand and supply depends entirely upon the type of

Let them eat cake?

● WE LIVE in the small village of Shakhen in the Karaganda province. We have three children, the youngest is one year old. My husband works in the Shakhtinskaya Mine. I am also employed by the mine but am at present on maternity leave.

So why am I writing to you? I read Pravda regularly. One column in particular, Vital Problems, interests me greatly. The letters that get published there are life itself. So I thought to myself, "I've never written to a paper before and now's as good a time as any to start." So here I am.

Take yesterday, for example. It was Sunday and I went shopping. I left the older children at home and took the little one with me. I needed butter. You should have seen the shop! It was packed with people. You would think that it was wartime and people were queuing for bread. Here was I, with a small child, at the far end of this commotion! Some hope. I turned away and went back home.

In our province there is a famous sweet factory which was given a national award, yet you cannot buy any decent sweets for children. Only "Snowdrops", and even the children are getting fed up with them.

Things should be getting better everywhere, yet in our little village everything seems to disappear. No cakes, no biscuits, no wafers. There are shortages of basic things, too. There is no sausage, no cheese, no margarine. And if you were to believe the papers, our food and agricultural industries are producing more and more food every year.

So where does it all go? Why are our shops empty? The only product that is always available, is tinned fish. My sincere thanks to the Fish Processing Industry for that.

You can occasionally buy meat too. However, it is sold in cooperative stores only, and it's very expensive.

Just think about it, how are we supposed to feed our children in this situation? Children are growing, they need proper nourishment. And so does my husband, who goes to work every morning. And he doesn't work in an office, but in a mine. – Dudareva, Shakhen, Karaganda Province.

Figure 10.16 Letter to a newspaper regarding bread shortages.
Source: Pravda International.

competition within which suppliers are operating. There are various degrees and types of competition, from those industries in which firms are very competitive to those producers who could be in a position to distort the competition and control the market for their own benefit.

A perfect market would be one in which competition between firms in the market would know no restrictions. Features of this perfect competition would be that all consumers were aware of all the prices being offered by different producers and all producers would make and/or supply identical products. As we move away from this 'perfect' situation we get more and more restrictions to competition (imperfections). Examples of imperfections are the lack of knowledge by consumers of price differences and differences between the products themselves. Sometimes these differences between products are real, e.g. differences in taste, shape and colour. At other times the differences may be artificially created by advertising hype.

A market in which there are a large number of small producers, each of whom sells a similar commodity, and which is easy for firms to enter would be highly competitive. In this type of competition producers have little control over price. They need to charge similar prices to their competitors if they are to survive. Even a 1p difference in price per unit can lead to lost sales.

On the other hand, a producer who controls an industry is known as a *monopoly*. A monopoly may control the supply of a raw material or be so well developed technologically that no other company is in a position to compete. Though it cannot control a market completely and is to some extent dependent upon consumer demand, it can set prices and its powers are often considerable.

There are many stages between a highly competitive market and monopoly (see Figure 10.17). There may be four or five firms dominating a market or hundreds. Firms will often seek to capture larger market shares by trying to make their product different from their rivals', e.g. through advertising and packaging.

■ Coursework activity

Figure 10.18 gives you some indicators as to the factors which influence the demand for tea. In class you should discuss the main factors which you think would influence the demand for Typhoo.

You should then prepare a questionnaire to carry out some primary research. This would involve finding out who buys Typhoo in your local area. Try to build up a profile of Typhoo drinkers. You should also find out why other people do *not* drink Typhoo. Try to make estimations of what will

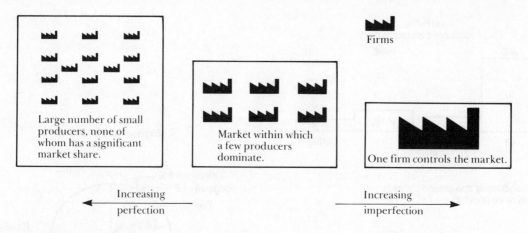

Figure 10.17 Types of competition.

happen to the demand for Typhoo in future years.

Carry out some further research concentrating on Typhoo drinkers to find out how they would respond to increases in its price. Try to explain the general relationship between the price of Typhoo and the quantity consumed.

What further information would you require in order to develop your local study into a national demand pattern?

■ Coursework suggestions

1. Choose a particular industry. Identify as many producers in this industry as you are able to find. Try to indicate what form of competition exists within this industry and justify your answer.
2. Produce a survey which asks consumers about their choice of consumables and the alternatives they may or may not turn to. Test the survey on a target group. Indicate which commodities have many substitutes and a high elasticity of demand and which have few substitutes and a low elasticity of demand.
3. Write to local firms. Ask if they can change their production levels by 10%, 20%, 30%, etc., in the short term. Make conclusions about their elasticity of supply. What factors influence their ability to increase or decrease output quickly?
4. Look at the financial pages of newspapers. Try to identify a firm which has recently had its circumstances changed. This change might

either be in its market share or in factors affecting its supply or demand for products. Find out as much as you can about this change in circumstances by following events in the press and by writing to the firm. Compile a report on these changes.
5. Prepare a survey which attempts to discover where gaps exist in markets. This would be where demand is strong, but supply is limited in both numbers and choice. Present your conclusions to the class.

■ Revision

Complete the following sentences using the words below:

producers	market
resources	larger
shift	movement
less than	free
desire	monopoly
left	excess supply
elasticity	more
subsidies	right
supplied	quickly
inelastic	perfect competition

1. Air and sea-water are _____ goods.
2. Demand is a _____ for a commodity and the ability to pay for it.
3. Consumers will buy _____ as price falls.

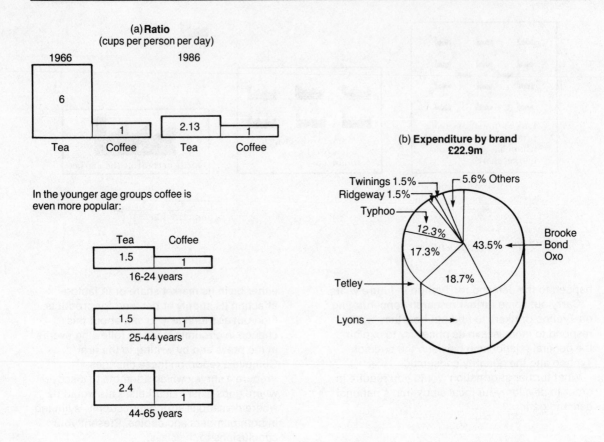

<![CDATA[
(a) Ratio
(cups per person per day)

| 1966 | 1986 |

6 — Tea / 1 — Coffee

2.13 — Tea / 1 — Coffee

In the younger age groups coffee is even more popular:

Tea / Coffee

1.5 / 1
16-24 years

1.5 / 1
25-44 years

2.4 / 1
44-65 years

(b) Expenditure by brand
£22.9m

Twinings 1.5%
Ridgeway 1.5%
Typhoo
5.6% Others
12.3%
17.3%
43.5% — Brooke Bond Oxo
18.7%
Tetley
Lyons
]]>

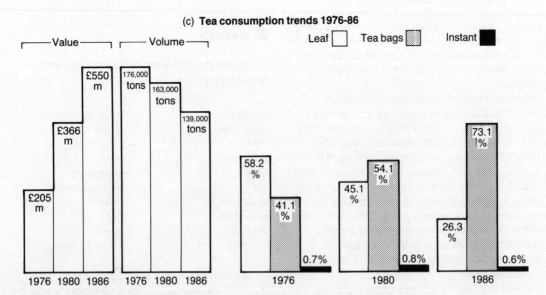

(c) Tea consumption trends 1976-86

Leaf ☐   Tea bags ▒   Instant ■

Value — Volume

£205 m / £366 m / £550 m
1976 1980 1986

176,000 tons / 163,000 tons / 139,000 tons
1976 1980 1986

| 1976 | 1980 | 1986 |
| 58.2% / 41.1% / 0.7% | 45.1% / 54.1% / 0.8% | 26.3% / 73.1% / 0.6% |

Figure 10.18 National statistics relating to tea consumption.
Source: (a) National Drinks Survey; (b) MEAL; (c) Trade estimates/National Drinks Survey.

4. If producers can obtain higher prices they will direct more _____ into production.
5. A _____ is any situation where sellers come into contact with buyers.
6. If the supplier produces more than the consumer wants at a particular price there is _____.
7. The equilibrium price relates consumers' wishes to the amount _____ are willing to sell.
8. A _____ along a demand or supply curve takes place when a price changes.
9. Sometimes events can bodily _____ the demand or supply curve so that more or less will either be demanded or supplied at every price.
10. An extensive advertising campaign would shift the demand curve to the _____ .
11. If the birth rate fell the demand curve for baby products would shift to the _____ .
12. _____ have the opposite effect to taxes and would shift the supply curve to the right.
13. Economists use the term _____ to describe the relationship between price changes and the market.
14. For a commodity with many substitutes the elasticity of demand will be _____ than 1.
15. If demand responds very little to price change it will have an elasticity of demand of _____ 1.
16. Elasticity of supply measures the extent that the quantity _____ changes if the price is altered.
17. If suppliers respond _____ to small price increases by producing more, supply will be elastic.
18. A firm which finds it difficult to vary its output levels will have an _____ supply.
19. In _____ firms must accept the market price.
20. If a producer controls an industry, it is known as a _____ .

CHAPTER 11
Income and wealth

Wealth

Wealth is the term used to describe a stock of valuables. For example, an individual's stock of wealth would include the money, stocks and shares, paintings, house and other possessions he or she had at a particular moment in time.

The wealth of a *country* is the stock of material possessions such as houses, factories, investments and other valuables which are owned by members of that country at any one time. In addition to the material wealth of a country we also must account for *human wealth*. This is the skill and business expertise developed by its members.

Wealth can be seen as a stock. The creation of new wealth will add to this stock; the using up and wearing out of wealth (*depreciation*) will run down this stock. This relationship can be likened to water flowing into a sink with the plughole open (see Figure 11.1). At any given moment there is a stock of water in the sink. Water pouring from the tap will add to this stock. Water going down the plughole will reduce the stock. If water enters the sink at a faster rate than it leaves then the stock of water will increase. If a country is to become wealthier it is important that investment in new goods and training for skills is greater than depreciation and the wastage of skills.

Income

Income is a flow. It is the flow of new wealth which is created over a period of time. If we measure the quantity of water in Figure 11.1 leaving the tap in a minute we could record its *flow* over this period. Flows of income are measured over a period of time; for example, Mr Brown earned £150 this week, while the national income (the sum of everyone's earnings from all sources) of the United Kingdom in 1986 was £323.3 billion.

Personal income comes from a variety of sources. Individuals can earn wages for providing their labour, rent for hiring out land, interest from lending out money, and dividends if they own a share of a business enterprise. For example, I can calculate my annual income in the following way:

		£
My pay packet comes to £12,000:	Wages	12,000
My share dividend from British Telecom came to £100:	Dividends	100
I rented out my garage for £20 a week:	Rent	1,040
Total annual income =		£13,140

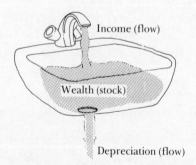

Figure 11.1 The wealth creation process.

Wealth creation

We live in a highly specialised community that is dependent on the efforts of both individuals and organisations for its well-being. Members of this community want the best for themselves and their families.

Some people define *standard of living* as the material possessions you can obtain with your money. However, many others would argue that living in a pleasant environment, the provision of good health care and being able to share in the benefits provided by a fruitful community are just as important.

Industry and business play a vital role in creating wealth and ultimately improving living standards. They bring together productive resources and create incomes for employees and employers. In creating products and providing services industry adds to the value of its products at each stage of production, e.g. a shoemaker will convert leather into shoes. The difference between the value of the raw materials and the price of the finished goods will represent the value added to that product.

Improving living standards

During the 1980s average earnings have increased considerably and though prices have gone up they have not increased by as much as average earnings. This represents an increase in average real incomes and, as a result, spending upon luxuries such as new cars has gone up. However, there have been inequalities such as:

1. *Unemployment rates.* Unemployment has been a major problem of the 1980s. Those out of work have to live meagrely on state benefits. Early in 1988 unemployment figures were running at approximately 18% in Northern Ireland, approximately 14% in the North and yet were only approximately 7% in the South East. Clearly average incomes in areas of high unemployment are likely to be lower and their inhabitants are likely to have a lower standard of living.

2. *Earnings of male and female employees.* In 1987 the average earnings of full-time male employees were nearly £200 per week whereas the average earnings of full-time female employees were significantly lower. Though many women do not see their careers as the most important aspect of their lives and some take on jobs which entail menial tasks irrespective of their abilities, it is another inequality.

3. *Location of industry and capital.* In recent years certain industries have suffered severe setbacks. Many of these industries have been traditional staple industries providing a large proportion of the employment in a limited area, e.g. Consett in the North of England and the steel industry. In areas where these industries have declined communities have suffered severe setbacks. At the same time high technology industries in areas such as the Thames Valley have been booming. Some of the reasons for industries moving to or developing in the South East have been the large nearby market, good communication links and skilled labour force. Some might argue that the forces of demand and supply seem to encourage the growth of industry in areas of low unemployment and limit the growth of companies in areas of high unemployment.

■ Case Study: The quality of life

Look carefully at the figures given in Table 11.1 and then answer the questions below.

Table 11.1 Quality of life statistics

	1976	1981	1986
Dwellings per 000 population	368	386	400
TV sets (licences) per 000	316	331	330
Private cars (licences) per 000	251	272	307
Telephones per 000 (March)	372	494	520
Refrigerators, % of households owning	88.1	96.1	97.6
Civil servants per 000	13.3	12.2	10.5
Pupils per teacher (January)	19.9	18.2	17.5
Real personal disposable income per head 1985 prices	£3,683	£4,084	£4,578

Source: Lloyds Bank 1987.

Questions

1. What can you say about the changes over time in:
   (a) the number of dwellings per 000 population;

Table 11.2 Method of transport used in various areas.

	Derwentside	Chester Le Street	Wear Valley	City of Durham	Easington	Teesdale	Sedgefield	Darlington	County Durham	England & Wales
Households with no car 1981 (%)	50.7	41.9	49.2	42.7	56.7	33.3	48.1	44.8	47.6	38.5
Households with one car 1981 (%)	40.2	46.5	40.5	45.3	36.8	47.5	42.6	43.6	42.1	45.6
Households with two or more cars 1981 (%)	9.1	11.6	10.3	12.0	6.5	19.2	9.3	11.6	10.3	15.9
Mode of travel to work 1981 (%)										
Car	51.7	60.1	50.7	56.0	40.6	54.5	50.5	49.2	50.6	51.2
Bus	23.5	22.4	17.9	20.9	25.3	7.0	19.1	19.1	20.6	15.3
Train	0.2	0.4	1.2	0.4	0.4	—	0.6	2.1	0.8	6.0
Motorcycle	1.2	1.4	1.4	1.8	1.5	1.9	1.7	1.9	1.6	3.0
Pedal cycle	0.3	0.3	1.1	0.7	0.3	1.0	1.1	4.3	1.3	3.9
On foot	16.8	11.9	20.4	15.7	27.1	24.2	22.6	18.5	19.8	15.0
Work at home	2.4	1.3	4.3	2.2	2.0	8.5	2.0	2.2	2.6	3.4
Length of highways April 1987 (kms)										
Motorway	—	7	—	14	—	—	15	9	45	2,602
Trunk	—	6	—	12	18	24	16	16	92	9,378
County roads – classified	261	74	248	148	126	367	165	181	1,570	119,097
County roads – unclassfied	350	183	264	292	323	219	292	250	2,173	166,894

Source: Durham County Council 1988.

(b) the number of private cars per 000 population;
(c) the number of telephones per 000 population.
2. Approximately what number of people share each house?
3. How many telephones are there per person?
4. Has our standard of living increased since 1976? Explain.
5. What other information would you need to show more fully the changes in our standard of living?
6. What has happened to the numbers of civil servants per 000 of the population over this period? Which groups and individuals are most likely to have gained/lost out from this change?

■ **Case study: Transport in County Durham**

Look carefully at the figures in Table 11.2 which refers to various aspects of transportation in County Durham, and then answer the questions that follow.

Questions

1. In which area of County Durham was the number of households with no car in 1981: (a) greatest; (b) lowest.
2. How do these figures compare with the national average of households with no car in 1981?
3. Compare the modes of travel to work in 1981 in County Durham with the figures for England and Wales and comment upon your findings.

■ **Case Study: Comparison of house prices**

Figure 11.2 compares house prices in the Greater London area with those in Yorkshire and Humberside. Look at it carefully and then answer the questions below.

Questions

1. What has been happening to relative house prices over the period shown?

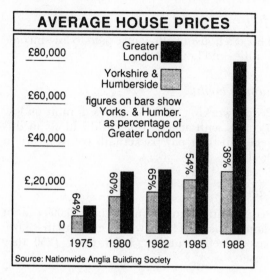

Figure 11.2 Average house prices.
Source: Nationwide Anglia Building Society.

2. What possible explanations could you put forward for this change?
3. Why might these figures encourage someone to seek work in London rather than in Yorkshire and Humberside?
4. Why might these figures encourage someone to seek work in Yorkshire and Humberside rather than in London?
5. Why might an employer find it an attractive proposition to move from London to Yorkshire and Humberside?
6. What further information would the employer require before making such a decision?

Factors of production

Factors of production are used to convert resources into products. Economists recognise four main factors of production: land, labour, capital and enterprise.

1. *Land* includes all the resources which are gifts of nature. As a result it does not just include the land surface but would also include the fishes in the sea, minerals under the earth's surface, forests and oceans.
2. *Labour* includes all forms of physical and mental effort that go into production.

3. *Capital* is a man-made resource. It includes machines, factories, schools and hospitals which people have produced in order to produce other goods and services. A modern economy possesses vast stocks of capital, and the capital stock is continually increasing. Increases in capital stock are called *investment*.
4. *Enterprise*. Some economists think that the entrepreneur is really another form of labour. An entrepreneur is a risk-taker who brings together the other factors of production to create goods and services.

Distribution of income and wealth

The United Kingdom economy like most others is characterised by obvious inequalities in wealth and income. *Wealth* is particularly unevenly distributed and over half of the wealth of the country is owned by just a small number of people (under 5% of the population). *Income* is not so unevenly distributed but even here vast differences occur so that some people can earn from one hour's work as much as others can earn in a week. (Up-to-date information on the distribution of wealth and income can be obtained from the Central Statistical Office's *Social Trends* survey.)

A society must choose whether to have inequality or not, and how much inequality to have. Different people think differently about the subject. Margaret Thatcher for instance once said: 'May all our children grow taller, but some grow taller than others!'

■ Question

What do you think that Margaret Thatcher meant?

The government influences the distribution of income and wealth through its policies in relation to handing out benefits and taking money from citizens in the form of taxes.

Benefits

In 1988 32% of government expenditure went on social security. Of this 50% went on the elderly, 17% on families, 16% on the unemployed, 14% on the sick and disabled and 3% on widows and orphans.

For most of the twentieth century governments have felt it increasingly necessary to create a network of welfare services. However, in the 1980s the emphasis changed. The government has simplified the system of welfare and reduced the amount of benefits. John Moore, the Conservative government minister responsible for introducing changes to the benefit system in 1988, said: 'We believe that dependence in the long run decreases human happiness and reduces human freedom. We believe the well-being of individuals is best promoted when they are helped to be independent, to use their talents to take care of themselves and their families.' In crude terms the government has been putting pressure on individuals to go out and get a job by cutting down on benefits.

■ Question

Jenny says: 'Reasonable benefits are necessary in a civilised society. People who work for the community should have something to fall back on in hard times.'

Greg says: 'People should stand on their own two feet. If they keep expecting handouts they will never learn to be independent.'

1. What questions would you ask Jenny and Greg to find out more about their views?
2. Who do you agree with? Why?

Some of the more important benefits in 1988 are listed below. These levels will change over time.

Income support

This system helps the poor and those out of work. A single person aged 25 or over gets £33.40 a week and a couple £51.45. There are additional payments for people with children, disabled people and old people.

Loans

The government runs a loans scheme for poor people who have special needs, such as for a cooker or clothing. Loans are paid back by deductions from other benefits.

Housing benefit

This is a housing allowance paid to low-income families and households.

Family credit

People working 24 hours a week or more on low incomes with at least one child can claim this benefit if their pay packet falls below a certain level.

Savings

People with savings of more than £6,000 cannot claim benefit. Those with more than £3,000 have benefits cut by £1 for every £250 they possess.

Pensions

State pensions for people under 50 in 1988 will be paid at a rate of 20% of their average earnings for their working life.

Child benefit

This benefit is paid at £7.25 per child to 7 million mothers.

Taxation

In order to finance public expenditure the government needs income and this comes mainly from taxation. In the United Kingdom there are two main methods of taxation.

Direct taxation

This is where taxes are directly assessed on income and capital and are paid by the taxpayer to the Department of Inland Revenue. Examples include:

1. *Income tax*, which is a personal tax on income earned.
2. *Corporation tax*, which is a tax on company profits.
3. *Capital gains tax*, which is a tax on increases in the value of certain assets. For example, if you buy a painting for £5 and sell it a week later for £1 million you would pay a tax on the gain in value.

4. *Petroleum taxes* are levied upon the income from the extraction of oil and gas.
5. *Inheritance tax,* which applies to income from gifts and transfers of wealth.

Indirect taxation

This is where the person who makes the tax payment passes the payment on to another person before it is collected by the Department of Customs and Excise. These are often called expenditure taxes as they affect spending. Examples include:

1. *Excise duties* added to the price of tobacco, alcohol, petrol and gaming.
2. A general sales tax called *Value Added Tax* (*VAT*), which applies to a range of goods and services. VAT at 15% must be charged on all items, except those zero-rated or exempt, by companies whose turnover exceeds a certain limit. The VAT has to be paid to HM Customs and Excise every three months. Firms whose turnover exceeds a certain limit add VAT to outputs and deduct VAT paid on inputs in order to calculate their VAT bills. For a small company VAT can involve a lot of paperwork and calculation.
3. *Protective duties* levied on imports to the United Kingdom.
4. *Motor vehicle excise duty and licences.*

The way in which these taxes are levied has a direct effect on our standard of living. For example, income tax is levied at two rates. A household with a large income will pay income tax at the higher rate. The tax has therefore taken into account the inequalities between individual circumstances. This type of structure is called a *progressive* one because those with higher incomes or more wealth pay proportionately more than those with lower incomes or less wealth.

A *proportional tax,* on the other hand, will take the same percentage of income, wealth and spending in taxation. All companies making profits over a certain limit pay a similar proportion of their profits in corporation tax.

A *regressive tax,* finally, works in the opposite way to a progressive tax. Those with lower incomes or less wealth would pay proportionately more to the authorities than those with higher incomes or more wealth. It could be

argued that the TV licence is a regressive tax as those on lower incomes pay proportionately more than those on higher incomes for whom the licence fee is only an insignificant proportion of total income.

■ Coursework suggestions

1. Look at all of the changes that took place in the last Budget. List them and point out who were the gainers and who were the losers. Indicate whether the Budget has created more inequality or less inequality.
2. Try to find out the sort of hardships that families upon subsistence incomes have to suffer. Show how the state tries to relieve their plight.

The Budget

Each year the Chancellor of the Exchequer presents a financial statement called the Budget to Parliament. The Budget forecasts national income and expenditure for the year ahead and is used as a major tool of economic policy. The Budget is also used to implement government policy with regard to taxation and benefits and so has an effect on the distribution of wealth and income in the country.

Local government taxes

Local authorities are responsible for approximately one-quarter of public expenditure. These authorities are largely financed by central government grants and by local taxes called *rates.* However, a new system of local taxation called the *community charge* (or more popularly 'the poll tax') is currently being introduced to replace the old rating system.

The community charge

From April 1989, canvassers will knock at the doors of every home in England and Wales with a poll tax form. The form will ask for the name, address and date of birth of people living in the house, plus reasons for any exemptions from payment. In this way each council will build up a poll tax register on computer.

Everyone over 18 will be legally required to

register, even if they are exempt from paying. Everyone on the register will have to pay the full poll tax set by their local authority, unless they are entitled to a rebate or an exemption.

Before the community charge was considered, local taxes were operated through the *rating system*. These were taxes levied by local authorities on occupiers of property. Rates were calculated according to the rateable value of the property. There were a number of major problems with this system. For example, if a single old-age pensioner lived in an identical property next door to six young professional people he or she would have paid the same rate. Under the new scheme the old-age pensioner will pay one-sixth of the community charge paid by the residents of the young professional household.

Under the new poll tax system far more people will have to pay local taxes. About 17 million people pay rates, whereas about 35 million will have to pay the poll tax. The amount of poll tax that individuals have to pay will depend on how much their council wishes to spend. If a council needs or wishes to spend a lot of money on providing local services then local residents will find these expenditures reflected in their community charge bills.

The system for taxing businesses for local services will, however, be different. The new system is being based on a fresh valuation of business property. Business rating will not be done on a local but on a national basis at a standard rate.

The effect of introducing a new taxation scheme such as the community charge is that there are a wide range of winners and losers. Some households and businesses will gain while others will lose out. On top of this there will be a wide range of other important considerations including:

1. The rise or fall in the cost of administering the new system.
2. The extent of evasion under the old and new systems.
3. The improvement or deterioration of local services as a result of changing the system.

■ Coursework suggestion

How has the new poll tax and uniform business rate affected individuals and groups in your locality? Who are the winners and who are the losers? What have been the benefits and costs of the new system? What advantages and disadvantages are there to the new system? This task will involve a group questionnaire put to a wide range of individuals and groups. You will also need to look at the existing literature. Find out information from local councillors of different political persuasions.

■ Case Study: Introducing the community charge

Table 11.3 shows the winners and losers from the introduction of an imaginary poll tax of £205 per person in Darlington in 1987/8. Look at it carefully and then answer the questions below.

Questions

1. Make a list of those (a) who gain; (b) who lose.
2. Whom does the change (a) affect least; (b) affect most.
3. Why do you consider that such a change is being introduced?
4. Explain how the community charge will have a redistributive effect.

■ Case Study: Labour election poster

Study the poster given in Figure 11.3 and then answer the following questions.

Questions

1. Why might Mrs Thatcher say about the new tax: 'It's a much better, much fairer system'? What sort of evidence would she use to back up her argument?
2. What is the main thrust of the argument presented in the poster to contradict Mrs Thatcher?
3. What do you think is meant by 'fair'?

Table 11.3 Effect of a hypothetical community charge.

Household	Type of house	Rates in 1987/88	Community charge (using £205)	How much households would have gained or lost in 1987/88
Two adults	Detached house (Edinburgh Drive)	£1,377	£410	+£967
Three adults	Terraced house (Fairfield Street)	£169	£615	−£446
One adult	Terraced house (Greenwell Street)	£182	£205	−£23
Four adults	Detached house (Town Farm Close, Bishopton)	£810	£820	−£10
Two adults	Semi-detached house (Rochester Way)	£552	£410	+£142
Three adults	End-terraced house (Teesway, Neasham)	£585	£615	−£30
One adult	Flat (Knoll Avenue)	£361	£205	+£156
Four adults	Semi-detached (The Mead)	£348	£820	−£472
Two adults	Terraced (Beaconsfield Street)	£182	£410	−£228
Five adults	Semi-detached (Honeywood Gardens)	£517	£1,025	−£508

Source: Darlington Borough Council.

4. What do you think is meant by 'better'?
5. How would you construct a local tax system so that it is 'fair' and 'better'?

The world situation

Standards of living and quality of life for individuals vary widely both within and between countries. We frequently hear references to rich world/poor world and North/South divides in news reports and everyday conversations. These issues are often highly complex but it is important to try to understand the range of possible causes and cures for such situations. The way that resources are allocated frequently depends on the division of power. What is 'fair' or 'unfair' is a matter of opinion and people's views are often based on a limited amount of evidence. An important part of doing a course in industrial studies is to consider a range of views and how these views are formed. An important consideration is 'what information is required' to understand an issue. Wherever possible you should try to frame questions that help you to investigate better the way that society operates.

Three-quarters of the earth's population live in the developing or Third World, and only a

WHAT WOULD YOU SAY ABOUT A TAX THAT COST A COUPLE IN A SMALL FLAT TWICE AS MUCH AS A MILLIONAIRE IN A MANSION?

The Poll Tax is Mrs Thatcher's plan to replace the rates. It will not be based on your ability to pay, but on the number of adults in your house. Even Edward Heath and Michael Heseltine have called it unfair.

Already this year the Budget has given huge cuts to the

"It's a much better, much fairer system"

very rich while the new Social Fund has cut benefits for the low-paid and forced claimants with special needs to appeal to charity.

In the local elections next month you will have a chance to tell Mrs Thatcher what you think of her Poll Tax. Fair and square.

VOTE LABOUR IN THE LOCAL ELECTIONS ON MAY 5

M 030 87. Published by The Labour Party. 10th H148, 150 Walworth Road, London, SE17 1JT and printed by Bell Press/TU, 5 Jeans Lane, Bells Hill, Bishop's Stortford, Herts. CM23 2NN.

Figure 11.3 Labour Party view of the community charge.
Source: The Labour Party.

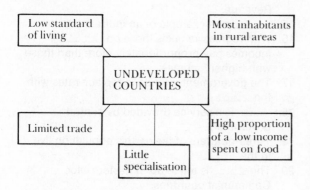

Figure 11.4 Some characteristics of underdeveloped countries.

quarter live in the developed First and Second Worlds. The First World consists of rich, mainly Western, industrially developed countries. The Second World is made up of Eastern-bloc Communist countries such as Poland and East Germany. The Third World consists of very much poorer countries in Africa, Asia and South America. One of the main problems for developing countries is that of population growth. Each year about 80 million people are added to the world population, and over 70 million of these are born in Third World countries.

Figure 11.4 illustrates some of the typical features of underdeveloped countries. However, no two developing countries are the same and we must be careful not to generalise. Most of the problems faced by developing countries are inter-dependent. For example, because many citizens have a low income, most of it will need to be spent on food. Because there is little income available for saving, few capital goods can be purchased. Because few capital goods are bought, output will be low.

Other features of developing countries include:

- a less-well-educated population
- poor housing
- poor sanitation (e.g. lack of access to clean piped water for drinking and washing)
- poor health standards

In recent years we in the West have become increasingly aware of starvation and famine in countries like Ethiopia and Sudan.

Two of the major reasons for famine are that:

1. Many of these countries do not have the money to buy food.
2. In many countries the land is not sufficiently fertile to grow food intensively and there is a limited supply of water.

For Third World countries, dependence upon rich nations has become a reality. At a time when they have limited natural resources to cater for their population's needs, they have also been saddled with large debts. Perhaps their future is now dependent upon their ability to specialise, trade internationally and develop their economies.

■ Revision

Complete the following sentences using the words below:

unemployment	direct taxes
rewarded	public sector
short supply	value added tax
South East	skills
Third World	standard of living
wealth creation	inflation
real income	Second World
earn	piece work
private sector	defence
community charge	lower

1. The term _____ would include the level of material comfort enjoyed by a personal group.
2. The difference between the value of raw materials and finished goods represents _____ .
3. The wealth of any country is the stock of material possessions and the _____ developed by its members.
4. _____ refers to the quantity of goods and services that can be purchased with a person's money income.
5. _____ might erode money income.
6. In British society some employees _____ more than others.
7. Those who have trained for a number of years will expect to be _____ for their skills.
8. _____ is where workers are paid for the number of items they have contributed to.

9. Employers will be prepared to pay higher wages if demand for that type of labour is strong and if labour is in _____ .

10. Many employers provide allowances to their employees to compensate for the cost of living in the _____ .

11. _____ has been a major problem of the 1980s.

12. Governments provide _____ goods and services.

13. The state intervenes in the _____ to ensure that its activities are not harmful to the public.

14. _____ are paid to the Department of Inland Revenue.

15. _____ is an example of an indirect tax.

16. With regressive taxes those on _____ incomes pay proportionately more than those with higher incomes.

17. The government intends to replace rates with the _____ .

18. _____ is a service provided by central government.

19. Three-quarters of the earth's population live in the _____ .

20. The _____ is made up of Eastern-bloc Communist countries.

CHAPTER 12
Government and industrial society

Government and business

The government is very much involved in business activity in this country. It tries to encourage certain activities such as training and tries to discourage other activities such as the creation of pollution or unfair trading practices. It taxes businesses and buys and sells goods and services from and to businesses. The government also sets out the rules under which business activity can take place.

Encouragement of business activity

The government can and does encourage business in a wide number of ways. For example, during the 1980s the government produced a whole series of measures including subsidies and tax relief to encourage the growth of small businesses. The government has also encouraged the development of industry-related training schemes, and has tried to influence education in the direction of producing more job-orientated courses. An example of this has been the change in the way that Design and Technology are taught at school. There is now far more emphasis on industrial applications than on producing chairs and tables to take home.

Another example of the way that the government has tried to steer industry has been in the creation of regional locational incentives. Businesses can get government subsidies to set up in areas of high unemployment and industrial decline.

■ Case Study: The Highlands and Islands Development Board

The Highlands and Islands Development Board is a government agency set up to encourage development in the Highlands and Islands of Scotland. In recent years the Board has helped about 1,400 enterprises per year.

Half of the Board's annual budget of around £36 million is invested in private businesses in loans, grants, and shares, and much of the rest goes to providing factories, workshops, help with marketing, research and industrial promotion.

New businesses in the Highlands and Islands can benefit from an HIDB financial package amounting to up to 50% of development costs.

The incentives offered may include one or more of the following:

1. Low interest loans for the construction, change or improvement of buildings, purchase of machinery, or for working capital.
2. Special grants – unique to the area – going towards projects of particular economic importance.
3. Equity finance, where the Board buys up to one third of the shares in a company.
4. Businesses can rent out special factory units built by the HIDB to encourage business. The rents are lower than in the rest of the country, particularly in the early years of setting up.

The effect that assistance from the Highlands and Islands Development Board can have is illustrated by the following example of Norfrost Ltd, a company manufacturing freezers. Read through the story of Norfrost carefully, and then answer the questions below.

A million Norfrost freezers around the world

It has often been said if you want a sure-fire loser, invest in the manufacture of white goods: refrigerators, freezers and washing machines. A troubled industry in recent years, the field has been characterised by closures, bankruptcies and amalgamations, and the market is now dominated by a few big names.

To suggest, in such a scenario, that a small company in the North of Scotland – next door to John o'Groat's in fact – could find a profitable niche in that highly competitive international market would seem to be stretching the imagination. But it can be done, as Norfrost Ltd highlighted in the autumn of 1987 with the manufacture of a symbolic gold-plated freezer, the millionth to roll off the production line at its Castletown factory in Caithness.

Norfrost is now one of the world's major manufacturers of compact freezers. The company's success highlights what can be done in the Highlands and Islands. Following a recently completed two million pound expansion Norfrost now produces 4,200 cabinet freezers a week – soon to increase to 8,000. About 55% of output goes for export.

The company was formed in 1971 by Pat Grant and her husband Alex. They made their first freezers in the bedroom of the flat above their TV shop in Castletown. The combination of Mr Grant's talents as an electronics engineer in designing and making much of the production equipment and Mrs Grant's self-taught marketing skills created a dynamic business. The help of their bank, and almost half a million pounds worth of loans and grants from the HIDB over a nine year period, really set the company up.

Questions

1. Locate the Scottish Highlands and Islands on a map of the UK. Draw a map highlighting major communications links and centres of population.
2. List five problems that you would foresee in trying to encourage industry to this region.
3. Make a list of major incentives offered by the HIDB to Norfrost.
4. What sorts of business ar most likely to locate in the Highlands and Islands?
5. What do you consider to be the main advantages of locating in the Highlands and Islands?
6. What do you consider to be the main disadvantages of locating in the Highlands and Islands?
7. How has the HIDB helped Norfrost to establish itself?
8. Write out a business report for the management of either a processing company or an electronics company thinking of locating in the Highlands and Islands. Give a detailed explanation of why they should set up in this area.

Discouragement of business activity

There are also various ways in which the government can *discourage* certain business activities.

1. *Declaring certain activities illegal.* The Monopolies and Mergers Commission, for example, can prevent the joining together of large companies if this will lead to them controlling too large a section of the production or market of a commodity. Price fixing is illegal in most markets. The production of harmful substances is against the law. Certain items cannot be sold over the counter to children.
2. *Prosecution and fines.* Traders and companies that break the law will frequently be prosecuted. This would apply, for example, to industrialists who dump more than the allowed quantity of waste into rivers and streams. Traders who sell certain goods on Sundays are also frequently taken to court.
3. *Taking government contracts away from a company.* The government has been known to blacklist companies that carry out activities which the government disapproves of.

Business taxes

Industry pays a range of taxes. A business rate is paid to the local council and corporation tax is paid to the government on profits over a certain size. National insurance is collected and paid by firms to the government for all employees.

Businesses also collect value added tax and customs and excise duties for the government.

The provision of services

Central and local government provide a range of services that benefit businesses. The government plays a major role in creating the *infrastructure*, i.e. the backbone of services and facilities to help business run smoothly. This includes the building and maintenance of roads and other forms of communication, and the provision of various sources of energy and power. There are also a wide range of other services provided, including the collection of refuse, street cleaning, the gritting of roads, and the provision of training facilities and education.

Buying and selling goods and services

The government is the biggest single purchaser of goods and services in the United Kingdom. A wide range of businesses sell their goods and services to the government including advertising agencies, insurance companies, banks, laundries, munitions manufacturers – the list is endless.

The government also sells goods and services through nationalised industries and other enterprises.

Setting out the rules

The government, through Parliament and local councils, sets out the law of the land. Laws frequently change and when the rules change individuals and businesses will feel the effects of these changes in widely different ways.

■ Coursework suggestion

Rule changes are an excellent source of coursework activities. In a situation where the rules change a number of people will benefit and other will lose out. It is worth finding out the implications of rule changes on a local community.

A student set out to investigate the following question: Has the privatisation of cleaning services been a good thing for my town? The student set out a short introduction to the work showing a brief history of the privatisation, i.e. how the service was run before and after the council privatised the service. The student then collected data by interviewing various people – councillors, owners of and workers for the new company, businesses, citizens and other consumers of the service. In order to try and involve as many groups as possible the student also found out all the previous suppliers of the old municipal enterprise and the new privatised company, e.g., the garage that serviced the vehicles, the suppliers of spare parts, etc.

The student used this local data to examine the national issue of privatisation and showed that different groups have different views and that such data can be used to show different things in different ways. The student was able in this way to show the good and bad points of the policy, and went on to evaluate the policy given the information he had been able to collect.

Try to select a situation from your local paper where there has been a rule change and investigate the effects.

The effect of the European Community

In 1973 Britain joined the then European Economic Community. The European Community (EC) is now made up of 12 nations (see Figure 12.1) and a large proportion of Britain's trade is with these countries. From 1992 this trading area will constitute a single market of 320 million consumers. British businesses will face competition at home from other European businesses. In 1993 the Channel Tunnel will join us physically to the rest of Europe.

The effects of all these changes are discussed below.

European standards

Many goods which companies produce must meet national standards and rules. Today other countries often impose their own standards and rules on the goods they import. Indeed we often do the same. The barriers which national standards put in the way of trade will be removed by:

1. setting the level of quality and safety which products must meet within Europe

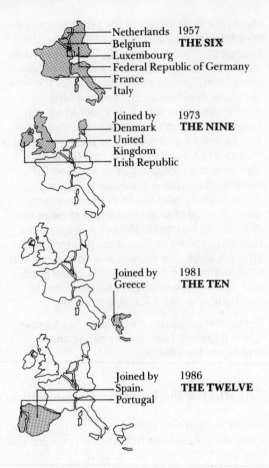

Netherlands 1957
Belgium **THE SIX**
Luxembourg
Federal Republic of Germany
France
Italy

Joined by 1973
Denmark **THE NINE**
United
Kingdom
Irish Republic

Joined by 1981
Greece **THE TEN**

Joined by 1986
Spain. **THE TWELVE**
Portugal

Figure 12.1 The growth of the European Community.

2. agreeing common standards
3. agreeing to accept other member states' tests and certificates.

Such changes will affect a wide range of products:

1. individual areas such as machines, personal protective equipment, toys
2. high technology products
3. medicines and drugs
4. food.

Many other products will also be affected.

British businesses must make sure that they meet European standards if they are going to sell in the European market.

Public purchasing

Selling to governments and public bodies accounts for about 15% of all the goods produced in the Community. The single market will mean that public bodies should buy on the basis of fair competition. In other words the British government, for example, should buy the goods and services which it thinks gives it best value for money rather than giving orders to British companies simply because they are British.

Open markets

In the past information technology systems and telecommunications equipment have been made to national standards. This has meant, for example, that it has not been possible to combine a British system with an Italian one. It must now be possible to combine systems through a Community Standard.

Financial services

By 1992 there will be freedom for the movement of funds throughout the Community. This will mean, for example, that there will be no restrictions on a business raising funds in another EC country. There will also be free competition between Community institutions such as banks and insurance companies.

Transport services

By 1992 transport companies will be able to provide transport facilities in other Community countries without having to have permits or other restrictions. There will be more competition in the provision of shipping, aviation and road haulage.

The professions

Many countries restrict the freedom to carry out a profession (e.g. doctor, lawyer, solicitor, etc.) to those with qualifications gained in their own country. A Community proposal, if accepted, would end such restrictions through a system whereby all Community countries recognise a common qualification of 'Higher Educational Diploma'. Everyone would then be able to practice his or her profession throughout the Community.

Competition

Restrictive agreements and practices and the abuse of monopoly powers are already forbidden when they may affect trade between member states. The European Commission has the power to investigate suspected breaches of the rules and unfair practices can be stopped and fines imposed of up to 10% of an undertaking's turnover.

Companies affected by such unfair competition will be able to take action through the UK courts or complain to the European Commission.

Trade marks

After 1992 protection of trade marks should be given by one application to a central Community Trade Marks Office.

Physical barriers to trade

Frontier safeguards like those restricting firearms, drugs and plant and animal diseases will continue for security, social and health reasons. But restrictions on the legitimate movement of goods and people should be abolished where possible, and where not possible reduced.

■ Coursework suggestion

Members of the class should each take one of the major changes being introduced in 1992 and find out:

1. How aware are local firms of this change?
2. How do firms expect to be affected by the change?

Who are the winners and losers? What opportunities and problems are presented?

Public sector expenditure

We live in a mixed economy. The goods and services which help to make up our standard of living come either from the private sector or are provided by the public authorities. These authorities are responsible for providing a wide range of goods and services. Nationalised industries – companies owned entirely or partly by the government – are also part of this public sector.

In 1988 government expenditure was as follows:

Social security	32%
Health	14%
Education and science	14%
Defence	12%
Law and order	5%
Transport	4%
Other	19%

Central government is responsible for making important *national* decisions. Its activities are largely financed by taxation. It is also responsible mainly for providing nationally administered services, such as:

1. Social security, e.g. pensions, other benefits.
2. Defence, e.g. army, navy, air force.
3. Industry, energy, trade and employment, e.g. training schemes.
4. Overseas aid, e.g. aid to developing countries.
5. Agriculture, fisheries, food and forestry, e.g. subsidies to farmers.
6. Health, e.g. National Health Service.
7. Government lending to nationalised industries.

Central government is also involved jointly in running a number of activities with local government such as some educational initiatives.

Local government is responsible for making important *local* decisions. It receives the bulk of its income from central government grants and from local taxes. It is mainly responsible fur running locally administered services, such as:

1. Transport, e.g. local roads.
2. Housing, e.g. council housing, repairs, etc.
3. Environmental services, e.g. refuse collection, parks.
4. Law, order and protective services, e.g. police, fire, prisons.
5. Education, e.g. schools, colleges.
6. Local social services, e.g. home care for the elderly.

■ Activity

For this activity you will represent county councillors for Midshire. The County Council had previously approved the following increases in expenditure for the coming year:

1. An extra 106 teachers in schools to reduce class sizes further. It has recently been noted that Midshire has a very poor pupil/teacher ratio when compared with the national average.
2. An extra £350,000 (15%) in home care for the elderly. Midshire has a rapidly ageing population. The home care service has not been improved for the last five years.
3. An extra 13 policemen in Middletown and more dog-handlers. The crime rate of Middletown has risen by 100% in the last year and the Chief Constable is 'seriously worried' by this development.
4. New grants available to starters in industry. This policy has been found to be very successful in reducing the unemployment figures.
5. More money for books in schools. A survey has recently shown that many of the books used in schools are out of date.
6. Better services for the under-fives. At present there are only two pre-school nurseries in the whole of Midshire.
7. An extra £100,000 into special education, e.g. to assist handicapped pupils who have special needs.
8. More money to combat child abuse.

The County Council has now discovered that it has seriously overspent on its previous year's budget. Unfortunately it must scrap one of the above projects as it needs at least £80,000 to balance its books. However, the project will be restored as a priority in the following year.

Two members of the class will be responsible for defending each of the above proposals from being cut. You have twenty minutes to prepare your defence. Each pair will then speak for five minutes. A chairperson will run the meeting. At the end of the session the chair will arrange a vote for which project to cut back on.

Decision-making

Decisions about public expenditure are made through the political system. These decisions are all about trading off one programme against another to make the most effective use of scarce resources.

Decisions made by government usually relate to the following areas:

1. *Provision of goods.* These will include many of the state-run nationalised industries such as coal, steel and railways.
2. *Provision of services.* A large proportion of government spending includes areas such as education, health, pensions, defence, etc. Governments aim to protect the population and prevent any of its members from suffering undue hardship.
3. *Influencing the private sector.* The state intervenes in the private sector to ensure that its activities are not harmful to the public, e.g. the Sale of Goods Act, Monopolies and Restrictive Practices Act. In order to influence the structure, performance and location of firms in the private sector tax reliefs, grants and subsidies can be used.
4. *Controlling the economy.* It is the role of government to undertake the responsibility of influencing economic activity. It has a variety of means at its disposal but influencing the economy through its own expenditure is an important aspect.

Public versus private sector

One of the major disagreements between individuals, groups and political parties in the United Kingdom is over who should be responsible for providing goods and services, how they should be produced and who should get them.

Up until 1979 the government took an increasing responsibility for providing a range of welfare and other industrial products. A wide range of key industries were nationalised and the government controlled and administered the bulk of educational, health and other social services.

Since 1979 a number of industries have been privatised and various activities have been returned to the private sector. For example, whereas until recently a hospital might have run its own laundry service, now this activity might be contracted out to a private firm. Whereas a council ran its own bus service, this is now likely to be in the hands of a private firm.

Table 12.1 sums up the arguments for and against both privatisation and nationalisation.

Table 12.1 Nationalisation v. privatisation.

Arguments in favour of nationalisation	Arguments in favour of privatisation
One large enterprise is able to benefit from economies of scale. The costs of a lot of small companies would be a lot higher. For example, having one large postal service will lead to greater output per worker and make possible the use of more specialist equipment.	Privatisation means that there will be a lot more competition. Firms will have an incentive to keep their costs down to a minimum. There will be less time wasting, waste of materials and badly used equipment.
The government will always look after the interests of consumers. If there was a large private firm it would be more likely to try and abuse its power to maximise profits.	Privatisation will lead to more choice. Different firms will produce a range of different goods and services. Although nationalised industries provide a range this will be fairly limited.
Nationalisation makes it possible to improve the running and operation of industries. The government is in a position to put a lot of investment funds into industries, taking a long-term view of profit.	Because of competition firms will produce better-quality products. If somebody else has a better-quality product yours will not sell. Therefore there is a spur to efficiency.
Nationalised industries are able to take a broad 'social view'. They are not just out to maximise financial profits. For example, they will provide post, electricity, gas, etc. to out-of-the-way places at a financial loss.	Private firms are much more sensitive to what consumers want. If they do not keep abreast of their market there will be no state subsidy to keep them afloat.
The 'commanding heights of the economy', i.e. the basic industries such as coal, steel and fuel, need to be in government hands because these products are so important to all other industries.	By privatising industries and giving citizens the chance to own shares you are giving people the opportunity to own a share in industry.

■ Case Study: The way forward for British Coal?

Read carefully through the article in Figure 12.2 and then answer the questions below.

Questions

1. What is going to happen to the coal industry according to this article?
2. Who is currently responsible for running the coal industry?
3. What changes have recently occurred in the coal industry?
4. How will the fact that British Coal is expected to break even in the near future make privatisation easier?

5. What other public corporations have recently been privatised?
6. What advantages can you see resulting from the privatisation of the coal industry?
7. What disadvantages can you see resulting from the privatisation of the coal industry?
8. Make a list of people you expect to (a) gain, (b) lose out from the privatisation of British Coal. Explain why.

■ Activity

Study the article in Figure 12.3 carefully and answer the following questions.

1. What is the main point that this article is trying to get across?

Government to end British Coal's mining monopoly

By Michael Harrison
Industrial Correspondent

THE PRIVATISATION of British Coal was yesterday put firmly on the agenda as the Government signalled its intention to strip the state-owned company of its monopoly over coal reserves and open up the country's pits to commercial operators.

In a forerunner to what will almost certainly be the eventual sell-off of British Coal, ministers are planning to take back its mining rights and award licences to private firms, in the way that the offshore oil industry is run.

Whitehall sources confirmed yesterday that ministers are "very seriously considering radical legislation" to bring about a fundamental change in the structure of the coal industry.

This followed a carefully-worded speech in London by the junior energy minister, Michael Spicer, in which he said: "We certainly ... have ambitions to privatise the coal industry. We have, however, no plans actually to sell off British Coal as such this side of the next General Election."

This is the first time a minister has publicly indicated the Government's intentions towards British Coal after repeated denials that there were any present plans for its privatisation.

With gas and telecommunications privatised, and both the water and electricity industries heading for the private sector, ministers have now clearly turned their sights on ending British Coal's monopoly.

Legislation is likely to be introduced in the Commons in 1989-90 to end British Coal's monopoly.

It has not yet been decided whether commercial operators will be able to bid to take on British Coal's existing collieries as well as future fields, but this is clearly an strong option.

The aim of ministers is to open up the coal industry within the next three years allowing private concerns to compete directly with British Coal, possibly selling their output direct to private power station operators. Should the Conservative Party win a fourth term of office this would allow it to begin selling off the coal industry.

British Coal's heavy closure programme has seen the industry axe nearly 80 collieries and more than 100,000 jobs since the national strike of 1984. Although British Coal is thought to have suffered a loss of £500m last year due to high redundancy and restructuring costs and the overtime ban, it has now lost the cushion of government deficit grants and is expected to break even. Its improving productivity and financial position will make it a more suitable candidate for sale.

As well as taking away British Coal's monopoly over reserves, vested in it at the time of nationalisation of the pits in 1946, the Government is considering scrapping or easing the tough limits imposed on private licensed deep and opencast mines.

This would encourage large private concerns such as RTZ and BP to enter the coal mining industry, particularly the highly lucrative opencast end of the market.

At present licensed deep mines are only allowed to employ a maximum of 30 men and licensed opencast is restricted to output of 25,000 tonnes a year. This effectively limits private mining to small-scale operators.

British Coal yesterday refused to comment on Mr Spicer's remarks although its senior executives have been aware of the proposals through informal contacts with the department.

Officials at the Department of Energy are now close to completing an internal review of British Coal. Because it will be a complex, technical and lengthy task to end British Coal's monopoly, the department will need at least 12 months to prepare legislation.

Figure 12.2 The future of British Coal.
Source: The Independent, *17 May 1988.*

MIRROR COMMENT

Unsafe in her hands

Mrs Thatcher said the National Health Service is safe in her hands. Baby Alexander Davies wasn't.

He died, aged two days, because the hospital which delivered him hadn't the equipment or the staff to save him.

Mrs Thatcher boasted in the House of Commons yesterday that the National Health Service is operating better and treating more patients.

Consultants at the hospital where Alexander lived so briefly say they can't fully guarantee the safety of any mother in labour or her baby because they haven't the money to do so.

Mrs Thatcher has said there is no crisis in the National Health Service.

Mockery

It's more than a crisis — it is utter and total chaos and a shambles that makes a mockery of the dedication of GPs and overworked hospital staffs. *There is a rebellion by nurses, a revolt by doctors, a declaration of civil war by consultants — and a spreading anarchy.*

Mrs Thatcher, with the National Health Service on the brink of collapse, has reluctantly found an extra £100 million, of which £65 million is for English hospitals.

The taxpayers' purse isn't bottomless and managements will have to be more efficient — but Mrs Thatcher's money is too little, too late.

If he could, baby Alexander would have told her that.

Figure 12.3 The National Health Service.
Source: The Daily Mirror, 18 December 1987.

2. Do you think that the newspaper is justified in presenting its case in this way? Explain your reasoning.
3. Find a recent example from a national newspaper of an issue involving government expenditure or lack of expenditure. What sorts of evidence are used? Is there enough evidence for the paper to make a statement of 'right' and 'wrong'? How much evidence is necessary to make such a statement?

Management of the economy

In the nineteenth century the government played only a small part in the control of the economy. Today, the role of government is open to debate but most people accept that the government should at least try to influence economic activity. Why has this change in attitude taken place?

There are a great number of reasons but some of the more important ones could include:

Widespread unemployment in the 1920s and 1930s

In some towns in the 1920s over half of the potential labour force were unemployed. Many people felt in the light of the terrible suffering during this period that the government should play a central role in creating and sustaining employment.

Rapid inflation in the 1970s

The 1970s was a period of rapid increases in prices. People felt the effects of inflation in different ways depending, amongst other things, on how much power they had to raise their own incomes to cope with price rises.

The general effect of price rises is to distort the workings of the price system. Trading needs to take place in settled price conditions. If you expect to be paid £100 in three months' time you will be very disappointed to find that when you receive payment you can only purchase half of the goods that you would have been able to buy today.

If people become reluctant to trade, then fewer goods will be produced to sell. If fewer goods are made, fewer people are employed in production.

Price disturbances can therefore cause the whole economy to stagnate.

The growth of the Welfare State

The twentieth century saw a rapid expansion in the public provision of goods and services. Examples of this were the development of state education, the National Health Service and the social security system. The Welfare State was designed to produce a safety net for all citizens that gave them some form of protection (social security) from the 'womb to the tomb'. Citizens would pay money into a National Insurance Fund and in return receive support at special times or at times of hardship. These benefits would particularly help the old, young, sick and unemployed.

The destabilising effect of trade

The United Kingdom is and always has been a major trading nation. This has particularly been a problem in the late twentieth century. When prices of a typical basket of imported raw materials and manufactures rise then prices rise in this country – we import inflation. There is strong agreement that rising world prices were a major cause of price rises in the 1970s and price falls in the 1980s.

The decline of direct control

Direct control of the economy by the government increased throughout the twentieth century up until 1979. The government had increasingly controlled sectors of the economy and directly provided more goods and services.

Since 1979 the emphasis of 'Thatcherite' policies has been on reducing direct government controls. However, the government is still very much involved in a wide field of economic policy-making.

The main objectives of government economic policy

In an ideal situation there would be no price increases, no unemployment, a steady growth of national output, a healthy balance of payments, and a steady and predictable exchange rate. In the real world prices increase, there are

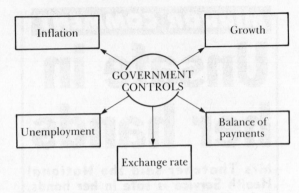

Figure 12.4 The five economic variables.

'unacceptable' levels of unemployment, national output increases in stops and starts, there are frequent balance of payments problems, and the exchange rate goes through highs and lows.

These five variables, illustrated in Figure 12.4, are the central focus for government economic controls and are considered in detail below.

Inflation

To the government, inflation means a general increase in the level of prices. Statisticians use the *Retail Price Index* (RPI) as a measure of inflation. It is an *average* of price changes and shows the general change over a period of time. Some items in the index will rise, some will remain the same, and others will fall.

The RPI is calculated in the following way. About 7,000 households throughout the UK keep a record of all their spending over a two-week period. This gives a picture of the 'typical items' bought by an 'average household'. The items will be recorded in the index. Each month, government officers make a record of about 150,000 prices of some 350 different items up and down the country. The average price of each of these items is calculated.

Using this data the average inflation rate can be calculated. Each individual price change is given a 'weight' which depends on how important it is in the 'typical household's' spending pattern. For example, food makes up about one-fifth of a typical household's spending. A 10% rise in the price of food would raise average prices by 10% × one fifth = 2%.

Price changes are measured over a period of

time. This is so that it is possible to compare changes in inflation from one period with another. This is done by setting a base date. The matter of choosing a starting date for an index is important. The aim is to choose as a starting point a time which is 'normal', i.e. when nothing abnormal or unusual was happening.

The base date is given an index of 100. We can then say, for example, that if in 1974 the RPI stood at 100 and today it is 350, prices on average have risen three and a half times over the period.

■ Case Study: Calculating a simple price index

Citizen Average spends half his or her income on food, one quarter on clothing and the remaining quarter on entertainment. (We can thus give these items weightings out of 10: food = 5, clothing = 2½, entertainment = 2½.) In 1974 (the base year), food cost on average £1 per unit, clothing £5 per unit, and entertainment £2 per unit.

In 1990 food cost on average £2 per unit, clothing £7.50 per unit, and entertainment £3.00 per unit. We can calculate the changes in prices as follows:

Item	Original index	New index	Expenditure weighting	Weighting × New index
Food	100	200	5	1,000
Clothing	100	150	2½	375
Entertainment	100	150	2½	375
			Total	1,750

The total of the new indexes for each item × their weights is 1,750. In order to find out the new RPI we must divide this total by the total number of weights (10), so:

$$\text{New index} = \frac{1,750}{10} = 175$$

This shows that on average prices rose by 75%. (Food doubled in price, whereas the other two items only increased by one and a half times. However, food was the most significant item in the index because Citizen Average spends as much on food as on clothing and entertainment combined.)

Questions

1. In Redland the average consumer spends seven-tenths of his or her income on wine, two-tenths on bread and one-tenth on cheese. In 1954 (the base year) the price of all these items was £1 per unit. In 1989 wine had fallen to 50p per unit, bread had gone up to £2 per unit and cheese had risen to £4 per unit.
   (a) What is the new index for 1989?
   (b) Has it risen, fallen or remained the same? Explain why.
   (c) Give at least three reasons why the weighting might need to be altered in 1989.
2. Is there such a thing as the Average Citizen? Does this matter: (a) to an individual family, (b) to the government?
3. In Blueland the public buy four items – eggs, cheese, bread and salt. Four-tenths of their income is spent on cheese, and two-tenths on each of the other three items.
   Between 1960 (base year) and 1990 eggs double in price, cheese goes up 50%, bread remains the same and salt goes down by 10%. Calculate the new index relative to the base year.

Growth

Growth statistics measure changes in national income which in turn measures the total value of the output of a country in a given period of time. One way of measuring national output is to add together the values added by all the individual industries, for example:

	Value added by coal industry	£100m
+	Value added by fishing industry	£100m
+	Value added by agriculture	£300m
+	Values added by manufacturing industries	£1,500m
+	Values added by service industries	£3,000m

Total value added £5,000m

Growth of national output is then used to make comparisons. Figure 12.5 is typical of the sorts of charts which are used to look at the performance of a country's economy.

1. Comparisons can be made over a period of time – 1982, 1983, . . ., 1987, etc.

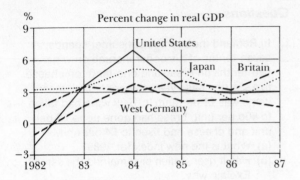

Figure 12.5 Comparison of economic growth rates.

2. Comparisons can be made with other countries – Germany, Japan, etc.
3. Growth is measured in terms of output. GDP means *gross domestic product*, i.e. the value of the output (product) of a country in a given time period. (You will notice that the term *real* GDP is used in the figure.)

If we measure output simply in money terms this does not give us a clear picture of changes in output. If Algeria produces £100 million worth of food in 1988 and £200 million worth in 1989 this does not necessarily mean that it is producing twice as much food. If the price of food has doubled then it will be producing the same quantity in 1989 as in 1988. To measure growth rates in real terms you need to account for inflation.

Other important considerations need to be considered when comparing growth rates between countries and over periods of time.

1. To calculate output per head of population you need to divide the GDP by the population. This is necessary because nations with similar national incomes might have vastly different populations.
2. You need to bear in mind that in some countries there is a lot more inequality than in others. Therefore a high national output is not shared by everybody.
3. Another important consideration is that it is very difficult to calculate the GDP. Because of tax evasion some people do not admit to their real production levels. Also, in some countries a large amount of output is not sold.

The balance of payments

The balance of payments is an account showing a country's trading with the rest of the world in a given time period. It is made up of three sections:

1. *Section 1* shows the value of all goods and services traded in a given time period.
2. *Section 2* shows the flow of money into and out of a country in a given time period. (Money flows for trading activities, and in addition it flows for investment and speculative purposes. For example, money may flow out of Britain when a Toyota car is bought; it also flows out of Britain when it is invested in an American company.)
3. *Section 3* shows how the account is balanced. Once all the inflows and outflows of money have been recorded it will show the sources of funds that have been used to make up an outflow of cash, or what has been done with excess funds if there has been an inflow of cash.

In this book we are only concerned with Section 1 of the balance of payments. This section is called the *Current Account*.

The Current Account

The Current Account is the most important part of the balance of payments and the one to which attention is mainly focused in the media and in parliamentary debate. The Current Account will be in surplus if a country's exports are worth more than its imports, and in deficit if its exports are worth less than imports. These situations are illustrated in Figure 12.6.

In the short term it is not a problem to have a surplus or deficit. Problems arise in the long term if a country runs a surplus or deficit year after year. Remember, exports earn money for the *sale* of goods or services, whereas imports lead to an outflow of money to *buy* goods or services.

The Current Account itself is made up of two main parts:

1. The visible trade balance – showing trading in goods.
2. The invisible trade balance – showing trading in services.

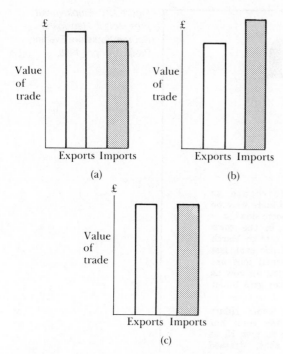

Figure 12.6 Current account situations: (a) balance of payments surplus; (b) balance of payments deficit; (c) balance.

Visible items include a wide range of goods including motor vehicles, machinery, paper, drinks, clothes, food, etc. *Invisible* items include a wide range of services including insurance, finance, transport, etc.

The Current Account is set out in the manner shown below (+ indicates money flowing into the country, – indicates money flowing out):

The Current Account

1. Visible exports +
2. Visible imports –
3. Visible balance + or –   (+1 – 2 = 3)
4. Invisible exports +
5. Invisible imports –
6. Invisible balance + or –   (+4 – 5 = 6)
7. Current balance + or –   (+ or – 3 + or – 6 = 7)

The account is simply calculated by adding the value of exports and subtracting the value of imports.

The exchange rate

The exchange rate is the rate at which a currency will be exchanged for other currencies. In 1988, for example, one pound could be traded for roughly two US dollars.

Exchange rates in recent years have been changing frequently and by quite large amounts. As a trading nation Britain is particularly interested in changes in the exchange rate against other currencies.

Unemployment

There is considerable disagreement over the exact figures for the number of unemployed people in the UK at any time. Only those receiving state benefits and registered for work are counted in the official statistics. This misses out most married women who, if their husbands are working, cannot receive benefit. People on the various training schemes are not included. Men over 60 who are long-term unemployed are also not included. The unemployment figures therefore depend very much on the way they are collected.

Which groups are most likely to be unemployed?

Unemployment is felt most by the young and the old. In the mid 1980s, for example, the unemployment rate for the under 25s and the over 55s was twice the national average. The ethnic minorities also have higher than average unemployment rates.

There is disagreement about the unemployment figure for women. Because so many women are employed in part-time work, underemployment may be as big a problem as unemployment. (Of course some people would argue that part-time work is not a problem because it enables women to combine work with home commitments.)

Unemployment can also be seen as a regional problem in that some areas, e.g., Northern Ireland, Wales and the North, have much higher than average unemployment figures.

However, as with any average figures we must be careful not to generalise. For example, there are a number of examples of boom towns in

*Figure 12.7 Employment
prospects in Harrogate.
Source:* Yorkshire Evening
Press, *14 April 1988.*

jobs in boom

by Simon Parry

JOB prospects in booming Harrogate are so bright employers are struggling to fill the vacancies.

The town's JobCentre has 1,000 full-time and part-time posts going begging after a three per cent drop in unemployment over the past year.

And a Job Club set up to help the long-term unemployed back into work is crying out for new members after seeing numbers tumble to just half of capacity.

Harrogate MP Robert Banks said after a visit to the Beulah Street JobCentre: "It is getting to the stage where some employers are having problems filling posts in Harrogate."

Shortage

JobCentre deputy manager Sue Jozefowicz confirmed employers were having to wait longer to fill vacancies, especially for part-time jobs and skilled labour.

"There is a shortage of skilled labour for construction works," she said, "and part-time vacancies are becoming difficult to fill because when unemployment is low people move from job to job more often.

"We have to explain the position to employers but they do realise what the problem is."

Mrs Jozefowicz described the economy in Harrogate as bouyant, and said there were no signs of the jobs boom slowing.

Unemployment in the town fell from 8.5 per cent in March last year to 5.4 per cent last month, and seasonal jobs are beginning to spring up now as the holiday season gets under way.

But Job Club leader Hilary Rucroft, who has seen her membership fall to just 12 as unemployment ebbs, stressed there were still people in need of help who were not using the club.

The fall in numbers corresponded with the booming economy, she said. More than 20 members were using the club's facilities a year ago.

But many people looking for work were not joining the club, often because they believed they were not eligible.

Housewives and anyone out of work for more than six months were welcome. "The club is here for anyone who wants to return to a job," she said.

The club, open four days a week at the JobCentre, provides free advice, stationery and facilities.

"We think there is a market of people who are not in receipt of benefits but still technically unemployed and looking for work in Harrogate," said Mrs Rucroft. "They are the ones we are having problems reaching."

zones of higher than average unemployment. However, within these towns there will be streets – and households – where unemployment is a serious problem.

■ Case Study: Unemployment in Harrogate

Find Harrogate on a map of the UK. Find out which region of the UK Harrogate is in and what the current unemployment figure is in that region. Then read the article in Figure 12.7 carefully and answer the following questions.

1. Is unemployment a problem in Harrogate? Explain your answer.
2. What services are available in Harrogate to help the unemployed find work?
3. What problems were employers having in Harrogate in recruiting labour?
4. What were some of the causes of these problems?

Does unemployment hit everyone equally badly?

Different people will feel differently about unemployment. The experience of unemployment for a man of 55, for example, who has worked all his life may be devastating. Somebody else who thinks that he or she can quickly get another job may not see unemployment as being a problem.

Young people without a lifetime of work behind them may well find the result of unemployment very different from older people. It could be argued that living on social security, freed from the boredom of a routine job, could at least for a short time be a pleasant life. However, there are a number of hidden problems. The first problem is that they may need to stay at home, continuing to receive financial support from their parents. It becomes more difficult to move out, buy a flat and get married. A study of youth unemployment in the Midlands found that some girls deliberately get pregnant in order to escape from their family, whilst getting benefits from the state.

■ Coursework suggestion

Different people feel the effects of unemployment in different ways. Do a group survey of family and friends to find out how they view unemployment. You need to take a cross section of ages, occupations, etc. The aim of the assignment is to find out if 'unemployment' is more of a problem to some groups and individuals than to others.

■ Activity

As a follow-up suggestion to the above piece of coursework, cut out some pictures of different individuals from a magazine. Use these photographs as a basis to construct an 'unemployment special' feature for a magazine. The magazine feature will focus on different reasons why people might be unemployed. For example, 'Geoff Davis was a computer operator for a firm working in Birmingham. When his firm moved to the South of Scotland, Geoff was not prepared to move with them since he had family and other ties in Birmingham. He has now been looking for a similar job in the area for the last six months'.

Set out the photographs and the stories that go with them on a piece of A1 card. You can make up your own name for the magazine. Write in bold letters 'Unemployment Special'. You should leave space on the card for an editorial comment which should mention the main causes of unemployment. Try to match these causes up with policy solutions to the problem. You will find that the section in Chapter 5 on finding employment helps you with this task.

Objectives of government policy

This is a very difficult topic because government economic policy is based on its understanding of how the economy works. Nobody has a clear understanding of how the economy works because there are so many factors involved and they are always changing. What might be an appropriate economic measure in 1989 will not necessarily be so in 1999 because people might behave in a completely different way by this date. Government policy therefore depends on their *view* of how things work and what is fair.

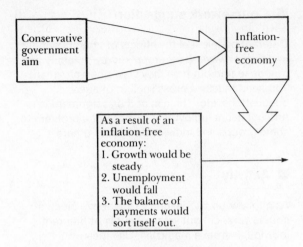

Figure 12.8 Deciding priorities.

Government policy deals with setting targets. For example, the Conservative government of the 1980s had as its major priority to get inflation down to zero. In order to meet this target it set out a number of policies.

Policy-making is all about deciding priorities. The government believed that by getting inflation down and enabling the price system to work smoothly then other objectives would sort themselves out (see Figure 12.8). A wide range of measures were employed to achieve this end. When some of them did not work they needed to be modified. (No government will ever have enough information about how its policies will work out.)

Another government, however, may have a different aim. For example, a Labour government might concentrate on reducing unemployment. Because the targets would then be an unemployment-free economy a wide range of measures to achieve this end would be employed.

To achieve its aims a government can use fiscal policy, monetary policy or direct controls over the economy. In the real world these three options are very closely connected and it is difficult to separate them.

Fiscal policy

Fiscal policy is the government's policy with regard to public spending, taxes and borrowing. The government can try to influence the level of demand in the economy through directly altering the amount of its own spending in relation to its total tax revenues.

A *deficit* budget arises when a government spends more than it takes in taxes (see Figure 12.9(a). The government can then borrow money on the Stock Exchange or from banks and other sources in order to carry out its expenditure policies. The difference between government spending and tax revenue is known as the Public Sector Borrowing Requirement. The logic of the deficit budget is simple. If there is not enough spending in the economy to create enough demand for goods to give everyone that wanted to work a job, then the government can boost spending itself. This is not seen necessarily as a problem – households in Britain frequently spend more than they earn in a given time period and pay back the money from future earnings.

Such a policy seemed to work very well from 1945 to the early 1970s. However, at this time world prices started to rise steeply and the world output of goods began to stagnate. Government deficit budgets were seen to be adding to these price increases.

A *balanced* budget is a situation when the government matches its spending with taxes (see Figure 12.9(b)). The balanced budget was practised by government up to 1945 and has been seen as a desirable policy objective of the current Conservative government. The idea behind the balanced budget is that the government should not encourage price increases. There is also a

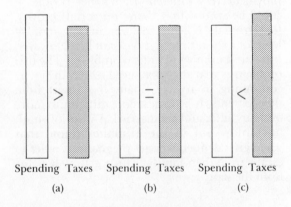

Figure 12.9 Budget strategies: (a) deficit budget; (b) balanced budget; (c) surplus budget.

belief that the government should spend as little as possible because private individuals and groups are in a better position to make their own spending decisions than if a third party does it on their behalf.

A *surplus* budget is a situation where the government takes in more revenue than it spends (see Figure 12.9(c)). This is generally regarded as being an unsound policy because it would take demand out of the economy – a situation referred to as *deflation*. However, in 1988 and 1989 the government actually achieved surplus budgets.

Multiplier effects

Changes in demand in the economy are likely to have what are known as *multiplier effects*. This means, for example, that if the government changes its expenditure a little the total effect will be much larger.

As a simple example, let us assume that the government spends £100 million in investment in a new colliery. This expenditure will be received by construction workers, firms carrying out the construction work, suppliers of these firms, etc. The recipients of this income are likely to re-spend some of that income on buying other goods and services. This expenditure will then be someone elses income, and the process goes on.

However, the multiplier process is not actually quite so direct. In fact income recipients will save some of their income, lose some of it in the form of taxes, and spend money abroad by buying imports. It has been estimated that in the UK a lot of income earned does not generate fresh demand in the UK. If the government, as suggested, spent £100 million on a new colliery, this is likely to lead only to an extra £50 million of expenditure according to current statistics. We can see therefore that the initial new £100 million of government expenditure effectively increases UK expenditure by £150 million, i.e. the multiplier is 1½:

$$\text{Multiplier} = \frac{\text{Total increase in spending}}{\text{Original increase in spending}}$$

$$= \frac{150}{100} = 1\frac{1}{2}$$

If unemployment is a major problem then a deficit budget can be used as a tool to stimulate demand. The effect of the deficit budget will also be boosted by the multiplier effect. This is known as *tackling the economy from the demand side*.

Major problems, however, are attached to how the government spends and borrows money in a deficit situation. If it spends money, it needs to do so in a way that creates real jobs and boosts future outputs. If it borrows money, it needs to do so in a way which is least likely to cause price rises.

Alterations in tax rates

Changes can be made in the structure of the tax system and in the way that particular taxes work. For example, there are differences in opinion as to whether the government should emphasise direct or indirect taxes.

Some economists argue that if *direct* taxes (i.e. taxes paid directly to the government such as income tax corporation tax, etc.) are too high this will discourage work and effort. Such economists argue that the total supply of goods and services in the economy will be increased if people have the incentive to work harder and if individuals and businesses invest more. This is called *supply-side* economics as opposed to boosting output from the *demand side* by means of deficit budgets. Supply-side economists argue that taxes on income and profits have been too high for much of the period since the Second World War.

The curve in Figure 12.10, developed in the 1960s by Art Laffer, an American supply-side economist, shows the problem of high tax rates. Tax rates are measured on the vertical axis and revenues from taxes on the horizontal. As rates

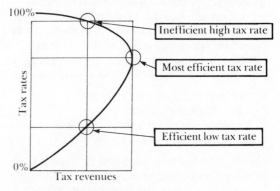

Figure 12.10 The Laffer curve.

rise, at first revenues will increase. However, when taxes rise too high people will:

1. start dodging payment;
2. work fewer hours, and work less hard;
3. invest less.

As a result the government will get less tax revenue, and the growth of national output will slump.

Supply-side economists generally argue that high income and profits taxes are undesirable because of their disincentive effects. They also say that such direct taxes interfere with freedom of choice. People who earn more than a certain income or make more than a certain level of profit *have* to pay these taxes. With indirect taxes (VAT, customs and excise duties, for example) people have greater freedom of choice. If they choose to smoke cigars and cigarettes and drink whisky and Pimms then they also choose to be taxed. If they prefer to spend their money on bread, children's clothes and books they do not pay tax.

However, other economists take a different view. They argue that most of the items available in shops today have some form of indirect tax on them. For example, you pay VAT on fish and chips, sandwiches and soft drinks. You even pay VAT on toilet paper. As a result, indirect taxes tend to hit the poor harder than the rich as poor households pay a higher percentage of their income in VAT than do richer households. Such taxes are said to be *regressive*.

■ Activity

People have different views about what makes a 'good' tax. One person's view might be that a good tax is one that does not take much money out of your pocket. Another person might say that a good tax is one that raises a lot of revenue.

Make a list of what you think the following individuals might consider to be a good tax:

1. The Chancellor of the Exchequer.
2. A hospital administrator.
3. Someone setting up a small business.
4. Someone who is unemployed.

Why might different groups and individuals have different views about what is a 'fair' tax system?

Look up the latest income tax rates. What percentage of income would be paid by a single person with no extra allowances earning the following incomes:

1. £5,000?
2. £10,000?
3. £20,000?
4. £50,000?
5. £100,000?
6. £250,000?

Illustrate the percentage rate of income taken in tax from people on these different incomes. How progressive is the tax?

Monetary policy

Monetary policy is concerned with controlling:

1. the *quantity* of money in the economy;
2. the *price* of money in the economy.

Monetary policy has been regarded of particular importance in the 1980s because the government believes that there is a strong link between money and inflation. The view is that if people start spending money at a faster rate than new goods come onto the market then prices will rise. Monetarists believe that it is essential to eliminate general price rises because of the way they destabilise industry and the economy. Uncertainty about prices means that industry cannot concentrate on its main task – producing goods. People become dissatisfied and the whole economic order starts to crumble – people fail to pay up on time, businesses are reluctant to invest, there is more industrial unrest, etc.

Quantity of money

It is very difficult to define *money*. People use different things to make purchases at different times. If citizens simply used notes and coins to make purchases calculating the *quantity* of money would be easy. Instead people use a variety of forms of money which are acceptable as ways of making a purchase. These include notes and coins, cheque payments, credit cards, and other forms of credit payments. Today it is also common practice for people to draw money out of building society and other accounts to make purchases. A wide range of new facilities for making payment are also developing. So if the government wants to know how much money is available to citizens to spend on goods at a particular moment in time it is an almost impossible task.

The government currently uses at least five definitions of money:

1. M0 – mainly notes and coins
2. M1 – M0 plus current accounts at banks
3. M2 – M1 plus any deposits (e.g. in building societies) which can be quickly withdrawn
4. M3 – M1 plus money in bank deposit accounts
5. PSL2 – M3 money in building society, and other similar accounts.

In order to control the quantity of money the government must decide on the definition of money which it thinks most accurately determines people's likely expenditure. It will then seek to control changes in the supply of money according to this definition. It might, for example, seek to prevent the quantity of money from rising at a faster rate than that of increases in the production of new goods in the economy. (The reason for doing this might be a belief that if the quantity of money increases faster than the quantity of goods then prices will be pushed up.)

The Bank of England has an important part to play in controlling the lending of high street banks and other financial institutions. The range of measures available to the Bank for limiting increases in cash and lending include giving advice and instruction to other banks on how much to lend and whom to lend to and raising interest rates to discourage borrowing (by making it more expensive).

The lending institutions, such as the high street banks, need to be carefully supervised by the government because of their tremendous powers of lending. They can grant overdrafts and loans and a wide range of other lending arrangements to customers. Only later do customers have to pay the money back.

A bank's customers will carry out a relatively small part of their transactions using cash. For example, a large oil company will use a cheque rather than cash if it is involved in a million-pound deal. Financial institutions, by creating credit instruments such as cheques and credit cards, make it possible for individuals and organisations to borrow money and make payments by means other than cash. The more these credit instruments are expanded, the more purchasing power there will be in the economy. It is essential that the government does not let this spending get out of hand. It therefore sets targets and builds up a framework for controlling the financial system. The Bank of England plays an important part in policing this system; it licenses financial institutions and keeps a watchful eye on their lending practices.

Price of money

As well as controlling the quantity of money in the economy the government will also control the *price* of money. The interest rates can be quickly altered by the Bank of England and the change will rapidly spread to all financial institutions such as banks and building societies. This is a way of controlling the amount of money borrowed. If interest rates rise people will be more reluctant to borrow.

In recent years the interest rate has become an important means of controlling inflation. If interest rates rise, borrowing and spending will fall, and vice versa.

■ Case Study: Interest rate as a weapon of monetary policy

Read the article given in Figure 12.11 carefully and then answer the questions below.

Questions

1. Who is responsible for raising interest rates?
2. Why was it thought necessary to raise interest rates?
3. What are the likely effects of an increase in interest rates?
4. What is meant by 'tightness of monetary conditions'?
5. Why is the interest rate regarded to be a good weapon in controlling price rises?
6. What is likely to happen to the balance of payments in a period of increased spending? Explain your answer.
7. Which groups and individuals are most likely to gain/lose out when interest rates are raised?

Interest rates up amid inflation fears

Interest rates were increased for the second time in less than a week yesterday in response to mounting evidence of growing inflationary pressures. In the City, there are expectations that another rise may soon follow, and leading building societies warned that this would probably mean higher mortgage rates.

Both the Treasury and the Bank of England made it clear that keeping inflation under control was the main aim.

The signal for higher interest rates was given by the Bank of England. The clearing banks quickly raised base rates from 8 to 8.5 per cent.

Government figures published yesterday underlined concern that demand in the economy is growing at a rate which may be stoking inflation. Consumer spending in April was at a peak for the fourth consecutive month, while consumer credit grew by 9 per cent in the latest three months. Car sales rose a record 10 per cent, with imported models rising from 50 to 55 per cent of the market.

The Confederation of British Industry also reported yesterday that pay settlements were accelerating, while other recent warning signs have come from rapidly rising house prices and rising imports.

The Bank of England said yesterday's interest rate rise demonstrated that 'It is important to maintain the tightness of monetary conditions and to ensure there is no resurgence in inflation in the economy.'

Figure 12.11 Rise in interest rates. Adapted from The Independent, *Tuesday 7 June 1988.*

Exchange rate policy

In recent years the international picture has had a tremendous impact on national economies. When world prices rise the global economy rapidly feels the impact.

Because Britain is an important trading nation it must pay close attention to the world market. The exchange rate has become particularly important because of its impact on inflation. If the price of the pound increases then imports become cheaper. If the price of the pound falls imports become more expensive. A falling pound can be inflationary because import prices are an important cost. The Bank of England must be careful therefore to make sure that the exchange rate does not trigger off inflation.

Direct intervention

The government can also influence the economy more directly, for example by limiting wage and price increases. It can either ask businesses and trade unions to hold back increases to a certain figure in a certain period of time, or alternatively, it can pass a law insisting on these limitations. Such measures were in fact used in the late 1960s and early 1970s when price rises were getting out of control as a result of rapid increases in the price of oil and wage and price increases across the board.

The government can also directly intervene in the economy by setting up bodies to deal with and passing laws against monopolies and restrictive practices.

The effects of government policy

Government economic policy has wide implications for industry and business:

1. Taxes are an important business cost. They also affect consumer spending. Industry is therefore very interested in budgetary changes.
2. Government expenditure helps to provide the infrastructure and community services in the economy. Industry is therefore very interested in changes in expenditure policy.
3. The quantity of money in the economy is an important determinant of how much people spend.
4. The interest rate is an important determinant of how much people borrow and spend. Interest repayments are also an important cost for households and businesses.
5. The exchange rate is an important determinant of import and export costs.
6. Direct controls limit the way firms, groups and individuals interact with each other.

■ Activity

Find out how the following are affected by

changes in government taxes, expenditures, and interest rate changes. Interview friends and family.

1. A pensioner
2. A local business person
3. A skilled worker

Trading off government policies

At the beginning of this chapter we saw that an ideal situation would involve no unemployment or inflation, a steady rate of growth and a healthy balance of payments. However, this sort of ideal has rarely been achieved in modern economies. Normally a government is faced by pressing problems such as high unemployment, a high rate of inflation, stagnant growth or a balance of payments crisis. Often there is a combination of problems.

At such times the government has to establish a set of priorities, i.e. which problem demands most urgent attention. The difficulty is then that a measure aimed at clearing up one problem might make one of the other factors worse:

1. An increase in expenditure to reduce unemployment may create rising inflation.
2. A reduction in expenditure to reduce inflation may create rising unemployment.
3. Trying to raise growth by increasing demand in the economy might suck in imports and cause a balance of payments problem.
4. Raising taxes to cut down on imports may reduce growth.

At any one time there will be a range of trade-offs, the nature of which will vary from period to period. For example, the way in which the economy works in the 1980s and 1990s is radically different from the way it worked in the 1950s. To help them, economists need to gather as much data as possible, though they will never have enough. There is no way that we can accurately predict how people – and therefore the economy – will behave.

It is politicians who make decisions about priorities and policies. The way that policies are shaped depends on people's values and their opinions about what is 'fair', 'unfair', 'good', 'bad', 'efficient', 'inefficient', etc.

■ Revision

Complete the following sentences using the words below:

profits
government
goods
services
expensive
privatisation
Bank of England
surplus budget
supply side
demand side

Monopolies and Mergers
  Commission
United Kingdom
Spain and Portugal
social security
direct government controls
retail price index
fiscal policy
deficit budget
multiplier effect
monetary policy

1. _____ involves the transfer of state-owned enterprise to the private sector.
2. _____ is primarily concerned with government expenditure and revenue.
3. The _____ can prevent the joining together of large firms if this will give them an unfair advantage.
4. The visible trade balance shows trade in _____ .
5. The invisible trade balance shows trade in _____ .
6. A _____ involves the government spending more than it takes from taxes.
7. If the price of the pound falls imports become more _____ .
8. _____ economics concentrates on measures to incease output.
9. The _____ joined the European Economic Community in 1973.
10. _____ joined the European Community in 1986.
11. The _____ supervises government monetary policy.
12. A _____ involves the government spending less than it takes in from taxes.
13. The largest government expenditure goes on _____ .
14. The _____ is an average of price changes.
15. _____ is concerned with the price and quantity of money.
16. _____ economics concentrates on measures to alter total spending in the economy.
17. The size of the _____ depends on how much is re-spent by recipients of income.
18. Corporation tax is a tax on _____ .
19. The _____ is the biggest single purchaser of goods and services in the UK.
20. Since 1979 the emphasis of 'Thatcherite' policies has been on reducing _____ .

CHAPTER 13
The impact of change

If you look around your local town or city you will soon notice the changes that have taken place in the last ten years. New shops have opened up, others have disappeared; new types of industry have started up, others have declined.

Industry needs to be constantly aware of changes around it. Major changes that particularly affect industry are:

1. Changes in demand for products
2. Changes in population
3. Changes in technology (the methods used to make products)
4. Changes taking place in other countries.

Impact of changes in demand

A business that is not aware of the state of demand for its product will be very lucky to survive. Pedigree Petfoods, the leading producers of petfood in this country, state that:

'We work constantly towards identifying and satisfying consumer needs. It is the activity from which all else springs. We never forget that we cannot influence millions of consumer choices until we have convinced first one, then a second and a third consumer that our product is worthy of purchase. Our success is based on thorough research of the wide range of needs for pet animals and their owners. The knowledge which we gain is translated into a range of quality products which satisfy these needs better than any of our competitors.'

Firms are constantly looking for a product that will be the 'next best thing' (NBT). Shell's NBT, for example, is a service station with easier to work pumps which allow you to fill up from both sides, computerised information about routes, a shop that will even take in your dry cleaning, and a machine that allows you to pay by credit card. (By the time this book comes to print Shell will be looking for their new NBT.)

■ Case Study: Consumer spending

Look carefully at the figures given in Table 13.1 and then answer the questions below.

Table 13.1 Consumer spending per head of population*

	1976	1981	1986
Food	528	540	564
Alcoholic drink	278	275	290
Durable goods	252	291	410
Rent and rates	448	485	513
Energy	276	294	325
Total spending	3,244	3,535	4,087

Source: *British economy in figures* (Lloyds Bank).

*At 1986 prices: this means that spending is calculated at the prices that the goods would have cost in 1986. (It is necessary to make this adjustment because prices go up from year to year.)

Questions

1. Try to present the information above by some other means than a table.
2. Which item has shown the greatest percentage increase in expenditure since 1976?

3. How has the percentage of total expenditure on food changed over this period?
4. (a) What has happened to the percentage of total expenditure spent on durable goods.
   (b) Give four examples of popular consumer durables.
   (c) Why has there been this change in total expenditure spent on consumer durables?
5. Why might a table like the one shown above be of use to producers?
6. What further information might be of use to producers?

Impact of changes in population

Some people regard changes in the population as having been the single most important factor in causing changes in society over the ages. It is important to distinguish between changes in the size of the population (i.e. the total number of people), and changes in the structure of the population (e.g. ratio of men/women, ratio of old/young, etc.).

The total population of the UK in 1987 was 56.6 million. It is projected to rise to 59 million by the year 2001.

The most dramatic changes in population structure which have already begun to affect us are:

1. The increasing number of old people. By the end of the century there will be ten million pensioners, including four and a half million over the age of 75.
2. A fall in the proportion of young people.

Changes in population are important for industry because of their effects on:

1. the supply of labour;
2. the demand for goods.

Supply of labour

During the 1970s and for much of the 1980s there were increasing numbers of people of working age. For example, in the ten years up to 1986 there was an increase in the population of those of working age of almost 2 million.

In the late 1980s there will be very little increase in the working population. In the 1990s it is estimated that the working population will be constant at 34 million.

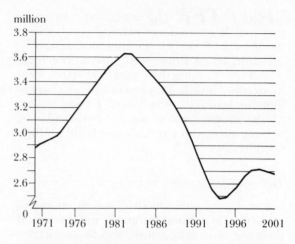

Figure 13.1 Changes in the number of 16–19-year-olds, 1971–2001 (projected).
Source: Office of Population Censuses and Surveys, and Government Actuary's Department

Most importantly, the number of 16–19-year-olds in the population will fall a lot. From a peak of 3.7 million in 1983 the number of 16–19-year-olds fell to 3.5 million in 1986 and will fall further to 2.6 million in 1994 (see Figure 13.1).

■ Questions

1. How do you think that it is possible to calculate the number of 16–19-year-olds who will be around in the year 2001?
2. What advantages will 16–19-year-olds gain in the 1990s as a result of the smaller number of people in their age group?
3. What disadvantages will there be to 16–19-year-olds?
4. What advantages/disadvantages will there be for people in the 40 to 50 age group as a result of the fall in numbers of 16–19-year-olds?
5. What advantages will there be for the government from the fall in 16–19-year-olds? What disadvantages will there be?
6. What advantages/disadvantages will there be to employers?

The rapidly falling numbers of 16–19-year-olds mean that many employers used to hiring young people will find increasing competition in recruiting and keeping young staff. They will need to make sure that they offer young people an attractive career. This is a major reason why many of Britain's large employers have been trying to improve their training programmes.

Employers in future will have to put more money into training their workforce if they want to increase its skill. Employers will also have to look increasingly to ways of getting unemployed people back to work, in particular by helping them to learn skills and build up their confidence.

Demand for goods

Changes in population also have an important influence on demand for goods and services. If there are more people there will be an increase in the demand for all goods. If there are increases in certain sections of the population then the products that these people buy will be more in demand.

■ Questions

1. List six products for which demand would rise if there was an increasing number of:
   (a) old people
   (b) babies
   (c) teenagers
   (d) people living in London
2. Why might the demand for some products fall even when there is a general increase in population?

■ Case Study: Changes in age structure

Look carefully at the figures given in Tables 13.2 and 13.3 and then answer the questions below.

Questions

1. What major changes are taking place in the age structure of the population of the UK?
2. What major problems are caused by this change?
3. In what ways is Andertown untypical of the UK?
4. What extra problems does and will Andertown have?

Table 13.2 Age structure of the population in the UK.

	Under 15	15–64	65 and over
1987	19%	66%	15%
2001 (projected)	20%	60%	20%

Table 13.3 Age structure of the population in Andertown.

	Under 15	15–64	65 and over
1987	17%	60%	23%
2001	15%	52%	33%

5. What possible reasons can you think of for the problems of Andertown?

The implications of population changes for the market

The European Community (EC) is a market of some 320 million people. It has a far larger share of world trade than the United States and by 1992 it will be completely open to British firms to compete on equal terms with other EC countries.

Some British companies have already taken advantage of the opportunity. For example, Rowntree found that French consumers were bored with the range of chocolate on offer. They therefore launched Lion Bar in France and today it is the second biggest seller in the market. By 1989 they will be selling over 300 million bars in France.

If you can reach a large number of people you can benefit from all sorts of advantages which we called economies of scale in Chapter 2. The best-known products on a global scale are Marlboro cigarettes and Coca Cola, which earn astronomic profits for the businesses that produce them.

Once the market for a product reaches a certain size it is possible to introduce new technology which will make possible cost cutting measures, the possibility of wider scale advertising, and the growth of monopoly powers. This is true whether a firm operates in a local, national or global market.

Impact of changes in technology

Technology means using scientific discoveries to solve problems. When technology is mentioned in this chapter it refers to methods of producing goods and services.

New technologies introduce new goods and services as well as change the ways in which existing ones are made. New jobs are created; new production methods and new markets are opened up.

■ Case Study: New technology in sugar beet production

Sugar beet is one of the main crops produced in Britain. In recent years there have been a number of important changes in the techniques used to produce beet sugar which at one time involved the use of a lot more labour and several more stages of production.

The sugar beet seed is made up of three parts which need to be separated (singled) before individual beets can be grown. However, the plants can only be separated once the seeds have germinated in the ground. As a result, the seeds need first to be planted and then singled out a few days later.

In Russia in the 1940s a freak experiment produced a sugar beet that could be produced from a single seed. However, the beet that was produced from this seed yielded a very low sugar content. It then took years of further experiments to build up the sugar producing ability of the seed germ. Today the seed has been perfected and is in common use.

Modern farm equipment is then used to plant the beet at the right spacing and depth to produce the most plentiful and best quality crop. In the old days a rhyme went:

'One for the mouse, and one for the crow,
One for to rot, and one for to grow.'

Farmers spread their seed plentifully to produce a crop. This was wasteful in terms of the quantity of seed used and because, if too many seeds germinated in part of a field, the beet plants would stop each other from growing.

A modern sugar beet farmer like Burtts of Lincolnshire can prepare a 120-acre field in a day.

Three tractors work together. The first tractor prepares the field in one sweep, the second tractor plants the seed and the third sprays the crop.

Questions

1. Describe in your own words one technique that has been used to increase the production of sugar beet.
2. Give two reasons why the farming of sugar beet in the old days might nowadays be regarded as wasteful of resources.
3. List three groups of people who you think have benefited from improved technology in beet production. Briefly explain how they have gained.
4. List three groups of people who you think might have lost out. Explain how.

■ Case study: New technology in newspaper production

The *Batley News* is part of a group of local papers produced in West Yorkshire. The area is famous for the production of heavy woollen goods. Local industry has recently been going through a technological revolution in production methods.

The Reporter Group (the group to which the *Batley News* belongs) felt that they too needed to go through a technological revolution that would secure their future in the twenty-first century. In 1988 the Reporter Group became computerised. Direct input was introduced at a cost of nearly £200,000, and now journalists write and print their own stories using modern computers (see Figure 13.2).

Questions

1. In what ways do you think that using new technology will help the Reporter Group to secure its future into the twenty-first century?
2. In what ways do you think that computers would make a journalist's work easier?
3. Who do you think might object to the increased use of computers in newspapers? What reasons might they give?

Figure 13.2 Getting out the news on a computer at the Reporter Group.

New technology in production processes

Like any other part of society, industry is being altered by new technology. As in many other areas, the computer is used more, but there are also many other changes. Industry must keep up to date with these changes to be competitive. The main areas where these changes are happening are, amongst others, computer-aided design, control and robotics.

Computer-aided design

The designer of an item working twenty years ago worked on a drawing board. Many skills were used from the creative (conceiving the ideas used in the design, styling, etc.) through the analytical (calculating the strength, weight, etc.) to the 'mechanical' (drawing the design on paper). Although the real role of a designer was to carry out the creative and analytical work, much of the time was spent on the drawing. With the coming of computers, it became possible to use a computer screen instead of a drawing board, saving time.

Computer-aided design (CAD) systems are based on either a powerful desktop computer or a 'workstation' attached to a minicomputer. The designer uses a keyboard, a high resolution monitor and a graphics pad. The graphics pad consists of a special board with a blank area in the middle and boxes containing symbols at the edge and a magnetic 'pen'. The designer can move the 'cursor' (position marker) around the monitor screen by moving the pen on the pad, and by touching the symbols can select various options (drawing lines and shapes, adding dimensions and text, changing scale, etc.). Having drawn the design, the designer can see a view of the item from different positions, and view it as a solid object instead of a series of lines.

Having developed the design, it is possible to use the computer to check its strength and calculate its mass and centre of gravity. For other than simple shapes, the strength is calculated using 'finite element analysis', a technique that requires a very large number of calculations and which is therefore virtually impossible without a computer. Other advantages of using CAD are:

1. It is much easier and quicker to make changes to the design than when it is drawn on paper.
2. Components that have been designed on one workstation and stored on the computer can be called up by another designer to check if the part fits with his or her design.
3. Modern storage technology enables a large quantity of drawings to be stored in a small space.

The use of CAD in industry has revolutionised almost every area of industrial design, from supertankers to microchips. The pressure on firms to reduce costs and the increased rate of change in products has made it essential for companies to use techniques such as CAD to remain competitive. The designer's job is made more enjoyable, as much of the drudgery is removed. However, one possibly less beneficial implication is that the ability to modify and redesign more quickly is reducing the lifetime of products. Customers quite rightly expect their purchases to last a long time, but with frequent changes they soon find that they have an 'old' version and that spares are no longer available. This particularly applies to domestic items like hi-fi and washing machines.

■ Case Study: Gatwick Airport

Architects are now using CAD to a large extent. For example, the new North Terminal at Gatwick Airport, opened in March 1988, was designed by the YRM partnership using CAD systems. The benefit gained from CAD improved over the period it was used (six years) as the sophistication of CAD systems increased. Starting with two dimensional plans, the use of CAD developed until all external elevations and floor plans for individual areas were being designed on the CAD system. Apart from the time savings,

another benefit was the ability to hand over accurate information to the airport authority for use in running the airport. The first is now using software capable of producing 3D views from any angle in order to evaluate designs and present proposals, and hopes to develop the ability to use the same data for structural calculations.

Questions

1. What evidence is shown in the above extract that technology improved during the use of CAD at Gatwick?
2. List three benefits of CAD that are mentioned above.
3. List three other industries that benefit from the use of CAD. Explain how they use CAD.
4. Why is it essential for some large firms to use CAD?

Control

The word 'control' literally means 'the ability to direct or restrain'. In the sense we are using it here it means that some kind of device, called a 'controller', performs a certain function automatically. A familiar example at home is an automatic washing machine. Once a program has been set, the controller takes over, switching the heater on and off, controlling the supply and pumping out of water and controlling the motor that rotates the drum. The basic elements of control are shown in Figure 13.3.

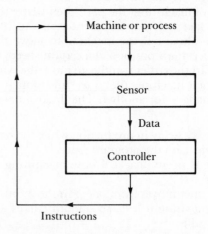

Figure 13.3 Basic elements of control.

The principle of control is used in many ways in modern industry, for example:

1. environmental control
2. process control
3. numerically controlled machine tools
4. robotics

Numerically controlled machine tools

Part of the reason for the increase in living standards in the developed countries of the world is the steady improvement in the tools available to industry. Throughout the whole industrial period of history, machines have been developed to make a specific item in large quantities, but the ability to make a machine that can be reprogrammed to produce a *variety* of items *automatically* is a more recent invention. These machines are used for cutting metal (or less commonly other materials) and for a range of other production tasks. They are called *numerically controlled machine tools*, the 'numerical' part of the name indicating that numbers are used to give instructions to the machine (i.e. control is digital rather than analogue).

Numerically controlled machine tools come in two types:

1. ordinary numerical control (NC) machines
2. computer numerical control (CNC) machines

NC machines are programmed using paper tape with holes punched in it. Working from the design drawing the programmer decides on the best way of machining the part, then writes the program as a series of instructions to the machine. These tell the machine to move the cutter to a certain position at a certain speed, to stop or start the cutter spindle, to move the part, etc. On some machines the cutter can automatically be changed for another. The disadvantages are:

1. There is a delay in production while the tape is loaded and the program tested.
2. There is no feedback of how machining is going.
3. The cutter moves from one point to another along a straight line, so smooth curves are impossible.

CNC machines contain a microprocessor, so the machine is capable of far more flexibility. They are programmed in one of two ways. In a factory where most of the items manufactured are 'one-offs' (i.e. made on only one occasion), for example by small subcontractors or in development workshops, the machines are programmed by the operator using a keypad and a VDU screen. Working from the design the operator programs the machines, defining cutter paths and speeds, and the screen shows a diagram of the component and the cutters so that the result can be checked. Once the program is complete, the parts are machined. The benefits of this type of programming are:

1. Reduction in throughput time (no delay between programming and machining);
2. No separate programming department;
3. If problems occur the program is easily changed;
4. Machining is still a skilled job, so job satisfaction is improved.

In a factory producing complex items in larger quantities, CNC machines are programmed from a central computer. This has the following benefits:

1. The time the machine is idle is minimised, as reprogramming is extremely quick.
2. The same program can be loaded easily to more than one machine.
3. It is no longer necessary to have one operator per machine.

CNC machines also have the following two advantages:

1. If given a defined curve (e.g. a semicircle of a given diameter and given centre), the machine will move the cutter smoothly along the defined path without steps.
2. Most CNC machines include toolholders, so that the machine will automatically change the tools over to carry out different operations. For example, given a casting, a CNC vertical milling machine can load a facing cutter to mill the top smooth, then load a succession of drills to produce holes.

The introduction of NC and CNC machines has great benefits for industry. They reduce labour costs per part by speeding production and enabling more than one machine to be controlled by one man. They also often improve quality because the chance for operator error is reduced. However, they also have potential disadvantages for society. First, the level of operator skill required is often greatly reduced, and traditional craft skills can be made worthless. An operator can become simply a loader of parts and machine watcher. Secondly, the introduction of these expensive machines means that to recoup their high cost they must be run as much as possible. If money has been borrowed to buy them they are effectively losing the company money whenever they are not working. This means that shift work is more likely to be used, resulting in inconvenient working hours.

Robotics

One of the best known examples of automatic control is in robotics. Robots are different from purpose-built automatic machines in that they are reprogrammable and hence multi-purpose machines. The use of robots is of benefit if the job is repetitive and does not require human manipulative skills. It is especially useful when:

1. the work area is dangerous or unpleasant, or
2. the item cannot be manipulated by hand (it may be very heavy, or hot, or radioactive, or even 100 metres under water).

Robots consist of a controller and the mechanical components and can be categorised in several ways.

1. *Power supply.* The transmission of power to the mechanical components can be pneumatic (by compressed air), hydraulic (by pumping fluid) or electric.
2. *Closed or open loop control.* In open loop control the controller gives instructions (for example, 'move the arm 30 degrees to the left') but has no way of knowing if the instructions have been carried out. In closed loop control measurements are continuously taken of the position of the robot (see Figure 13.4), so in the above example position sensors mounted on the arm or the base give feedback as to where the arm is. This reduces the damage done if for some reason the robot cannot obey its instructions (if the object it is

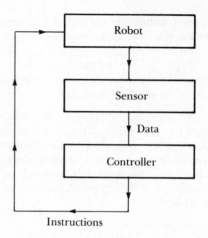

Figure 13.4 Closed loop robot control.

working on is the wrong shape or in the wrong position, for example).

Robots also vary in the method in which they are programmed. Some are programmed by keying in instructions on a keyboard in a similar way to programming a CNC machine. This is laborious and liable to error. However, with closed loop control robots where the position of the robot can be measured by the controller, the robot arm can be 'led through' the correct motion by a human operator, and the controller 'remembers' the movements. This is especially suitable where the robot is directly replacing a human operator. It is ironic that the operator teaching the robot is the person likely to be replaced by it.

The mechanical part normally consists of a base, a vertical trunk, an arm, and either a hand or a tool (welding gun, paint sprayer, etc.) attached to the arm by a wrist. As robots become more 'intelligent' they increasingly also have some kind of system for checking progress (probes or a camera, for example).

Robotics have taken a long time to achieve wide usage, but they are becoming more common in applications where repetitive manual tasks are concerned. While they cannot approach the flexibility of human operators they are becoming more able to adapt themselves to situations through vision processing. This ability to 'see' will greatly increase robots' effectiveness but has only recently become useful due to the combination of clever programming and the enormous computer power required.

The implications of the greater use of robots are, as always, both good and bad. The benefits, apart from the essential maintenance of competitiveness in the market place, are:

1. People can be displaced by robots in mundane jobs where human intelligence is not required but simple mechanisms are unsuitable (e.g. simple assembly work).
2. Robots can be used where working conditions are difficult or dangerous, as described earlier.

The disadvantages are:

1. Further erosion of craft skills may result.
2. Greater levels of capital investment increase pressure for shift working, as with numerically controlled machine tools.
3. A new danger is introduced into factories – the first fatality from an accident involving a robot has already happened.

■ Case Study: Robotics in the car industry

Robots are now used extensively in the motor industry. Because of the great number of options now offered on cars (different levels of trim, different engines, 2 or 4 doors, different colours, sunroofs, central locking, etc.) the possible number of different cars is vast. It is necessary to run different versions of cars down the same line together. In a modern car plant, therefore, a line producing the same model of car could have, in succession, a black 1.3 litre 2-door, a blue 1.1 litre 4-door with a sunroof, a white 2 litre with wider wheels and so on. Unintelligent machines could not cope with the variation, so robots are used to carry out painting, welding, assembly and so on. The specification of the car is read into the controller, which then runs the correct program for that car.

Questions

1. What is a factory robot?
2. In what ways do they help to improve production?
3. Why are robots said to be 'intelligent'?
4. What types of production line do they work well on?

CAD/CAM and CIM

Once design information is held in digital form on a CAD system, and NC machines are also using digital information to machine the product, the next logical stage is to ask if the data from the CAD system can be used to drive the machines. Although simple in theory this is not so in practice. However, CAD/CAM (as this combined operation is called) is being used to an increasing extent in many large, technologically advanced companies. The use started in industries like aerospace where the level of technology is already extremely high, but has filtered down into others like the car industry (see Figure 13.5).

The final stage of integration is called *computer integrated manufacturing* (CIM). This term is used for a situation where all the data used to run the manufacturing operation is integrated. In other words:

1. The product is designed on a CAD system.
2. That data is used to order materials.
3. The data is used to drive CNC machine tools.
4. Data on the progress of production is collected from the machines and used to drive a computer-based production planning and control system. (This system provides a centralised set of data for purchasing, accounts, sales and so on.)

No company has a 100% CIM system, but companies like British Aerospace, DEC (a computer maker), Westland Helicopters and Austin Rover have many of the elements installed.

The coming of CIM in industry will integrate the entire manufacturing process for the first time. The change is necessary to maintain competitiveness, and will help to improve flexibility and reduce costs. The social impact will also be great. The level of manning in manufacturing industry will decline further, there may be a trend towards shift working and some job types like unskilled machine operators and clerks may virtually disappear.

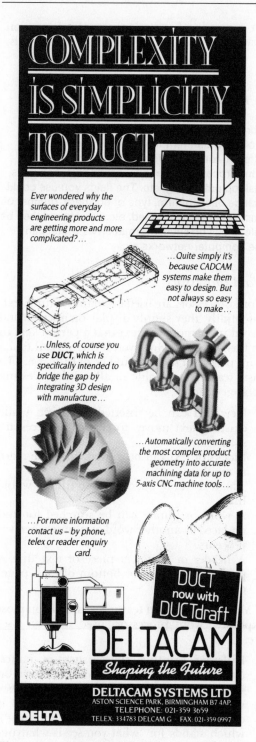

Figure 13.5 CAD/CAM: the shape of the future.
Source: Deltacom Systems (with permission).

Information technology in industry

It is obvious that the survival of any company depends on the efficient and accurate manufacture of its products. However, the survival of any medium- or large-sized company depends just as much on the rapid and accurate processing and distribution of information. As in other areas of commercial life, this is increasingly being carried out using new technology, principally computers.

Why is it that industry, which has apparently coped perfectly well without computers from the Industrial Revolution until recently, now suddenly needs computers? There are a number of reasons for this:

1. Competition between firms is more fierce; it is almost impossible for a company to find a market area that is not extremely competitive.
2. The rate of change in industry has increased (as in the rest of society). Firms must therefore be quicker in responding to factors such as technological change, market forces and better competition.
3. The level of technology used in products has dramatically increased, complicating the design and manufacturing processes.
4. Many of today's companies are very large. While it is possible to maintain a large organisation without computers (the Great Pyramid took 100,000 men 20 years to build, 5,000 years before computers), the efficient running of a large multinational company can no longer be achieved using manual methods.
5. Cost reduction at every stage of the design and manufacturing process has become very important. By using computer-aided design (CAD) and computer-based production control systems, the inefficient use of material, equipment, labour and energy can be minimised.
6. New materials and processes are being created at an increasing rate, and must be introduced as quickly as possible to maintain competitiveness.
7. Legislation relating to industry has increased greatly, leading to the requirement to hold and process more information relating to health and safety, employment law, tax, etc.

Some of the more important aspects of the new information technology are discussed in detail below.

Personal computers

The personal computer has now become common in industry. The work that it is used for is generally based around standard application packages, many of which are described below. More powerful versions of many of these programs are also used on mini- and mainframe computers.

Spreadsheets

A spreadsheet program is essentially a very large grid of 'cells' which contain text, numbers or formulae. It is used for numerical problems where a large amount of figures are to be calculated. The figure in any one cell can be calculated from the figures in any other cell (or combination of cells) using the spreadsheet to perform the calculations. If any one figure is changed, the result on all the other cells is seen immediately, saving long calculations. The spreadsheet is usually used as a financial tool, but can also be used by engineers, scientists and many others. Most spreadsheet programs also have the ability to produce graphs from the data.

Databases

Databases are programs that enable information of any kind to be stored in a structured form, selected, sorted and retrieved. The information is held in the form of 'records', made up of 'fields'. A field contains a specific item of information; a record contains all the fields relating to a given item. For example, a company's stock records would contain one record per part, and would have a field for name, part number, supplier, cost, selling price, last receipt and so on. So far, the database is doing nothing that can't be done on a piece of paper. However the database can now:

Multiply the stock of each part by the cost to give the stock value.
Produce a report of, say, all parts costing over £35, sorted into alphabetical order.
Raise all the selling prices 8% or £8, whichever is the greater, and so on.

For processing large quantities of information, a database is far quicker than manual methods.

■ Activity

Working in small groups, set out a database to show how different firms in your locality use different forms of information technology, e.g. word processors, personal computers, networks, desktop publishing, etc. The fields you use could include name of firm, type of business, number of employees, systems used, etc. You should then be able to call up such information as which banks use computer networks etc.

Word processors

Word processors are used for manipulating text. Essentially, they simply display on a screen and record in memory the text that a person keys in on the keyboard. However, if this was all that a word processor did it would be of little use. The basic features, available in all word processing packages, are:

1. New text can be inserted on screen while existing text moves to create the necessary space.
2. Blocks of text can be moved from one place to another.
3. The text can be spaced out to fill the whole line.
4. A word or phrase can be searched for and replaced by another word or phrase wherever it occurs.
5. A header or footer (a piece of text that is printed at the top or bottom of each page) can be added.

More sophisticated features available on most expensive word processors used in businesses are:

1. Different printing styles (such as italics, underlined text and so on), can be shown on screen either as different colours or as they would appear when printed. The latter is called WYSIWYG (pronounced 'wizzywig'), which stands for 'what-you-see-is-whatyou-get'.
2. Text can be written in more than one column, as in newspapers.

3. Graphics can be incorporated into the text.
4. A number of similar letters can be produced, with information added from a database on each letter. For example, if a company has a database of its suppliers and wishes to contact the local ones, the database can be used to select all suppliers who are situated in the same county. The word processor will then print a letter for each supplier selected, adding the individual information such as the name and address of the firm to the letter. This is called *mailmerge*.
5. A spelling checker may be provided. This checks all the text against a dictionary and points out any words that it does not recognise. Such a word may be spelt wrongly or it may be a name or technical word unknown to the program, so the option is given to change the word or to leave it. If it is a name or technical term likely to be used again, it can be added to the dictionary so that it will be 'passed' next time. Many packages suggest a replacement for a mis-spelt word, so that if the program finds 'suplies' in a letter, it may suggest 'supple', 'supplies' and 'surplus' as possible replacements.

■ Coursework suggestion

Use a word processor to prepare a business report showing the advantages and disadvantages to a local firm of introducing modern word processing equipment.

Desktop publishing

The improvements in word processing programs and the developments in computer power and graphics displays have resulted in a very new area of personal computing: *desktop publishing* (DTP). These programs offer the facility to produce pages of text and graphics, with the refinements previously only offered by typesetting firms – a large range of character designs ('typefaces') and sizes, the freedom to adjust the space between characters and lines, the ability to place a diagram or picture on a page then make text automatically 'flow' round it, etc. Pictures can be introduced into the document from a graphics program and stretched or shrunk to fit a space. DTP programs are being used to produce items such as newsletters, training manuals and advertisements.

Project planning

Project planning packages are used to plan and monitor a project consisting of a number of inter-related stages called 'activities'. First, the activities are defined and the time taken by each estimated. Then the way in which the activities depend on each other is defined. The computer then calculates the total time for the project and shows the activities which must be completed on time for the project not to be delayed.

A very simple example could be building a new factory. The activities and times may be:

1. Prepare land and build foundations   30 days
2. Build walls   30 days
3. Build roof   15 days
4. Install equipment   30 days
5. Equip offices   20 days

Activity 1 must be done first, then 2, then 3, but 4 and 5, although they must come after 3 has finished, can be done at the same time. Therefore, the total time for the project is only 105 days (30 + 30 + 15 + 30), not 125 days. The program will also tell you that number 5 is not 'critical', i.e. it can start late or take longer than planned without delaying the project.

This helps the project manager to determine the tasks that must be given top priority. Most versions of the program can also plan the use of resources on activities, record costs and produce a variety of reports. While this example is too trivial actually to require the use of a program, if a real project with 1,000 activities is taking place, it saves a lot of manual work.

Expert systems

Expert systems are a new family of programs. They consist of a set of rules based on the knowledge of a relevant expert, which can then be used to form conclusions on information the program is given. For example, one oil exploration company's geological experts have formulated the rules they use in deciding whether a certain area is likely to contain oil deposits. Data on different areas can then be fed in to the program and it will assess the chances of oil in a similar way to the human expert.

These programs are of particular use where a human expert is not available at the time. One interesting use is in medicine, where a program is being tested to aid diagnosis. It is used by the patient, not the doctor, the idea being that for personal and intimate problems a patient may answer questions more easily from a machine than from a person. It also means that trivial problems can be diagnosed without using the doctor's time.

One big problem with setting up expert systems is that it is often surprisingly difficult for human experts in a subject to define exactly how they reach decisions.

Communications

One flourishing area of computing is communications, principally using the telephone network. This facility can be used in three ways:

1. Direct communication of data between organisations or different branches of the same organisation.
2. Use of an 'email' (electronic mail) service such as Telecom Gold. To use this, a subscriber to Telecom Gold sends a message using the telephone line addressed to another subscriber. When the other subscriber calls the service he receives the message. The advantage over ordinary mail is speed and low cost.
3. Using remote databases. Several large computer databases have been set up for specialist use, covering rapidly changing areas like the law, information on companies and medical knowledge. For a (substantial) fee, companies can call up and do a search for specific topics. Searches can specify a combination of factors, e.g. an enquiry can be made for medical information referring to 'malaria' and 'France' to find only those items referring to both. The information is found rapidly and should be up to date.

Networking

If a company is using a number of personal computers, it is possible that some of the information on one is useful to another user. Rather than continually swapping data using floppy disks, it is possible to connect the machines together using a *local area network*

(LAN) (see Figure 13.6). This consists of a mixture of hardware and software which enables data to be transferred between the machines.

There are two basic ways of using a LAN. In one, the computers work using their own programs and their own data, but can exchange data when necessary. In the other, the program and data are held on one machine called a *file server*, and the others act as 'terminals', updating the data on the file server.

Minicomputers

Where an application exists that cannot be carried out on personal computers, minicomputers are used. These applications are generally where a personal computer would not be powerful enough (e.g. sophisticated CAD programs) or where an integrated system, where a lot of the information is to be available to all computer users, is required (e.g. production control systems). These systems consist of a central computer and anywhere between half a dozen and several hundred terminals. Common applications for businesses are given below.

1. *Production control.* Production control systems for manufacturing firms are available in two types:
   (a) An MRP (*materials requirements planning*) system is one that contains information on all the items that make up the firm's products, all the items currently in stock, and the requirement for finished products. It then can calculate the total requirements for all items that the firm uses, work out when they are needed, and tell the production control and purchasing departments to order them. This process would not be possible on a personal computer, and even on a minicomputer the calculations are normally carried out overnight.
   (b) An MRP2 (*manufacturing resource planning*) system extends this process by incorporating items such as cost information, the automatic scheduling of parts on the shop floor, monitoring of purchase orders, etc., so that the whole company is using the same set of data. Installing such a program and learning how to use it can take over two

Figure 13.6 In a large modern office workstations are often 'networked' together.
Source: Kim Hooper.

years, and they are expensive (tens of thousands of pounds) but the benefits can be very great.

2. *CAD*. CAD systems have been described elsewhere. Minicomputer-based systems are required where the items are complicated or where a centralised set of data must be used, e.g. in designing an integrated product such as a car, rather than individual items (e.g. clothes).

3. *Word processing and information distribution*. If a minicomputer is used as a word processing system, it can easily be used as a messaging system so that a letter can be written on the word processor, sent to a colleague for comments, returned to the originator for amendment, and then distributed to a number of recipients.

Other uses of minicomputers are generally integrated versions of personal computer applications so will not be described in detail. It is, however, worth noting the benefits of a minicomputer system:

1. Greater power for major jobs.
2. Centralised data available to all.
3. A common set of programs and data.

Mainframes

Large companies use mainframe computers for their data processing needs. These computers are powerful machines, occupying a room and requiring a team of operators and programmers. The companies using them have both major data processing requirements and resources, so the programs are often designed specifically for that company. One example of an application is in mail-order firms. These rely totally on mainframe computers to monitor and reorder stock, to bill customers and to control the whole operation. Since the firms are selling virtually identical products in an identical way to a single market, the computer system is one of the few ways to gain an advantage over other firms.

■ Case Study: Using information technology in a small business

Tariq Aziz owns a small newsagents business in Exmouth. The shop delivers newspapers and magazines to 1,200 customers. Tariq employs 20 local school pupils to deliver these newspapers and magazines. Each paper deliverer has a 'round' of roughly 60 customers.

Tariq uses a BBC microcomputer (complete with printer and double disc drive) to help with the administration of the business. Information about customers, the magazines and newspapers that have been delivered to them, the amount of money they owe, publication days for magazines, and the prices of magazines and newspapers is kept in a series of computer files.

Each morning Tariq inputs the number of papers and magazines delivered to the shop. The program then prints out the numbers of newspapers and magazines required for each 'round' and updates the amount of money owed by each customer.

Tariq has been asked to give a presentation to the local newsagents' federation highlighting the benefits of the system.

Questions

Imagine that you are Tariq Aziz and that you must produce a report for the Newsagents' Federation.

1. Outline the advantages of the system to shop managers.
2. Outline the advantages of the system to customers.
3. Describe other facilities you would like to see incorporated in the program.

Impact of industrial changes in other countries

Specialisation is an important feature of the world economy. Generally each country will concentrate on its best lines, leaving others to concentrate on areas where it is less strong.

At the end of the nineteenth century the United Kingdom was supreme in manufacturing industry. However, as other countries developed their manufacturing bases the United Kingdom lost this advantage. Today it is the new manufacturing nations that lead the world in many areas of manufacturing. After the Second World War it was Germany and Japan that led the field. Today we are looking to countries like Korea and Taiwan.

These countries specialise in producing modern consumer durables. They use sophisticated automatic machinery at full capacity. Products include microwave ovens, video recorders, television sets, cars and motorbikes.

With the move towards the single EC market in 1992 and the threat of European Community restrictions on imports, a number of companies from these countries are moving their manufacturing operations to the United Kingdom. Korean officials, for example, regard Britain as a favourable location for investment because of language advantages and low labour costs compared with other parts of Europe such as Germany.

The British government in recent years has encouraged a number of foreign companies to move here to set up operations or joint ventures with British companies. The advantages are the creation of employment and the revitalisation of local companies. The disadvantages include increasing competition for British companies, the lack of security resulting from the way that multinationals switch operations between countries, and the fact that profits go overseas.

As other countries have taken the manufacturing initiative British industry has moved increasingly towards a service base.

■ Case Study: The importance of paper to Finland

Paper was supposed to become redundant in the computer age. It has not. Demand for computer printouts and copying has helped to double the quantity of paper consumed in the world in the past twenty years.

No country is more dependent on its paper output than Finland. Of its exports 40% are forest products and 90% of the paper it produces is sold overseas.

Two-thirds of Finland is covered by forest. Because it uses its forests to full capacity, the only way to increase the value of its paper industry is by improving the value of its products. This means going glossy. Finland has moved away from the bulk products (mainly pulp and newsprint) to high value-added paper – the shinier material used by magazines, advertisers and offices.

Growth in upmarket sorts of paper has been running at 14% a year. Even newspapers now require improved newsprint, e.g. for colour reproduction.

It has also made sense for Finland to move into quality paper production because of the threat to the cheap end of the market posed by Japanese competition. Countries such as Japan, Germany and America now recycle a lot of their newsprint. The Germans have made recycling paper as cost efficient as buying Finnish newsprint.

Questions

1. What has happened to the demand for paper over the last twenty years?
2. In what ways has modern computer technology:
   (a) reduced the demand for paper?
   (b) increased the demand for paper?
3. What is meant by the 'paperless office'?
4. Why is the demand for paper of particular interest to Finland?
5. Give three reasons why it has been of importance to Finland to move into 'quality paper'.
6. List two alternative ways of producing paper.
7. Why must Finland pay close attention to:
   (a) demand conditions for paper in other countries?
   (b) supply conditions for paper in other countries?
8. Name one British product for which sales are very much dependent on the international picture. Which other nations are important

sellers/buyers of this product? What factors could weaken the performance of this industry? Who would lose out as a result of the decline of this industry?

■ Revision

Complete the following sentences using the words below:

mainframes	materials
networking	requirements
word processors	planning
robotics	databases
control	numerically controlled
European Community	computer-aided
next best thing	design
robots	ageing population
life cycle	CAD/CAM
spreadsheet	tools
electronic mail	project planning
three-dimensional	packages

1. _____ brings together a series of personal computers.
2. Gatwick airport uses software that can give _____ views.
3. _____ are powerful computers occupying a room and requiring a team of operators.
4. The _____ is a market of 320 million people.
5. Modern design methods mean that products have a shorter _____ .
6. _____ is the combination of modern design and manufacturing systems.
7. A _____ system contains information on all the items that make up a firm's products.
8. _____ are programs that enable information of any kind to be stored in a standard form.
9. _____ machines are programmed using paper tape with holes punched in it.
10. _____ are being used to replace repetitive manual operations.
11. Firms are constantly looking for the _____ .
12. Telecom Gold is an example of an _____ system.
13. _____ are used to plan and monitor a project.
14. _____ are different from purpose-built automatic machines in that they are reprogrammable.
15. _____ are used for manipulating text.

16. A designer using _____ will use a keyboard, a high resolution monitor and a graphics pad.

17. The word _____ means the ability to direct or restrain.

18. A major problem in Britain in the late twentieth century is its _____.

19. Part of the reason for our improved standard of living is the range of modern _____ available to industry.

20. A _____ is a large grid of cells containing text.

CHAPTER 14
The social consequences of business activity

Growth

In 1987 nearly 400 million bags of Hula Hoops were sold in Great Britain, and 1 million cans of baked beans were sold a day. It was a year in which a wide range of new products were being bought in vast quantities: Levi 501s, cordless telephones, Perrier water, jug kettles, steam and spray irons, video recorders and home computers.

Every year new products enter the market and more goods are sold. The quantity and value of goods sold keep on rising.

The 'growth' of a country is often measured in terms of the value of the goods it produces. People are said to be better off if they can afford to buy a bigger basket of goods than before. We can even measure the contribution of various firms and industries to a nation's output of goods.

■ Case Study: An economy based on bread

In this example the only product that is consumed in the economy is bread. Like many other products, bread must go through several stages of production before it reaches its final form. First wheat must be produced; then this must be ground into flour; the flour must be baked into bread; and finally the product must be retailed to the consumer. The total value of the national output will be the final expenditure on bread.

At each stage of production value is added to the product (see Table 14.1). The farmer produces wheat worth £1,000. The wheat is sold to the miller for £1,000. The miller grinds up the grain and sells it for £1,300 – the miller has added value of £300. The baker buys the grain for £1,300, bakes it into bread and sells the bread for £2,000 – the baker has added £700 of value. The retailer buys the bread for £2,000 and sells all the loaves for a sum of £2,500 – adding value of £500.

Table 14.1 The process of adding value in bread production.

Type of industry	Value of output	Value added
Farming	1,000	1,000
Milling	1,300	300
Baking	2,000	700
Retailing	2,500	500
Total of values added		2,500

Questions

1. Which of the above stages in the production of bread is most important? Explain your answer.
2. Make out a table similar to that shown above using the following figures. A forester produces £2,000 worth of trees; the timber yard saws them into planks and sells them for £3,200; a pulping mill pulps the wood into paper which it sells for £4,500; a book publisher makes books out of the paper which it sells for £6,000 to retailers who sell all the books for £7,000 to consumers.
3. At what stages is value added in bringing butter to the consumer?

Arguing the case for 'growth'

Growth means having more goods per head of population.

Three major arguments can be put forward in favour of growth:

1. People prefer to have more goods than less. In other words, the more possessions that people have, the happier they will be.
2. Without growth it would be impossible for one person to become better off without someone else becoming worse off.
3. Growth makes it possible to reduce poverty within the community.

■ Questions

1. Do you agree with each of the above statements? Explain your answer.
2. In a country where the number of products per head is increasing who will benefit most? Would everyone benefit? Explain your answer.
3. Do you think that growth would help to reduce poverty? What factors would increase/decrease its effect in reducing poverty?

Costs and benefits

When you try to weigh up the effect of any action or policy it is necessary to look at:

1. who are the winners and losers;
2. the size of their gain or loss.

This is very difficult because different people have different views and give different values to things. Whereas one person would not mind the property next door being converted to a fish and chip shop, another would regard this as an absolute disaster.

Even when it is possible to measure costs and benefits in money terms it is easy to underestimate the 'real' effects. For example, if a new office development creates 100 jobs paying average salaries of £10,000 it is quite easy to compute the increased earnings in the area. However, it is impossible to attach a value to the excitement somebody might feel who is being taken on to work in the office who has not worked for the previous five years. Attaching money values to costs and benefits, therefore,

can at best only be a very rough measure.

Costs and benefits can also be split up into *private* and *social* aspects.

Private costs and benefits

When an individual or group carries out a project he or she will calculate the costs and benefits to him or herself. For example, when you decide to buy an item of clothing you consider its price, what else you could spend the money on and how much satisfaction you will get from the item.

Social costs and benefits

Social costs and benefits go beyond the individual or group to consider *all* the individuals and groups who will be affected by an action or policy. If I build a new factory I would take into consideration the private costs and benefits to me. The local planning authority would, however, also take into consideration all the other groups and individuals who would be affected, e.g. the builders of the factory and their employees, the employees who would operate the new factory, people living near to the factory buildings, etc.

■ Case Study: Costs and benefits of relocation

Octavius Atkinson is a heavy steel engineering firm (producing girders, etc.) that has been based in Harrogate for over a hundred years. Its present site was located on the railway to make use of this transport system. It now needs to expand the site on which it operates if it is to be competitive as we move into the twenty-first century. It would like to remain in the Harrogate area for historic and financial reasons. The firm had earmarked a site close to Harrogate as being ideal for expansion and relocation. However, its relocation decisions had not been approved (April 1988) by the planning authorities. The site chosen by Octavius Atkinson had previously been set aside by the planning authorities as a 'greenbelt zone'. (Greenbelt zones are greenfield sites on which no building is allowed.)

Read through the newspaper article in Figure 14.1 before answering the following questions related to the proposed move to Highfield Farm.

Steel firm gets thumbs down

ANXIOUS steelworkers feel their jobs are on the line following Harrogate Council's decision to reject Octavius Atkinson's controversial re-location plans.

And they hope that only loyalty to the workforce will stop the company, which employs 400 people, from looking at alternative locations ''wider afield''.

After a two-and-a-half-hour debate, councillors eventually voted 35-16 against the proposed move by the steel fabrication firm to Highfield Farm — a 43-acre, green field site on the A59 Harrogate to York road.

The town's MP has supported the decision.

More than 100 workers from the Starbeck firm packed into the council chamber on Wednesday evening to witness the debate, which was adjourned for several minutes on two occasions.

The factory had closed early on Wednesday to allow workers to attend the meeting.

Coun Philip Allott called on planning committee chairman Coun Nigel Kitson to resign

By ROBERT WATSON

when the latter spoke against the decisions made by the full planning committee which had recommended rejection of the £12 million plan.

Coun Kitson said: "The site proposed is not an area of outstanding beauty even though we live in areas full of green fields.

"I know conservation is the flavour of the year, but our decision depends on the economy, and I therefore beg members to support the application," he added.

And he suggested that the plan should not be rejected but referred instead to the Environment Secretary for the final decision.

Coun Allott declared the Council had a moral obligation to identify a more suitable site for the firm, a point taken up by the majority of members.

The meeting accepted Coun Malcolm Ferguson's proposal that officers should get together with the firm to look for a better location within the area and safeguard the jobs for the district.

"I believe the firm should extend its search way beyond the areas they have so far explored. This is not the site and further ones

should be considered," he said.

After the meeting, workers expressed their disappointment at the way the vote had gone, and expressed fear and concern over the safety of their jobs.

Tony Nelson, 26, a plater, was just one of three workers involved in collecting a 4000-name petition in favour of the re-location plans.

He argued that councillors were playing Russian roulette with their jobs and their livlihoods at stake.

And Steve Abbott, 28, said if the factory moved from the area, many of the workers would be unwilling to go with it.

"We have lived here all our lives and want to stay here," he said.

The Managing Director of Octavius Atkinson, Mr Michael Reffitt, expressed disappointment at the outcome.

"We will have to look out our future development plans," he said, "but we intend to stay in Harrogate."

Harrogate's MP, Mr Robert Banks, said he believed the council's decision to reject the application was wise.

"On balance, I have felt that the number of jobs which would be preserved by the construction of a new building was outweighed by the size and impact of the planning proposal in an area of outstanding importance."

Young supporter

THIS young man with his eye to the future was among hundreds of Octavius Atkinson workers and their families who descended on the council offices to show their support for the proposed factory site at Highfield Farm, Knaresborough.

More than a third of the workforce had time off to take part in the demonstration before Wednesday's full council meeting, peacefully congregating to show councillors their strength of feeling.

"We were going to leave it to the council to take action, but then people started calling us thugs and yobs," said plater Tony Nelson. "We want to show that we are not yobs, but we are willing to fight for our jobs." (A1070)

Figure 14.1 Costs and benefits of relocation for Octavius Atkinson.
Source: The Harrogate Advertiser

Questions

1. What would be the main costs to Octavius Atkinson of moving to a larger site at Highfield Farm?
2. What would be the main benefits to Octavius Atkinson of moving to Highfield Farm?
3. What would be the main costs/benefits to an existing Octavius Atkinson employee with a house close to the existing works site of moving to Highfield Farm?
4. Which other individuals and groups would gain/lose out from the Octavius Atkinson move. Give a reason with each example.
5. What do you think are the main factors which the Environment Secretary would have to take into consideration in making a decision on whether to let Octavius Atkinson move to Highfield Farm or not?

Social losses from industrial progress

Product development can offer better, more reliable, more convenient, more accurate products. For example, a digital watch tells the time more reliably than a wind-up watch and can cost less.

However, it is important to look hard and carefully at the cost of new technology. Should we accept the pollution it can bring, and in some cases the destruction of the environment? Should we accept job losses and the break-up of communities?

New technology – New ways of producing items.

Environment – The things that surround us.

Environmentalist – Someone who seeks to protect or improve our surroundings.

Pollution

Air pollution

The advertisement shown in Figure 14.2 graphically illustrates the dangers of air pollution. It goes on to say: 'Acid rain causes death and damage to forests, lakes, wildlife, crops, buildings and ourselves.'

There are a number of causes of air pollution, including the way that products are made and the use of products. Coal-fired power stations in

Figure 14.2 Advertisement on the effects of acid rain. Source: Greenpeace.

Britain are regarded by many Western Europeans as a major cause of acid rain in Germany and Scandinavia. Other EC countries impose far stricter laws than the UK to control industrial pollution. Researchers have also estimated that if Britain is to meet the main EC targets to reduce sulphur dioxide pollution this will just put half of one per cent on average yearly electricity bills – about £1.

If poisonous gases can be removed from the air it may take twenty to thirty years before lakes and rivers can fully recover.

Prince Charles is reported to have banned aerosols from his house because of the possible damage some aerosols are causing to the ozone layer which protects our planet from the sun's rays. Some scientists believe that unless the use of aerosols is tightly controlled then there will be serious consequences, such as the climate of the planet being thrown out of balance, and an increase in the number of skin cancers.

The air pollutants that come from cars in particular are numerous. The one that has been the most talked about over the last ten years is lead. Lead has been recognised as a highly dangerous substance since Roman times, and yet there is now more of it in the air that we breathe than at any time in the past. Between 90% and 99% of it comes from vehicle exhausts.

Lead poisoning can lead to a wide range of bad health effects including brain, liver, kidney and nervous damage. Children are far more likely to suffer than are adults. Children may become hyperactive and slow at learning when exposed to the sort of lead levels often found near schools situated beside main roads.

Several countries including the USA and Japan have already got rid of lead in petrol. In the UK lead-free is rapidly becoming available, and from 1990 all new cars must be able to run on such petrol.

Several other ingredients in exhaust fumes also help to cause headaches and dizziness.

Noise pollution

Noise is experienced when the ear picks up unwanted vibration. Most vibration comes from machinery of some kind, and at its most intense, for example a jet plane taking off, it can cause actual physical pain.

New roads can bring the nuisance of traffic noise into people's homes, often in areas which previously enjoyed peace and quiet. The M25 motorway around the outskirts of London is a good example of this.

Noise is particularly annoying at night, when it can interrupt sleep. There is nothing new in this. In the times of the Roman Empire the capital's residents complained so vigorously about the disturbance caused by cart traffic that the Emperor Augustus put a ban on all carts leaving or entering Rome at night!

Water pollution

Water pollution is a serious problem in Britain's rivers and seas. It has been estimated that even a small seepage from a farm's waste tank is equivalent to the dumping of a day's untreated sewage from a medium size town into a river. Chemicals sprayed onto the land by farmers to increase crop yields are washed into streams and rivers killing fish and destroying plant life.

The Queen expressed her environmental concern over the North Sea last night. In a speech during a banquet at Windsor Castle, the Queen said that it was in Britain's best interests to keep the area free from pollution.

Her comments echo a similar concern expressed by the Prince of Wales, who, in a speech during a conference of environment ministers from North Sea states last November, described the North Sea as 'a rubbish dump'.

At last night's banquet, held in honour of King Olav of Norway, who is on a visit to Britain, the Queen said: 'In recent times we have co-operated to exploit its valuable oil and gas resources.

'It is therefore in the interest of both our nations to see that the health and cleanliness of the North Sea are maintained, and that its renewable resources are only exploited on a sustainable basis.'

The Queen's remarks will be welcomed by environmentalists, who have blamed many pollutants for damaging the life of the North Sea.

Their targets include sewage, sludge and industrial waste, toxic materials which are burned at sea, oil spills and agricultural chemicals washed out from rivers.

Figure 14.3 Extract from an article reporting the Queen's views on North Sea pollution.
Source: The Independent, *Tuesday 12 April 1988.*

■ Case Study: Royal agreement over pollution of the sea

Read carefully the article in Figure 14.3 reporting the Queen's views regarding pollution in the North Sea, then answer the questions below.

Questions

1. When the Queen said that 'renewable resources should only be exploited on a

sustainable basis' she meant that resources like fish (which replace themselves) should not be used up (e.g. fished) at a faster rate than the time necessary for the fish to replace themselves. Do you agree with this? Explain your reasoning.
2. List six groups which might have helped to cause North Sea pollution and explain one way in which each might have done so.
3. Why have Britain and Norway a particular responsibility to conserve the North Sea? Try to give three reasons.
4. Why will the Queen's remarks be particularly welcomed by environmentalists?

Food pollution

Pesticides now treat our food as never before. Niney-nine per cent of all fruit, vegetables and cereals are sprayed at least once before we eat them, and some are sprayed up to 42 times in just one growing season. Since Britain joined the EC, pesticide use has probably increased about fourfold, as farmers try to grow more crops per acre.

Controlling pollution

There are a variety of ways of dealing with pollution including:

1. An increased awareness and concern about pollution so that individuals and groups are less inclined to cause pollution, or more prepared to control the amount they cause.

2. Members of the public can boycott products and firms that cause pollution.
3. The government can encourage firms to reduce pollution.
4. Penalties can be imposed on the creators of pollution.

Increased awareness

People are more aware today than in the past of the problems of pollution. Many people will think twice before dropping litter and will look carefully at the ingredients of the products they use (certain products such as some aerosols and leaded petrol can directly pollute the atmosphere.

Businesses are also more interested to show a concern for the environment. Many large companies deliberately spend a lot of money advertising their concern for the environment.

■ Case Study: Conservation through a unit trust

Read carefully through the newspaper article given in Figure 14.4 and study the accompanying advertisement in Figure 14.5, then answer the following questions.

Questions

1. What do you think are the aims of Merlin Ecology fund?

Unit trust hopes to clean up the environment

Environmental concern and the financial world do not always go hand in hand. Investors have tended to be more concerned about a company's profitability than about the pollution it might create.

Now the pressure of public opinion, and tougher environmental controls, are making environmental concern big business. British businesses involved in the control of pollution had turnovers of over £1 billion in 1987, and if the United States is anything to go by the trend will continue to expand.

Merlin Fund Management, a small unit trust company, is now launching the Merlin Ecology Fund which aims to 'invest in companies engaged in pollution control or which demonstrate a commitment to the long-term protection and wise use of the environment.'

The Fund aims to invest in shares which will yield good profits as well as those with a safe record of profitability such as water supply and waste management.

The Fund is confident that they will fill an investment gap for environmentally aware investors, charities, local authorities and other institutions.

Figure 14.4 Newspaper article on the Merlin Ecology Fund.
Source: adapted from The Independent, *15 April 1988.*

The new Merlin Ecology Fund.
Now you can profit from
a concern for the environment.

Day by day environmental concern is exerting a growing influence on industry and commerce.

Industry is increasingly recognising its responsibility for reducing pollution and using natural resources more wisely.

A major oil company has now developed a biodegradeable oil.

Aerosol manufacturers are starting to care about the ozone layer.

The 'environmental' sectors are growing – $70 billion was spent on pollution abatement and control in the USA in 1985. By 1987 UK companies in this sector had a turnover of £2.2 billion, twice that of the UK pharmaceutical industry.

And the demand for environmentally clean products and services is increasing.

The Merlin Ecology Fund enables you to profit from these new developments. By investing in well-managed and profitable companies who show a real commitment to the environment, the managers aim to provide a safe, secure investment capable of long-term capital growth and a rising income.

But you should remember that the price of units and their income can go down as well as up.

Merlin have combined the knowledge and experience of the investment and environmental worlds. Merlin's International Growth Fund has an impressive seventeen year history. The Merlin Research Unit, the first of its kind, will assess the environmental performance of investments. An Advisory Committee will ensure that the principles of the fund are followed.

You can buy units in the Merlin Ecology Fund at the fixed price of 50p until 18th April 1988.

Simply complete and return the coupon below.

MERLIN
ECOLOGY FUND

30 St. James's St., London SW1A 1HB.
Telephone: 01-925 1277.

Important Information

The Merlin Ecology Fund is a 'wider range' investment under the Trustee Investments Act 1961, and a UK authorised unit trust.

The managers are Merlin Fund Management Limited, 30 St. James's Street, London SW1A 1HB, and are members of the Unit Trust Association.

The trustee is Bank of Scotland.

An initial charge of 5% is included in the units' offer price. A rounding adjustment not to exceed the lower of 1% or 1.25p per unit is also permitted. An annual charge of 1% (plus VAT) is deducted from the Fund's assets to cover managers' expenses and trustees' fees. The managers may increase this charge to 1¹⁄₂% p.a. (plus VAT) by giving 3 months notice.

Units may be bought or sold on any subscription day (Wednesday each week). Certificates will be sent within 6 weeks. When selling units, a cheque will normally be sent within 7 working days of receiving your renounced certificate.

Prices and Yields are published daily in the Financial Times and Daily Telegraph. The estimated commencing gross yield is 2% p.a.

The managers will not invest in any company directly involved in the arms, tobacco or nuclear industries, or in South Africa.

Commission is paid to qualified intermediaries. This offer is not available to residents of Eire, or people under 18.

To: Merlin Fund Management Limited, 30 St. James's Street, London SW1A 1HB. Telephone: 01-925 1277.

I/We wish to invest £ _____ in Merlin Ecology Fund at the special price of 50p per unit, fixed until 18th April 1988.

I enclose a cheque payable to Merlin Fund Management Limited. (The minimum initial investment is £500 and subsequent investments at least £250.)

I wish to have the income reinvested. ☐ I wish to automatically receive the income. ☐

(Block letters please) *(please tick)*

Surname _____

(Please state Mr, Mrs, Miss or title)

Full Forename(s) _____

Address _____

_____ Postcode _____

Signature _____ Date _____

In case of joint holders, please sign and give details separately.   S1

Figure 14.5 Advertisement for the Merlin Ecology Fund (reproduced with permission).

2. What sorts of people would you expect to buy units in this fund?
3. Why do you think that environmental concern is becoming 'big business'?
4. Do you think that society will benefit from the existence of more Merlin Ecology Funds? Explain your answer.
5. How will investors in Merlin Ecology Fund benefit from their investment?
6. How might investors lose out?

Consumer boycotts

Twenty years ago it was fashionable to wear a fur coat; today it is regarded as being in bad taste. An increasing number of consumers are questioning the products that they buy – they want to know how they are made, what is in them, where they come from, what side-effects they might have, what is done with the packaging, etc.

The pressure group Friends of the Earth first hit the headlines in 1971 by dumping 1,500 throw-away bottles on the doorstep of Schweppes, the soft drinks manufacturers. Such direct actions by consumers have frequently put pressure on firms to change their practices.

■ Coursework activity

Working in pairs select an item that is sold by a supermarket. Find out how it is made, what ingredients it contains, where the products come from, what happens to the packaging, etc. Each pair should then make a presentation of their findings to the class.

Encouragement to reduce pollution

There are various ways of encouraging firms to be more environmentally conscious. The most obvious way is for consumers to buy products which are produced in an environmentally friendly way.

The local council and other government bodies can support businesses and offer prizes to schemes that support the environment. The government can impose penalties and fines on the producers of pollution, and subsidise schemes that reduce pollution. For example the government could support the conservation of the Lake District in the following ways:

1. By placing a conservation tax on all firms that benefit from the tourist trade in proportion to their profits.
2. By placing an environmental repair tax on the hotel bills of people visiting the Lake District.
3. By taxing the numerous publishers of walkers' and climbers' guidebooks.

■ Question

What other measures can you think of?

Many people are becoming increasingly alarmed about threats to the biosphere from industrial pollution. Scientists have raised a number of important questions related to the destruction of the layer of gases known as the ozone layer, which filters rays from the sun. One possible explanation for the reduction in the effectiveness of the ozone layer is that a number of the substances in household products such as aerosol hairsprays have a damaging effect when released into the atmosphere.

Biosphere – The regions of the earth's crust and atmosphere in which living matter is found.

Recycling

Many of the most important resources we use are non-renewable so that once they are used up they are finished. This is particularly true of fuels like oil and coal and metals like iron and copper. Re-using materials is a very important process for the long-term best use of scarce resources.

Rubbish

To throw something away suggests that it is worthless. In the case of waste from dustbins nothing could be further from the truth. Britain buries nearly all its waste in holes in the ground and buries £1 million a day by doing so. This is the possible value of the energy content in waste. The contents of your dustbin could be worth as much as £20 per tonne.

Over the last 50 years, the nature of household

waste has changed. In the 1940s a dustbin would have contained a high proportion of cinders and dust. Today, a typical dustbin in the course of a year will carry about 90 lb of plastic, all that remains of six mature trees (312 lb of paper), 310 lb of mixed food wastes, 40 lb of metals and 90 lb of glass. Multiply these figures by the 18 million homes in the UK and you have a lot of rubbish.

Because of the high cost of land in and around towns and cities waste has to be transported further and further to be buried. It is becoming a very costly business to bury waste.

There are three major ways in which household waste could be used to create energy. All these methods have proved to be successful:

1. Burning it to raise steam
2. Converting it into solid fuel
3. Collecting and burning the methane gas given off at existing landfill sites

Roughly speaking, 2½ binloads of rubbish contains the same heat energy as a bag of coal.

Glass

There is a strong case for recycling glass. Not only are there strong environmental arguments, but it also makes sense in money terms. Recycled glass melts at a much lower temperature than do the raw materials of new glass. Also, less energy is required to collect, process and deliver the glass from a well-organised recycling scheme than to produce and deliver an equivalent amount of raw materials. To make one tonne of new glass requires 12 tonnes of raw materials, or just a tonne of broken glass. In all, each tonne of broken glass added to the furnace means savings of about 30 gallons of fuel oil.

The process of quarrying for sand and limestone uses a lot of land, so replacing those materials with recycled glass saves countryside. In addition, every tonne of bottles and jars recycled means a tonne less rubbish to be disposed of, so less land is taken up by landfill.

Today 14% of glass comes from recycled sources, and bottle banks play a particularly important part in providing the raw materials.

Unemployment

Businesses can create jobs, and they can take them away. New products develop, old products die out. With these changes people find that their skills are no longer required. Many longer-term unemployed people lack the kind of skills needed to fill the jobs now becoming available. Many have limited experience of what is happening in new technology, and lack of skills is often made worse by a lack of qualifications. Over half of the unemployed adults who have been out of work for six months or more have no educational qualifications at all.

The inner cities provide a clear example of small areas where unemployment is very high, as do many council housing estates not necessarily in inner cities. The evidence suggests that to some extent people in such areas can be trapped in unemployment by their lack of skill, by their lack of knowledge about jobs, and by their past lack of success in getting work.

Twenty years ago there were far more factories and workshops operating in inner city areas, but because there was no room for expansion and rates were too high, such industries went into decline.

■ Coursework activity

A group of students were set an investigation into who should be made to pay for pollution caused by fast-food operations. They were given the following datapack which looked at the pollution caused by a local business Burger Chief. The datapack included a map of the area (Figure 14.6), a letter of complaint from a local resident (Figure 14.7), an article from the local paper (Figure 14.8), pictures showing the problem (Figure 14.9) and a copy of an interview with the owner of Burger Chief (Figure 14.10).

The students used the datapack to explore a series of questions and issues which are given at the end of this exercise. Once the students had explored the problem in the classroom they went out to carry out their own field research which they wrote up as coursework. This involved devising a group questionnaire for people of the town to answer, and separate questionnaires for the local council and fast-food operators.

Use the datapack as instructed on p. 230 to explore the issue in your own classroom before carrying out some field research.

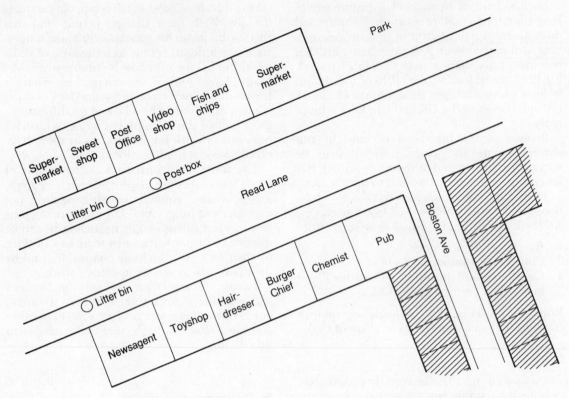

Figure 14.6 Datapack: map of area.

6 Boston Ave
Grantham
8 April 1989

Dear Sir

We the residents of Boston Avenue are writing to you to
protest in the strongest possible terms about fast-food
businesses in this town. Like many other streets in this town
which have the misfortune to be near fast-food takeaways we
daily suffer from their existence. This morning I removed 5
soft drink tins, 3 Burger Chief cartons, and 1 plate of mushy
peas and chips from my garden. Nearly every day myself and
my neighbours suffer similar misfortunes. We have
complained to the council several times but they have done
nothing. On the last occasion we presented a petition asking
the council to take action signed by over 1,000 people.

Yours

Simon Jones

Disgusted residents of Boston Avenue.

Figure 14.7 Datapack: letter of complaint.

Well served for fast food

FROM a pizza to a bag of chips, in Grantham we are spoiled for choice.

Want something to fill the gap between lunch and the evening meal? That's no problem in a town where fast food is on offer in variety. Tucking in to a take-away solves a lot of problems.

But does the towns' mass of fast and convenient food outlets create problems? Even the humble hot potato comes in a special box, that doesn't always wind up in the litter bin. Soft drink cans rattle in the gutters and roll across the road.

Has the price of convenience food become too much to pay — a town where chip papers blow in the wind, and insulated containers crunch under foot?

For a quick snack you just cannot beat chips, agree student John Rudd, and girl friend Teresa Warner.

In Grantham there is no shortage of outlets for that particular fast food. The couple agree that whatever you choose in Grantham to fill the hunger gap, you will get taste and value.

"From Chinese to pizza, the town is well served," said John.

But there is a gap in the food scene, that is just waiting to be filled. "That is a specialist burger bar," said Teresa. Something like McDonalds to replace our long lost Wimpy."

Getting people to tidy up after a snack in the streets, is very much a matter of education, believes Julie Parkinson from Earlesfield.

"We have a chip shop on the estate, and a mobile chip van and people to tend to take their litter home with them," she said. "But if you want anything other than fish and chips, you have to come into Grantham for choice. And it is a very good choice."

But she too highlighted the glaring gap. "How nice it would be to have a McDonalds," she said.

"Walking round with a burger is not the same as sitting in a proper burger restaurant."

Mrs Sharon Bright is an authority on the tasty burger. With her brother Mike Embling she runs the mobile burger bar that offers snacks to customers of the Phoenix night club.

"In a weekend we sell 400 burgers, and that is a lot of burgers."

"But I agree with other people you have spoken to. Grantham needs a specialist burger bar that is open right round the clock. It would do tremendous business."

With customers indoors, the wrappers and boxes should wind up straight in the litter bin.

"It's an idea we might take up," said Sharon.

"Certainly we could use a McDonalds, and perhaps a good kebab house," said Vincent Pattison, from Thames Road.

"Our chip shops and Chinese take-aways are good, but there are so many. I like a burger or a bacon butty."

Commuting from West Bridgford to work in Grantham, Alan Dare could only suggest that the litter is the price the town has to pay for having so many food outlets.

"The problem is just as bad in Nottingham," he said.

"Grantham is not lagging behind in the convenience food stake. What we have is very good."

But he did pinpoint one gap in the food chain.

"You've guessed it!

"We do need a Wimpy or a McDonalds restaurant."

Sharon Bright: "Round the clock burgers would be a hit."

Alan Dare: "Grantham fares well for fast food."

Julie Parkinson: "Take your litter home."

John Rudd and Teresa Warner: "Make ours chips."

Vincent Pattison: "No more Chinese or chipples, please."

Figure 14.8 Datapack: article in local newspaper.
Source: The Grantham Journal, *Friday 13 May 1988.*

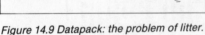

Figure 14.9 Datapack: the problem of litter.

The worst areas for litter (see Figure 14.6) are at the corner of Read Lane and Boston Avenue, the park, and the gardens along Boston Avenue. Letters of complaint have been sent to the council by the supermarkets, sweet shop, post office, video shop, newsagent, toyshop, hairdresser, and chemist. There has always been a problem of litter in the area, but it has become particularly serious since Burger Chief opened up two years ago.

... Yes, I have noticed the litter. I should think that it has always been here. It makes me laugh when people blame it on Burger Chief. They come in here for their food at all hours and then expect me to clear up the mess they leave. I know that they sometimes throw the wrappers in the streets and in gardens. But, I pay my rates to the Council and they should clear it up. I say that litter should be cleared up by the people that cause it. It is not my problem. You can see the service I am providing by the number of people that queue up for food.

Figure 14.10 Datapack: extract from interview with Burger Chief owner, Jane Morrell.

Activity

The following questions should be discussed in small groups before being discussed in class.

1. What is 'the issue' highlighted by the datapack?
2. Is it a problem? If so, why?
3. Who is it a problem for?
4. What is the cause of the problem?
5. Who is responsible for causing the problem?
6. How, if at all, should groups and individuals be made accountable for causing the problem?

Once these questions have been discussed you should construct a group questionnaire to enable you to investigate a similar issue in your local area.

■ Revision

Complete the following sentences using the words below:

growth	value
private cost	social cost
social benefit	cost benefit analysis
environment	acid rain
noise pollution	water pollution
pesticides	consumer boycotts
biosphere	recycling
bottle bank	unemployment
factory farming	increased crop yields
Greenpeace	Germany and Sweden

1. _____ is often used by government economists setting out the advantages and disadvantages to the community of certain policies.
2. _____ caused by traffic can reach extreme levels in city areas.
3. _____ is often blamed on coal-fired power stations in Britain.
4. The _____ of an economy is often measured in terms of the increase in national output of goods and services.
5. _____ are a major cause of food pollution.
6. _____ leads to a waste of human resources.
7. _____ involves the re-using of scarce resources.
8. The cost to a factory owner of hiring labour is an example of a _____ .
9. The things that surround us are referred to as the _____ .
10. _____ are an effective way of putting pressure on producers.
11. _____ increases the output of poultry farmers but at a cost to the animals.
12. Forests in _____ have felt the effects of acid rain.
13. The _____ is the term used for the regions of the earth's crust and atmosphere in which living matter is found.
14. _____ is added at each stage in the production of a product.
15. _____ includes private costs as well as the costs suffered externally to a business.
16. _____ cannot simply be measured in money terms.
17. A _____ is a sensible way of recycling glass.
18. _____ is an environmental pressure group.
19. _____ can be achieved by the use of pesticides.
20. _____ is often a consequence of the use of pesticides by farmers.

CHAPTER 15
Influencing decisions in a democratic society

Most modern Western governments are elected by the people. People's government is known as *democracy*. In Britain we have a system known as 'representative democracy', in which certain people known as Members of Parliament are chosen to represent their constituents (people who live in the area from which the MP is chosen). Members of Parliament typically represent about 60,000 people.

However, our democracy involves more than simply choosing people to represent us. We also have the freedom to express opinions which are critical of the government, other bodies and individuals. We also have uncensored media, free from the controlling hand of government, and an independent legal system.

Decision-makers can therefore be influenced by a wide range of individuals and groups including:

1. political groups
2. the mass media
3. pressure groups
4. other groups and individuals

Political groups

Political parties are organised groups of people who share similar sets of ideas and beliefs. These political parties set out manifestos laying down their beliefs and the sorts of policies they would like to see come into effect.

■ Case Study: Possible Labour Party plans

Look carefully at the article in Figure 15.1 which reports some of the proposals being made by a group of Labour Party members.

Political parties can have an enormous impact on decision-making. New laws are passed through Parliament and it is the party with the majority in Parliament which will be able to see a wide range of its policies become laws. These policies might include:

1. How large the public sector should be
2. Whether to emphasise direct or indirect taxes.
3. How to control pollution.
4. How much money to spend on various services such as education and health.

Opposition parties can also influence the decision-making process by voting against the government, by canvassing support, and by making the public aware of a wide range of concerns.

The mass media

The mass media include all forms of written communication to the public such as newspapers, magazines and books, and all forms of transmitted communication, such as radio, television and cinema.

The mass media play an important part in a number of areas of industrial society:

STATE-BACKED garages, estate agents and building companies should be set up by a future Labour government to challenge private enterprise, a Labour policy review group has told the party leadership.

The public sector should demonstrate its ability to offer high quality services in areas where the market often fails the consumer, promoting a "public enterprise culture", the group says.

"Examples include estate agency, car maintenance and garages, and house maintenance," according to the "consumers and the community" review group, headed by Jack Straw, Labour's education spokesman, and David Blunkett, a member of the national executive.

By Andrew Marr
Political Correspondent

The paper is one of seven being considered by Neil Kinnock and the home policy committee of Labour's national executive. It calls for a "right of reply" for individuals attacked in the Press.

Another paper, prepared by the policy review group on democracy, chaired by Roy Hattersley, the deputy leader, argues that Labour should set up a new ministry to carry out legal reforms, including a "fundamental" review of the way judges and magistrates are chosen and trained.

"Ministerial responsibility for these major reforms in the administration of justice must reside with someone other than the Lord Chancellor," the group says. Much of his power and responsibility would be handed to the new ministry.

The home policy committee last night endorsed by 18 votes to four the review group report on the economy, which suggests the setting up of "public interest companies" and other alternatives to renationalisation.

Mr Kinnock told the committee that the policy review, a two-year process which has now completed its opening phase, was not an alternative to facing tough choices. Nor was it "an attempt to mask deviations, or cover retreat".

Figure 15.1 Possible Labour Party plans.
Source: The Independent, *May 1988.*

1. In the transmission of information
2. In shaping and reinforcing opinions
3. As large employers, and as parts of larger media groups

The transmission of information

The mass media reach a wide audience. A single edition of a mass circulation newspaper may reach up to 10 million people and a popular television programme may be seen by 15 million viewers. It is estimated that 95% of the population became aware of the British Gas share issue through an expensive advertising campaign involving a fictitious character, Sid.

The obvious channel for getting messages across to the general public is through television and the popular press. Important public information can be communicated to large numbers of people, as was demonstrated by the factual information about Aids broadcast in a huge campaign in early 1987.

Shaping and reinforcing opinions

There is a lot of debate as to how and to what extent the mass media influence behaviour. However, advertisers are prepared to pump millions of pounds into media promotion of their products. These campaigns are often highly successful and similar adverts may be used for years. In recent years political parties have been prepared to pay huge sums in using advertising agencies to promote a party image.

The media are also major employers

Apart from the BBC, which is in the public sector, most of the other major media concerns are part of large groups with a range of media and non-media interests. Many also have multinational connections.

Pressure groups

A pressure group is a group of people that attempts to influence decision-makers. The decision-maker(s) may be an individual, group or government organisation.

■ Questions

Copy out the grid in Figure 15.2 and complete the final column with the action a pressure group might take in each of the examples.

There are thousands of local, national and

Decision-maker	Pressure group	Action
An individual burning rubbish in his or her garden	Local Residents Committee	
A supermarket putting up its car parking charges	Local Shoppers Association	
Local council closing down one of its children's day nurseries	Parents' Association	

Figure 15.2 Action by pressure groups.

international pressure groups. The formation of a pressure group is usually sparked off by a particular event.

■ Case Study: The Grantham Commuters Association

Read carefully the articles given in Figures 15.3 and 15.4 looking at the activities of a local pressure group, and then answer the questions below.

Questions

1. What event sparked off the formation of the Grantham Commuters Association?
2. How would this have affected commuters?
3. In what ways did commuters organise themselves to protest?
4. Who supported the commuters?
5. What concessions did the commuters win?
6. Does this article suggest that the GCA is a powerful group? Explain your answer.
7. Why do you think that British Rail did a 'U turn'?

Pressure groups can be:

1. Very loosely organised protest groups set up to fight a given issue;
2. Highly organised groups, which may start

Victory for town travellers

BATTLING commuters are today celebrating an important victory in the fight to maintain vital county rail links.

Under pressure from Grantham Commuters Association, British Rail has scrapped plans to cut out an important evening train from London used by more than 120 county commuters.

And the commuters have won the promise of full consultation from British Rail before any other major rescheduling of timetables.

Great victory

Grantham commuters formed their association two months ago when British Rail announced that the 5.55 p.m. weekday train would no longer stop at Grantham.

More than 1,000 people signed a petition calling for the train to be saved, and backing came from five MPs.

Figure 15.3 The activities of a local pressure group.
Source: The Grantham Journal, 17 October 1987.

off as protest groups but then go on to build up a more permanent organisation, developing a wider range of activities and interests.

■ Case Study: An organised pressure group – Friends of the Earth

Friends of the Earth is one of the leading environmental pressure groups in the UK.

Our message is a simple one: it is only in protecting the Earth that we can protect ourselves – against pollution, the destruction of our urban and rural environment, mass unemployment and the horrors of global famine and war.

It is our role to put the pressure on politicians and decision-makers at every level. Changes in the law and public opinion are examples of our successes.

Organisation

Friends of the Earth is a national campaigning organisation (Friends of the Earth Ltd) set up in

*Figure 15.4 Activities of a
local pressure group.
Source: The Sleaford
Standard, 15 October 1987.*

Travellers win a victory

SLEAFORD and Grantham commuters have won their battle to keep the 5.55 pm London train — at least for the time being.

Following key talks with senior British Rail managers the Grantham Commuters Association has been told they can keep their train at least until more surveys have been done.

In the meantime, talks will continue as to its future — with the association consulted every step of the way.

The step marks a remarkable U turn on B.R's original decision to axe the Grantham stop on the 5.55 pm train from London.

At that time, BR said it wanted to attract more first class passengers travelling to Yorkshire.

But Sleaford and Grantham commuters fought hard to retain their train in the face of having to arrive home an hour later than usual on an overcrowded train or leaving work half an hour earlier each day.

Sleaford and Grantham MP Douglas Hogg, joined in the fight and took part in the talks with B.R. along with Chairman of the Grantham Commuters Association, Mr Mike Kirton.

And on Tuesday, a jubilant Mr Kirton was told that the had won the day. The train would remain at least for the time being.

Mr Kirton said: "B.R. will be consulting with us in the future on all thoughts of rescheduling.

"And, while I obviously see it very much as a victory for the commuters and the travelling public, I think that it is also a victory for common sense.

"In a sense too it is a victory for British Rail senior management because they now have well over 100 satisfied customers and it does illustrate that, although they have a monopoly, they do listen to customers — providing they make enough noise."

Mr Kirton thanked everyone who had helped in the Save the 5.55 pm. Campaign particularly Mr Hogg and Grantham Chamber of Commerce.

Mr Hogg said that the meeting at Rail House, Euston with David Rayner the Deputy General Manager Eastern Region was most useful.

He said: "Mr Kirton and I stressed the great importance to Grantham and in particular Grantham commuters of having a fast train service leaving Kings Cross at about 6 pm.

"I think that Mr Rayner was impressed by our arguments and the figures produced."

Britain in 1971 with 250 local groups. Each group raises its own funds and decides its own policies. Groups support national campaigns, organised by Friends of the Earth Ltd, and also start campaigns on local issues.

Friends of the Earth Ltd has a Board of Directors, the majority of whom are elected by the local groups, which is responsible for the overall running of the organisation.

There are Friends of the Earth groups in 25 countries in four continents, all linked under the umbrella of Friends of the Earth International.

Finance

There are about 25,000 registered Friends of the Earth supporters who provide about 40% of the yearly income. Special fund raising events raise 25% and another 15% is received as donations. Campaign appeals and trading operations each contribute about 10%.

Campaign methods

Friends of the Earth first hit the headlines in 1971 by dumping 1,500 throw-away bottles on the doorstep of Schweppes, the soft drinks manu- facturers. With no money or public support, Friends of the Earth had hit on one of the best ways of reaching a wider audience. Since then, always backed by excellent research, we have used a variety of imaginative methods to get the environmental message across and to influence decision-makers. Thousands of people have participated in consumer pressure campaigns, protests against acid rain, direct action to stop the destruction of irreplaceable wildlife sites, public meetings to stop nuclear waste dumps, cycle rallies, and many more events. In addition, Friends of the Earth has published reports, promoted new laws in Parliament and been involved in public inquiries.

Friends of the Earth staff and groups are constantly addressing public meetings, giving radio, TV and newspaper interviews, and meeting politicians, civil servants, local government officers and representatives from industry.

(Reproduced with the permission of Friends of the Earth)

Questions

1. What do you think is the main aim of Friends of the Earth?
2. List four methods which they use to get their point across.
3. Which of these methods would you consider to be the most effective to:
   (a) Try to stop rain forests being destroyed by business expansion in the tropics.
   (b) Try to control aerial spraying of pesticides.

(c) Try to stop the government from building a new nuclear power station.
Explain your answers.
4. List four groups of decision-makers mentioned in the text that Friends of the Earth tries to pressurise.
5. How would you go about testing whether Friends of the Earth is a powerful organisation or not?
6. Arrange for a speaker from the local branch of Friends of the Earth to visit your school or college.
   (a) Where is the organisation based?
   (b) How does it raise funds?
   (c) Investigate a local issue that it has campaigned on. How did it go about organising the campaign? How success- ful were Friends of the Earth in the campaign?

■ Coursework: Investigate a local issue involving pressure groups

In looking at any issue you must be careful to try to make sure that you examine a wide range of points of view. You must attempt to look at all sides in order to show the heart of the conflict of opinions (i.e. what people are disagreeing about, why they disagree, and how they show their disagreement).

It is so easy to get a one-sided view if you only listen to one group of people – those who are most willing to give their side of the story, or those most able to get their message across.

That there are many views on an issue is illustrated by the award winning advert shown in Figure 15.5 regarding nuclear energy.

Asking the questions

The groundwork for your piece of research starts in asking questions. Before you ask questions, you must consider:

1. Who to ask.
2. How to ask.
3. When to ask.
4. What to ask.
5. What you will do if you can't find out enough information.

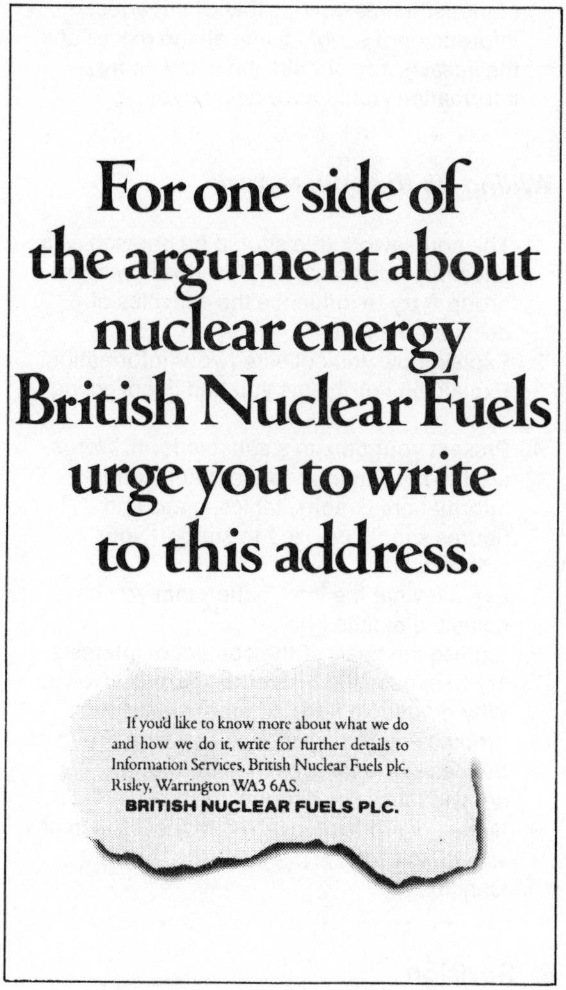

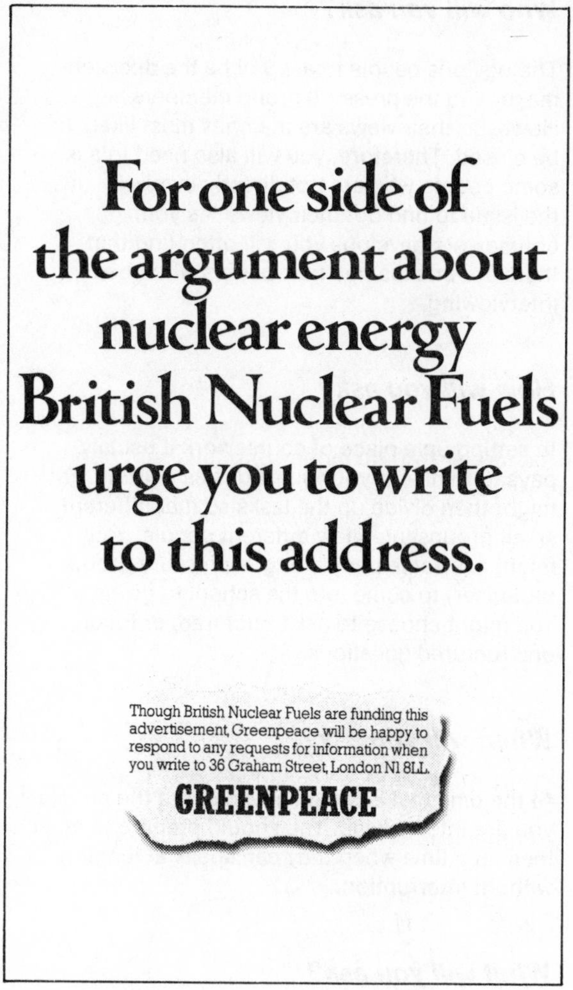

For one side of the argument about nuclear energy British Nuclear Fuels urge you to write to this address.

If you'd like to know more about what we do and how we do it, write for further details to Information Services, British Nuclear Fuels plc, Risley, Warrington WA3 6AS.
BRITISH NUCLEAR FUELS PLC.

For one side of the argument about nuclear energy British Nuclear Fuels urge you to write to this address.

Though British Nuclear Fuels are funding this advertisement, Greenpeace will be happy to respond to any requests for information when you write to 36 Graham Street, London N1 8LL.
GREENPEACE

Figure 15.5 Several ways of looking at an issue.
Source: British Nuclear Fuels.

Of course, a lot of information can be found in secondary sources such as letters in newspapers and newspaper articles. However, successful fieldwork depends on getting as many of *your own* questions answered by those people who *you* consider to be of importance to your research project as possible.

When you interview people, you will find that the best way of recording information is on a tape recorder. If you take written notes it is important that you write down as much as you can at the time of the interview.

If you prepare a list of questions, do not expect the questions to work perfectly. You will not always get the answers you expect. When you investigate real situations you will find that you are finding out new things that perhaps nobody has noticed before.

Some of the answers you get may be poor – always be ready to ask further questions to get more information.

Who will you ask?

The obvious people to ask will be the decision-maker and the pressure group members. However, their views are the ones most likely to be biased. Therefore, you will also need to ask some people who are not directly involved with the issue to find out their views. As your coursework develops you will often find that there are unexpected new people who need interviewing.

How will you ask?

In setting up a piece of coursework it usually pays to think out your questions as a group. You might then divide up the tasks so that different small groups interview different people. You might ask some people (e.g. a pressure group organiser) to come into the school to give a talk. You might choose to ask structured, or totally unstructured questions.

When will you ask?

At the time that is most convenient to the people you are interviewing. You should prepare to meet them at a time when they can speak at length, without interruption.

What will you ask?

The questions you ask will show your understanding of the task. When you come to write up your coursework you will show this understanding by explaining why you asked particular questions. The better the questions you ask, the better the information you will uncover. A fair bit of time should be spent on discussing and deciding on questions.

What do you do if you cannot find out the information that you are looking for?

1. Try harder.
2. Change your questions.
3. Be prepared to identify the problems you had in your write-up. A basic problem of any piece of industrial research is that of imperfect information (i.e. not having all the pieces of the jigsaw). You should show how more information would have helped you.

Writing up the coursework

1. The coursework title should be phrased as a question. For example: 'How does pressure group A try to influence the activities of decision-maker B?'
2. Explain how you collected your information.
3. Explain any problems you had in collecting data.
4. Present your data in a suitable form. Words are the best method for communicating information. Graphs, tables, maps and figures should be used to support your written work.
5. Explain what the information that you have collected means.
6. Expose the heart of the conflict of interests.
7. Try to expose the bias of the parties involved. Why do people have different views?
8. Who has more power – the pressure group or the decision-maker? What are the consequences of differences in power?
9. Is the government involved in the issue in any way? (How? Why?)
10. Conclusion.

■ Revision

Complete the following sentences using the words below:

mass media	advertising
BBC	pressure group
political party	democracy
new laws	British Telecom
Friends of the Earth	campaign
national press	decision-makers
protest group	particular event
policy	representative democracy
television	local radio
government	opposition parties

1. The formation of a pressure group is usually sparked off by a _____ .
2. The _____ is a state-owned corporation.
3. _____ is an example of a pressure group.

4. Pressure groups will attempt to influence a wide range of _____ .
5. _____ will only reach a limited audience.
6. _____ has tremendous powers to put its policy decisions into effect.
7. A _____ is an organised group of people who share similar ideas and beliefs.
8. A _____ programme can put a message into millions of homes.
9. In this country we have a system of _____ whereby we choose Members of Parliament.
10. People's government is known as _____ .
11. A _____ can often turn into a pressure group.
12. The _____ tends to be owned by a small number of people.
13. The _____ privatisation advert reached nearly every household in Britain.
14. _____ must be passed by Parliament.
15. _____ can put pressure on the government in Parliament.
16. _____ provides a lot of revenue for the mass media.
17. The _____ includes television, national radio and national newspapers.
18. Pressure groups will mount a _____ to put their views across.
19. Greenpeace is an example of a _____ .
20. _____ making is carried out by governments, groups and individuals.

Index